The poems of Elizabeth Siddal in context

Manchester University Press

Series editors: Anna Barton, Andrew Smith

Editorial board: David Amigoni, Isobel Armstrong, Philip Holden, Jerome McGann, Joanne Wilkes, Julia M. Wright

Interventions: Rethinking the Nineteenth Century seeks to make a significant intervention into the critical narratives that dominate conventional and established understandings of nineteenth-century literature. Informed by the latest developments in criticism and theory the series provides a focus for how texts from the long nineteenth century, and more recent adaptations of them, revitalise our knowledge of and engagement with the period. It explores the radical possibilities offered by new methods, unexplored contexts and neglected authors and texts to re-map the literary-cultural landscape of the period and rigorously re-imagine its geographical and historical parameters. The series includes monographs, edited collections, and scholarly sourcebooks.

Already published

Engine of modernity: The omnibus and urban culture in nineteenth-century Paris   Masha Belenky

Spain in the nineteenth century: New essays on experiences of culture and society   Andrew Ginger and Geraldine Lawless (eds)

Instead of modernity: The Western canon and the incorporation of the Hispanic (c.1850–75)   Andrew Ginger

Creating character: Theories of nature and nurture in Victorian sensation fiction   Helena Ifill

Margaret Harkness: Writing social engagement 1880–1921   Flore Janssen and Lisa C. Robertson (eds)

Richard Marsh, popular fiction and literary culture, 1890–1915: Re-reading the fin de siècle   Victoria Margree, Daniel Orrells and Minna Vuohelainen (eds)

Charlotte Brontë: Legacies and afterlives   Amber K. Regis and Deborah Wynne (eds)

The Great Exhibition, 1851: A sourcebook   Jonathon Shears (ed.)

Interventions: Rethinking the nineteenth century   Andrew Smith and Anna Barton (eds)

Counterfactual Romanticism   Damian Walford Davies (ed.)

Marie Duval: Maverick Victorian cartoonist   Simon Grennan, Roger Sabin and Julian Waite

The poems of Elizabeth Siddal in context

Anne Woolley

MANCHESTER UNIVERSITY PRESS

Copyright © Anne Woolley 2021

The right of Anne Woolley to be identified as the author of this work has been asserted by her in accordance with the Copyright, Designs and Patents Act 1988.

Published by Manchester University Press
Oxford Road, Manchester M13 9PL

www.manchesteruniversitypress.co.uk

British Library Cataloguing-in-Publication Data
A catalogue record for this book is available from the British Library

ISBN 978 1 5261 4384 6 hardback
ISBN 978 1 5261 7892 3 paperback

First published 2021

The publisher has no responsibility for the persistence or accuracy of URLs for any external or third-party internet websites referred to in this book, and does not guarantee that any content on such websites is, or will remain, accurate or appropriate.

Typeset by
Servis Filmsetting Ltd, Stockport, Cheshire

For Keith, because I couldn't have done it without your care and support.

Contents

List of figures	viii
Acknowledgements	x
Introduction: Siddal, Christina Rossetti and the literary context	1
1 Siddal, Dante Gabriel Rossetti and the duality of love	16
2 Siddal, Swinburne and the ballad tradition	89
3 Siddal, Tennyson, Ruskin and the feminist question	143
4 Siddal, Keats and Pre-Raphaelite relations of power	196
Conclusion: Contextualizing Elizabeth Siddal	257
Bibliography	264
General Index	278
Index of individual poems, pictures and collections	282

Figures

1. Elizabeth Siddal (1829–62) *Pippa Passes*, c.1855, pen and brown ink, © Ashmolean Museum, University of Oxford — 17
2. Dante Gabriel Rossetti (1828–82) *Found*, designed 1853, begun 1859, unfinished, oil on canvas (92.1 × 81.1cm) Delaware Art Museum, Samuel and Mary R. Bancroft Memorial, 1935 — 19
3. Elizabeth Siddal (1829–62) *Sister Helen*, 1851, pencil, Bryson Bequest, © Ashmolean Museum, University of Oxford — 22
4. Dante Gabriel Rossetti (1828–82) *Elizabeth Eleanor Siddal*, 1855, pencil and ink, © Ashmolean Museum, University of Oxford — 25
5. Dante Gabriel Rossetti (1828–82) *Portrait of Elizabeth Siddal Reading*, 1854, graphite, pen and ink drawing, © The Fitzwilliam Museum, Cambridge — 26
6. Dante Gabriel Rossetti (1828–82) *Rossetti Sitting to Elizabeth Siddal*, 1853, pen and brown ink, Birmingham Museums Trust — 27
7. Dante Gabriel Rossetti (1828–82) *Beata Beatrix*, c.1863–68, oil on canvas, © Tate London 2019 — 40
8. Elizabeth Siddal (1829–62) *Self Portrait*, 1853–54, oil on canvas, whereabouts unknown — 41
9. Dante Gabriel Rossetti (1828–82) *Astarte Syriaca*, 1877, oil on canvas, Manchester Art Gallery, UK/Bridgeman Images — 43

List of figures

10 Elizabeth Siddal (1829–62) *Lovers Listening to Music*, 1854, pen and brown ink, Bryson Bequest, © Ashmolean Museum, University of Oxford   44
11 Elizabeth Siddal (1829–62) *Madonna and Child (The Nativity)*, date unknown, watercolour, © Ashmolean Museum, University of Oxford   56
12 Elizabeth Siddal (1829–62) *Clerk Saunders*, 1857, watercolour, © The Fitzwilliam Museum, Cambridge   90
13 Elizabeth Siddal (1829–62) *Lady Clare*, c.1854–57, watercolour, private collection   147
14 Anna Mary Howitt (later Watts) (1824–84) *Elizabeth Siddall*, 1854, pencil, University of Delaware Library, Museums and Press   160
15 Barbara Leigh Smith (1827–91) *Elizabeth Siddall*, 1854, pencil, University of Delaware Library, Museums and Press   161
16 Dante Gabriel Rossetti (1828–82) *Profile Portrait of Elizabeth Siddal with Irises in her Hair*, 8 May 1854, pencil, Acc. #VICTORIAN15-L1.38, National Gallery of Canada (NGC)   162
17 Elizabeth Siddal (1829–62) *A Woman and A Spectre*, date unknown, pen, brown ink and some wash over pencil, © Ashmolean Museum, University of Oxford   197
18 Elizabeth Siddal (1829–62) *Study for St Agnes' Eve*, c.1855, pen and brown ink over pencil, © Ashmolean Museum, University of Oxford   202
19 William Holman Hunt (1827–1910) *The Eve of St Agnes*, 1848, oil on canvas, City of London Corporation   220
20 John Everett Millais (1829–96) *Isabella*, 1848–49, oil on canvas, National Museums, Liverpool   224

Acknowledgements

I would like to thank the staff of Keele University Library for obtaining numerous books and articles, and the archivists of the Special Collections Department of the Brotherton Library, Leeds University, of the Western Art Print Room of the Ashmolean Museum, Oxford, and of Girton College Library, Cambridge University for arranging access to manuscript sources and making my visits well organized and fruitful. I am indebted to the National Trust and House Stewards of Wightwick Manor, Wolverhampton, for allowing me to work for many hours in the library and borrow unlimited books from the Mander Collection of Pre-Raphaelite literature housed there. I thank the staff at the Ashmolean Museum, Art UK, Birmingham Museums Trust, Bridgeman Images, Delaware Art Museum, University of Delaware Library, the Fitzwilliam Museum, Cambridge, the National Gallery of Canada, National Museums Liverpool, Tate Images and Mark Samuels Lasner for sending me images and supplying the licences for their reproduction. I thank Anna Barton for suggesting I publish this book through Manchester University Press and then taking me so smoothly through the initial process of submission, and Matthew Frost, whose advice and reassurance has been sustaining, and his colleagues at Manchester University Press for bringing it out. I am beholden to Martin Hargreaves who has complied a truly accessible index, a task I was very glad to pass to a professional. I am hugely grateful to David Amigoni, Anna Barton, Constance Hassett, Jonathon Shears and Sarah Parker for their invaluable academic and moral support, constructive criticism, advice and friendship. To all those family members and friends who have given vital technical help, shown consistent interest and resurrected flagging enthusiasm, I hope you know how important you've been to this endeavour.

Introduction:
Siddal, Christina Rossetti and the literary context

On the evening of 10 February 1862 Elizabeth Siddal, her husband Dante Rossetti and Algernon Swinburne went out to dine at La Sablonière, a favourite restaurant in Leicester Square. Siddal was by turn semi-comatose and over-excited, but the meal went ahead as planned and without incident, Siddal in good spirits according to Swinburne, if a little weaker than usual. Around eight o'clock Swinburne left them, promising to return the following day for Rossetti to continue painting his portrait, and Siddal and Rossetti went home to Blackfriars where she retired to bed. They quarrelled before Rossetti left her there asleep to go to the Working Men's College where he had a teaching post, or possibly to meet another woman. When he returned at half-past eleven he found her snoring loudly and in disconcerting manner, a previously half-full bottle of laudanum now empty at her bedside and a note addressed to him pinned to her nightgown, asking him to take care of her disabled younger brother. Rossetti, having ineffectually tried to rouse her, called for the doctor who had attended Siddal during the stillbirth of her daughter the year before, who pumped out her stomach. She continued to slide into a coma, at which point three more medical men and Siddal's two other siblings were summoned, while Rossetti set out for Ford Madox Brown's house with the note in his pocket. Having read it, Brown destroyed the note on the grounds that suicide was not just scandalous, and likely to lead to social disgrace for her extended family, but illegal. Siddal did not regain consciousness and died at twenty past seven the following morning, just 32 years old, and pregnant again.

In the immediate aftermath her death was variously attributed to fear of another stillbirth, Rossetti's supposed involvement with other women, laudanum addiction and postnatal depression. Few friends expressed genuine sadness at her passing; the Rossetti family were apparently secretly relieved that such a troubled woman was out of his life for good. An inquest was held two days later amid fears that even without written proof Siddal's precarious mental state would bring in a verdict of suicide, but the coroner recorded one of accidental death, meaning that the Rossetti name was left unsullied. Rossetti was however inconsolable; the trials of their ten-year relationship were forgotten in an outpouring of grief that threatened to cripple his creative genius, compounded by rumours not of suicide but murder by his hand.

Much of the above account is of course unprovable; only the sketchy evidence that emerged from the inquest and subsequent newspaper reports and the distant reminiscences of some of those directly involved at the time of Siddal's death can throw any light on the events of that night, leaving those hungering for biographical detail to embroider an embellished story around her. As the suicide note was naturally not mentioned at the inquest, its existence has to be called into question. Almost every reference to Siddal was removed from Rossetti's diaries, so what private conversation passed between them or with their immediate acquaintances at any stage of their relationship can never be reported with confidence and must be regarded as apocryphal or at best anecdotal. Swinburne gave evidence at the inquest but none of it was recorded in the newspapers. Within days of her demise Siddal was to become the epicentre of a legend that continues to fascinate, one that has spawned a number of accounts of her life and the role she played in the Pre-Raphaelite (PR) circle as model, muse, artist, relative and (occasionally) friend. These accounts are often conflicting, a reflection of the emphases and prejudices of the time in which they were written rather than the result of the unearthing of new documentary evidence relating to a life-history by tradition shrouded in myth and mystery. Siddal has almost no primary record, so what is currently known about her is largely the result of the accumulation of secondary treatments which tend to advertise themselves as definitive truth, and when such treatments pursue a personal agenda accessing her through successive layers of subjectivity becomes difficult. Furthermore, it is ironic that despite this interest she remains an enigma, a woman whose lack of substance opens the way for multiple reconsiderations of her character and actions. Siddal's involvement with the Pre-Raphaelites, and Dante Gabriel Rossetti in particular, was undoubtedly unconventional and this has added to her allure; it is known that she lived unchaperoned at his lodgings and holidayed with him for several years before they were married in 1860, and she refused patronage from John Ruskin even though it was urged upon her, preferring artistic independence. However, only in the last forty years have her drawings, paintings and poems, vital aspects of her documentary record, come under critical scrutiny. The balance is therefore slowly shifting; Siddal is becoming known primarily as a creative force, not just because of the supposedly scurrilous nature of her life-history, and this book aims to forward that process.

Unlike Siddal's life-history, her poems have so far been given little attention. They were published posthumously and their writing appears to have been a completely secret activity as there is no mention of it in any surviving material from her lifetime. The manuscripts are in a fragmentary and confused condition and many parts are illegible, as Siddal's handwriting varies from the orderly to the chaotic according, perhaps, to her consumption of laudanum. They are generally without punctuation and in some cases consist of individual verses scrawled in pencil or ink on scraps of blue paper. Almost all have been heavily revised and corrected and it is impossible to say from what stage of the writing process they emanate. What remain could be early drafts, provisional and much-corrected attempts to put random thoughts on paper that were never thrown away when later revisions were destroyed personally or by a third party. By 1906 fifteen had been transcribed, given titles and punctuation and published, piecemeal, by William Michael (W. M.) Rossetti.[1] It is assumed none of the poems were meant for publication because she never made any mention of their existence, even to her few close friends. It is possible this might have been her intention had addiction, stillbirth and depression not intervened, or they may have been subject to further revision whilst remaining hidden. All her poems are enigmatic; they are timeless, and do not relate to any particular person or event. It is tempting as a result to read them purely autobiographically, in which case they appear excessively morbid and repetitive, but their apparent simplicity can be deceptive. The fact that Siddal's poems survive in so raw a state has opened up the possibility of multiple readings, an important aspect of the recovery of any 'lost' poet.

Once derided for its derivative and indulgently mournful content Siddal's poetry is now being mined for more than its personal associations and this – along with critical appreciation of her drawings and paintings – has helped to dismiss the earlier twentieth-century image of her as mere tabloid sensation. Publication has ensured her a permanent place in the Pre-Raphaelite canon, her skill as a poet and artist taking precedence over speculations about her contested biography, and work has been done to throw light on Siddal's aesthetic, but this book draws Siddal into a considerably wider literary arena.[2] If Siddal was prompted to write by other writings, then those writings and their contexts must inform the poems Siddal produced as much as the vagaries of her personal circumstances.[3] Being part of the Pre-Raphaelite circle she was subject to cultural influences that extended well beyond the immediate. Aspects of classicism, medievalism, romanticism and the Italian Renaissance informed the art, design and literature of the Pre-Raphaelite Brotherhood (PRB), giving them a dual, paradoxical, ethos that was both revolutionary and reactionary, a reflection of a desire to take creative endeavour in a new and challenging direction that was fundamentally a return to earlier traditions. Homer, Chaucer, Dante, Petrarch, Shakespeare, Raphael, Leonardo da Vinci, Milton, Keats, Wordsworth and Tennyson are among the fifty-seven 'Immortals', an eclectic list of names that constituted the Pre-Raphaelite creed, so as a productive associate of the PRB Siddal is likely to have been influenced by those figures they considered most inspirational. If Siddal is to be considered an integral part of the Pre-Raphaelite Movement rather than an accessory to it, then her work should be examined for the extent of such influence, thereby beginning the process of assessing the uniqueness or otherwise of her contribution.

As the only female Pre-Raphaelite poet/artist Siddal is already unique, and this both strengthens and challenges the hitherto gendered appraisal of nineteenth-century women's poetry. Modern scholarship has leaned towards the inclusion of female poetic voices in single-sex anthologies or accounts which stress their collective contribution and emphasize those aspects of Victorian society and politics that engaged women most. Until comparatively recently Siddal had no poetic voice, one step removed from those women poets whose previously published work had simply been ignored or fallen out of favour with a twentieth-century readership. Once in the public domain Siddal, adept in two genres, becomes a potential feminist figurehead, making it even more important that she be represented among the many other 'rediscovered' poetesses. On the other hand, such placement arguably reinforces cultural stereotypes and counter-productively shields women poets from over-rigorous comparison with the much larger male canon. Only Christina Rossetti and Elizabeth Barrett Browning are regularly included in combined collections, which automatically augments their critical reception. Siddal and her lesser-known counterparts suffer as a result of this exclusion, their contribution sidelined because their exposure to the acclaimed 'greats' of Victorian poetry is limited. This book considers the texts of Siddal's work alongside those of four male poets and one critic who were either personally known to her as members of the Pre-Raphaelite group, or who inspired or influenced it. This establishes an intertextual dialogue with visual and verbal contexts that enables fuller examination of poems that can profitably be read for more than their autobiographical content. Once the latter is set aside it is evident that the poems are attempts to balance conflicting forces that manifest themselves in a series of dualisms and paradoxes. This book examines these and the contexts that gave rise to them in order to extend the recovery of Siddal the poet/artist.

The rediscovery of nineteenth-century women means that Siddal is contextualized within a body of literary criticism that seeks to establish the nature of feminist poetry and the multiplicity of issues women felt drawn to write about. Romantic poetry was largely male-centred, and women were apparently unaware of the exclusion.[4] Furthermore, according to contemporary male critics women's poetry exemplified conventional ideas of femininity and was inherently different from what a man could write as it was impulsive, confessional, without reason or restraint, and reliant on sensibility rather than intellectualism.[5] This would be contradicted as part of the culture of an emerging women's movement so that Victorian female poetics would be one of self-definition and universalism, making poetry a powerful repository of collective feminine experience.[6] The latter constituted a narrative of suffering and resistance that demonstrated a linked network of female self-expression. Myths and fairy stories were used to dramatize subjectivity and self-awareness. Sexuality, gender and desire were explored, along with the experience of inequality in relationships between men and women, an articulation of the rebellious self, downtrodden by male dominance or patriarchy. Attempts were made to deconstruct masculine stereotypical representations of women, and domesticity and nurturing were extrapolated into the wider world of public issues. Factory conditions, slavery and its abolition, marriage, motherhood, sexual and religious passion, prostitution, militarism, nationalism, colonialism, dissent and deprivation are all discussed in the poems of such women. The role of silence and secrecy in a relationship came under scrutiny, as did the right to choose chastity, and some, like Christina Rossetti, found the ultimate submission to divine law transcended the mortal, physical love others sought to elevate.[7] Victorian feminist poetry was a movement whereby women removed 'masks' put over them by male writers: angel, monster, hysterical weakling, mad queen, Snow White. In a deliberate reversal of a dominant ideology which tended to distort and ignore women's experience, intuition and empathy contrast sharply with the attitudes of men trapped in this traditional repressive role.[8] Some female poets wanted a happy marriage as well as the opportunity to explore their gift, others were reliant on male financial support yet sought independent fame as a poetess. Romantic poets Felicia Hemans and Letitia Landon (L. E. L.) needed to work so had to compromise their art; L. E. L. wrote fiction as did the fictitious Aurora Leigh, later poets Augusta Webster and Matilda Blind produced journalism and many others put their work into annuals and gift books, facing up to a different, professional world. Those underwritten by privilege, education and inherited wealth, like Rossetti and Elizabeth Barrett Browning, were more fortunate.

Of the one hundred or so 'lost' voices a representative few are used here to show Siddal was not writing in isolation: Hemans and L. E. L., and Victorian poets Webster, Barrett Browning, Jean Ingelow, Adelaide Anne Procter, and (principally) Christina Rossetti. Whereas Siddal and her male counterparts will remain centre stage, reference to their work is made where it coincides thematically and technically with Siddal's in the chapters that follow. Hemans's poetry was nostalgic, trans-historical, international, drawing on literatures past and present and representing imperial and domestic ideologies. As such she could be considered an emblematic Victorian, so close is she to their needs and desires, especially in her focus on the female virtues of courage, self-sacrifice and maternal affection.[9] Her saintly reputation, cleverly manipulated, tempered her academic accomplishments and other contentious aspects of her private life to maintain an image of perfection, but by the end of the century her poems seemed overly sentimental despite some of her longest and most ambitious such as the 'The Forest Sanctuary' (1825) and those in *Records of Women* (1826) being full of strife, violence and protest.[10] Hemans was part of the later twentieth-century revival of interest in women writers but her standing was slow to advance because of close identification with a Victorian ideal of womanhood incorporating suffering and self-renunciation. New historicist and feminist critics subsequently hailed her poems as examples of dissonance in nineteenth-century cultural ideals, and fluctuations in reception of her poetry are credited with redefining what 'Romantic' actually means and with more accurately mapping how women's poetry is shaped by that gendered culture, its aesthetic value and its historical setting.[11] Landon frequently returns to the question of identity, very much a Romantic characteristic, in her poems. Improvisation, the reconstruction of a separate poetic self known as L. E. L., is perhaps the key to understanding her world view.[12] She cleverly wrote what she believed the public wanted: descriptions of exotic lands, mythological creatures, orphans, abandonment, solitude and alienation. Emotional responses are paramount and the language is energized and fulsome, but she also uses poems like the series *Subjects for Pictures* (1836) to subversively blur the boundaries between female and male poetics.[13] Her heroines are unhappy women like Sappho and Ariadne who are dissatisfied with institutions and customs which burden women, like marriage, which is shown as death or sacrifice. She challenged and subverted existing tradition while still acknowledging the boundaries assigned to the woman poet, and her poems were eventually sidelined as structurally over-simplistic and self-indulgent, which may account for her decline in popularity and subsequent failure to exert as much influence on Victorian poets as Hemans.[14]

The division between the Romantic and the Victorian literary era is not clear cut and spheres of influence overlap just as the web of cross-currents generated by so many women working at the same time becomes more complex as the century wears on. Hemans and L. E. L. left a legacy that would be adapted, extended and replaced, but the process was gradual and taken in multiple directions according to personal circumstance and association. Within this fluid and evolving picture Siddal's most significant literary contemporary has to be Christina Rossetti, her sister-in-law and fellow Pre-Raphaelite. 'In An Artist's Studio' (1856) obliquely refers to Dante Rossetti's workplace and the many drawings of Siddal produced and stacked there unsold. It uncovers a problematic, tragic relationship between a male artist and the beauty of his model, her identity gone, replaced by numerous reincarnations so that she becomes known only via his talent. He figuratively feeds upon her face, addicted to her beauty (as Siddal was to laudanum), but as he eats she disappears into the many images of her. 'Siddal' comes across as more than just an empty figure but she is still remote, and this arguably exemplifies the relationship between the two women. Christina once called her 'my beautiful sister-in-law', yet they appear not to have been close. In retrospect, however, their poems can be seen to share a number of traits. Siddal's work is full of paradox and both women wrestled with the ironic notion that writing as a communicative exercise conflicts with the essentially private and personal thoughts that give rise to it. Siddal's poems are also full of dualisms and Rossetti mixes opposites like pleasure and pain, detachment and belonging, restraint and overflow in *Goblin Market*. In 'My Dream' (1862) the skin of the king crocodile is rich and beautiful but beneath it lurks cannibalism and greed. Siddal's poems are enigmatic and open to interpretation and in *Goblin Market* female closeness and affection can be read as lesbianism and incest. Both write about secrecy and silence and extrapolate that into dialogue with the self, and both are experimental, Siddal with ballad construction and Rossetti in reversing gender roles in her sonnet sequence *Monna Innominata* (1881). They deal with common themes: the dead woman, betrayal of love, the superiority of religious love, allowing the female voice to speak of emotions and desires, and respect for the Romantic legacy of Keats and medievalism.

Rossetti had a prodigious output that encompassed several genres so to compare it with the few slight poems Siddal wrote is unfair and unrealistic. There are, however, some differences worth exploring that point to individuality. Rossetti chose to publish and has remained continually in print, the only nineteenth-century woman poet to occupy such a prominent position. She engaged in intertextual debate with mainly male forebears and corresponded with and supported contemporaries, which indicates confidence in her own ability and ideas.[15] She had a public persona beyond her writing, lending support to a refuge for women and in membership of the Portfolio Society which shared opinions and texts between women. Siddal's writing was, for whatever reason, an entirely secret operation, in no way a career or profession. Her poems are narratives of unknown protagonists experiencing doubt and uncertainty and rhetorical questions abound. Rossetti wrote of specific identifiable situations at home and abroad that covered politics, children's literature and explicit, constant Christian devotion. She references the Bible and Gothic novels that speak of other situations beyond the merely personal reality of the present. Siddal's poetry is always circumstantial, nebulous, non-specific and introspective. Her pieces are gender-fluid, lacking the definite sexuality present in Rossetti's verse; by contrast it is the adverse effect of a sexually charged relationship that dominates. A particular area of divergence is their attitude to death. There is a Christian message in 'Uphill' (1862) for example, in which Rossetti's speaker aspires to a place in heaven, but it's not necessarily a comforting place. Death may not be a release, more another perennially erected barrier to the happiness of humankind.[16] This is very different from Siddal whose speakers, certainly melancholic, long for death because it is the unquestionable answer to earthly concerns. Differences aside, initially, all these poems were read autobiographically, with failed love relationships at their epicentre, partly because of the editorial influence of W. M. Rossetti. Feminist literary criticism of the 1970s changed this and Rossetti's were then re-read for their challenges to political and economic authority, the nature of desire, and her relationship to earlier poets such as Dante and Keats. This book now undertakes the last part of that process for Siddal.

Creating an intertextual relationship with Dante Rossetti, Swinburne, Tennyson, Ruskin and Keats may enhance and consolidate Siddal's reputation as a poet, but it may also throw new light on mutual mid-century concerns, which is why the establishing of context is so important in the analysis of all the texts under scrutiny here. The issues and concerns challenging Siddal, such as the changing status of women and the role of religion in an increasingly scientific and secular society, are clearly not just the province of female writers. Siddal's response to the rapidly changing dictates and mores of industrialized Britain can throw light on the male response to those same sets of contentious and bewildering circumstances; amid growing demands for female economic, even political, equality, Dante Rossetti instigated and popularized a 'religion of beauty' in which women were worshipped for their physical attributes and sexual parity was considered the key to mutual understanding, while Siddal mocked such efforts to avert the impending social upheaval. Of course, such intertextual close reading is not intended as a competition. Siddal's poems are essentially different, impossibly slight when put up against the literary weight of Tennyson's *The Princess*, Rossetti's *The House of Life*, or Keats's *Lamia*, and simply being read side by side they run the risk of being enveloped and thus diminished by proximity. However, they can be put on the same interpretative platform, another reason for the emphasis on contextualization as a preliminary to any analysis of their content. Siddal and Keats were obviously not acquainted or part of the same poetic school but both were Pre-Raphaelite constructs whose image was manipulated to suit the doctrine and ethics of the PRB, and, as Chapter 4 elucidates, both appear to have believed they inhabited parallel existences. This commonality permits profitable comparison of texts which elucidate the spectral nature of the self and an experience of sensation beyond the physical. The process is one of symbiosis; Siddal's texts may well cast new light on the male perspective offered in poems long since in the public consciousness, but more importantly, reading her work alongside such pieces and sharing their literary and contemporary contexts opens up enigmatic poems that withhold their meaning despite their apparent structural and linguistic naivety. It will also encourage alternative readings of poems that at first glance can appear meagre, self-indulgent and unambitious.

Almost all Siddal's poems are very short as well as ambiguous, so their initial impression is visual, making the inclusion of certain of her drawings and paintings an informative entrée to each of the chapters that follow. She was an exhibited artist of some critical and commercial success in her lifetime and, as expected, her pictures are closely influenced by the prevailing Pre-Raphaelite style and favoured literary sources. In the absence of other primary evidence her work in both genres assumes even greater importance in the appreciation of Siddal the person, but it also allows room for intertextual analysis of a different kind because not only do her pictures illuminate often quite discreet aspects of a borrowed literary source, but they also relate directly to elements common to her poems. Many of her paintings graphically depict protagonistic women at moments of emotional crisis, an almost universal poetic theme. Similarly, most of these poems in some way or other refer to silence, particularly women's inability to express themselves, and the women Siddal paints are usually frozen in time, faces taut and curiously expressionless. It is therefore possible and desirable to use some of her pictures ekphrastically, which is why they are given prominent position at the start of each chapter. In the past Siddal's artwork has been largely used to illustrate aspects of her character or for some social commentary; they have generally not been read allegorically, yet her preparatory sketches in particular lend themselves to this. It is beyond the focus of this book where the primary objective is the analysis of verse-writing, but Siddal's paintings and drawings would benefit from the close reading and intertextual comparison to which her poems are subjected here. Like her poetry, her artwork is distinctive and thematically varied, and scrutiny reveals precision of touch and the illumination of minute detail, the visual equivalent of a short stanza in which almost every word becomes important to meaning. Such analysis would enhance Siddal's profile as a poet/artist, and draw further attention to her creative voice and away from an often apocryphal life-history. Pre-Raphaelitism was primarily an artistic movement but it cultivated strong literary connections; the poetry of Keats and Tennyson exerted powerful influence upon artists who chose to illustrate them extensively and Dante Rossetti believed poetry to be his true calling, only turning to drawing because he felt it unlikely he could earn a decent living as poet. Some of the pictures that follow are therefore by other Pre-Raphaelite artists, not just Siddal, and are included because they illustrate and illuminate the texts under consideration, comment on the contemporary concerns that inform such texts, and embody the ekphrastic philosophy of the group to which Siddal was allied.

The chapters that follow advance this thesis, but also seek to examine one of a number of dualisms present in Siddal's poems and in the chosen texts of her male counterparts. Her poetics is essentially one of finding a balance between opposing forces, a dilemma shared with Swinburne, Keats, Tennyson, Ruskin and Rossetti because these forces emerge from shared literary and contemporary contexts. Each of the four chapters considers a different poetic dialogue and exploits a particular literary and sometimes personal relationship. Each also refers to the work of female contemporaries, so that Siddal may be seen not as an isolated or exceptional case but as part of a more general poetic 'sisterhood' and her contribution assessed accordingly. The allocation of individual Siddal poems to each chapter is to a certain extent arbitrary. It is important that each of the sixteen poems is given fair scrutiny so they have been evenly spread between the chapters, but as will become clear, some readily lend themselves to the concerns of a particular discourse whereas others could be used to illustrate several concepts. In taking this course, the way is left open for further analysis of Siddal's work because grouped differently or when applied to a different set of contexts they may yield yet more meaning. The texts are those from the Lewis and Lasner edition, taken (with the exception of the titles) from Siddal's manuscripts rather than revisions worked by Dante or W. M. Rossetti.[17] Serena Trowbridge's timely new annotated edition of all of Siddal's poems illustrates the extent of these alterations, adding another layer to the complexity of the analytical task when a poet seemingly wishes to remain silent.

Swinburne was Siddal's only close personal friend, and both independently engaged with the ballad tradition and its ongoing methodology of adaptation and imitation. Chapter 2 explains how Siddal uses this historically oral medium to lament the inability of women to express themselves, allowing her ballad poems to be read as expressing a voice/silence dichotomy. They also point to a dialogue with the self that stretches throughout her work; indeed, the search for the autonomous self is postulated as driving her poetics. Siddal was nicknamed 'Ida' by the critic John Ruskin, her one-time patron as well as a champion of Pre-Raphaelitism, who took the epithet from the heroine of Tennyson's *The Princess*, a poem that questions the Victorian feminist movement as Ruskin does in his lecture 'Of Queens' Gardens' (1865). Thus, in Chapter 3, the writings of Ruskin and Tennyson are drawn together over the so-called 'Woman Question', the focus being on the advisability of female educational reform. Siddal's poems widen the debate to examine diverse attitudes to the question of feminism, but at their heart lies the problem of balancing it with the need, as a professional artist, for male patronage. Tennyson's poems were widely illustrated by the Pre-Raphaelites, Siddal included, who found his rich archaic language and medievalism inspirational, and this serves to strengthen the literary connection. Siddal appears to have cultivated a certain elusiveness which was remarked upon by her contemporaries, and many of her poems infer a sense of separation and removal, creating the possibility of fluidity between the physical self and the spectral nature of the self. Keats, the most profound source of personal and literary inspiration for the Pre-Raphaelites was of the same inclination, believing himself only half-alive and occupying a parallel existence that carried the transformative power of passion. The dualism between the spectral and physical bodies is examined in Chapter 4 through three of Siddal's poems and four of his, *Lamia*, *The Eve of St Agnes*, 'La Belle Dame Sans Merci' and *Isabella and the Pot of Basil*; all of them indicate the struggle to balance illusion with reality especially within a dying if erotic relationship. But first, the balance between erotic and divine love is the centre point of the opening chapter, in which *The House of Life* sonnet sequence by Dante Gabriel Rossetti is read alongside the first group of Siddal's poems. A volume likely to have contained the manuscripts of some of those sonnets written before 1869 was buried with Siddal whose love reputedly inspired them, so her connection with them is particular and personal.[18]

Rossetti's worship of female beauty and the mutuality of sexual love that leads to true emotional communion appears at first to be at odds with the more overt mystic and religious references in Siddal's work, but knowledge and understanding of the self is the ultimate goal for both Siddal and Rossetti in this struggle between human and spiritual passions.

This book undertakes appraisal of Elizabeth Siddal in a number of new ways, making this a rather different recovery project, one that allows her work to be viewed from perspectives not previously associated with her name. It close-reads all her complete poems but with an awareness of literary and historical contexts, and it focuses attention on male rather than female contemporary poets. It pulls away from her painting and drawing, using the latter purely to illuminate her poems while celebrating her unique achievement in both arts. It looks for consistent philosophical threads in her work: paradox, dualism and balance of power. It puts forward a methodology that can be extrapolated to fit other similar projects. Crucially, it moves Siddal away from the context of her life-history and places her in one that facilitates an extended analysis of her poems, but the dualisms that pervade her work, and those of the male poets she was associated with in life, extend beyond her texts to engage those who seek to undertake this task. An essential power struggle remains unresolved; for whatever reason, Siddal's was, paradoxically, a deliberately silent poetic voice, and her poems were a dialogue with herself, not an outside reader. In bringing what appear to be quite random and undeveloped thoughts to public awareness the Siddal critic is caught in a moral dilemma: whereas it is important that Siddal be afforded recognition as a 'good poet', these works represent private deliberations that were intended to remain so, a paradox perhaps more difficult to resolve than those postulated in the poems themselves.

Notes

1 Serena Trowbridge, *My Ladys Soul. The Poems of Elizabeth Siddall* (Brighton: Victorian Secrets Limited, 2018) has a full publication history along with annotated texts.

2 Jan Marsh is the acknowledged biographical authority and has written extensively on Siddal's art. *The Legend of Elizabeth Siddal* (London: Quartet Books, 1989) has a chapter devoted to her poems.
3 Constance W. Hassett, 'Elizabeth Siddal's Poetry: A Problem and Some Suggestions', *Victorian Poetry*, Vol. 35, No. 4 (1997), 443–70, p. 446.
4 Jan Montefiore, *Feminism and Poetry. Language, Experience and Identity in Women's Writing* (London, Chicago, Sydney: Pandora, 2004), p. 8.
5 Glennis Stephenson, 'Letitia Landon and the Victorian Improvisatrice: The Construction of L. E. L.', *Victorian Poetry*, Vol. 30, No. 1 (Spring 1992), 1–17, p. 4.
6 Montefiore, *Feminism and Poetry*, p. xv.
7 *Ibid.*, pp. 12–55 has extended discussion of all these issues.
8 Sandra M. Gilbert, and Susan Gubar, *The Madwoman in the Attic. The Woman Writer and the Nineteenth-Century Literary Imagination* (New Haven and London: Yale University Press, second edition, 2000), p. 17.
9 *Ibid.*, p. 3.
10 *Felicia Hemans. Selected Poems, Letters, Reception Materials*, ed. Susan J. Wolfson (Princeton and Oxford: Princeton University Press, 2000), p. xxi.
11 *Ibid.*, p. xiv.
12 Stephenson, 'Victorian Improvisatrice', p. 2.
13 *Ibid.*, p. 5.
14 Virginia Blain, ed., *Victorian Women Poets. A New Annotated Anthology* (Harlow: Pearson, 2001), p. 5.
15 Kathryn Burlinson, *Christina Rossetti* (Plymouth: Northcote House Publishers, 1998), p. 8.
16 Isobel Armstrong, *Victorian Poetry. Poetry, Poetics and Politics* (London and New York: Routledge, 1993), p. 363.
17 Elizabeth Siddal, *Poems and Drawings*, eds Roger C. Lewis and Mark Samuels Lasner (Wolfville, Nova Scotia: Wombat Press, 1978).
18 Dante Gabriel Rossetti, *The House of Life. A Sonnet Sequence* (Variorum edition), ed. Roger C. Lewis (Cambridge: Boydell & Brewer, 2007), p. 230 lists 25 titles from the sequence as having been written before 1869.

1

Siddal, Dante Gabriel Rossetti and the duality of love

Pippa Passes and *Sister Helen*

In June 1857 Siddal was among the contributors to the small Pre-Raphaelite salon exhibition organized by Ford Madox Brown at Russell Place in Fitzroy Street. She submitted three subject watercolours, an oil on canvas self-portrait, some drawings from Tennyson, and *Pippa Passes* (figure 1) a pen and brown ink illustration executed in 1854 of Scene III from Robert Browning's 1841 poem of the same name. The latter is set in and around the town of Asolo near Venice where Pippa the silk winder spends her day's holiday wandering the streets, singing songs and thinking of the four local people she considers the most blessed. In reality they are very different from her innocent imaginings and are caught up in an inter-related web of intrigue, but her songs effect a moral revolution in each of them, even if Browning does not divulge the outcomes. As Pippa approaches the dwelling of the last person on her list, a visiting bishop, she passes a group of four 'loose women', prostitutes. Their presence in the poem is no accident; Bluphocks, an English vagabond, has been paid by Uguccio, the bishop's Intendant, to locate Pippa and the prostitutes have been looking out for her at Bluphock's behest. The bishop has discovered she is his long-lost niece, daughter of his brother whose funeral he is in Asolo to organize. Rather than potentially lose the fortune he stands to inherit he wants Uguccio to find and kill Pippa, which explains the role in the plot of these minor characters accustomed to street life.

Siddal's drawing captures the moment when Pippa walks past

Siddal, Dante Gabriel Rossetti and the duality of love

1 Elizabeth Siddal, *Pippa Passes*, c.1855, pen and brown ink

the (now three) women as they sit on steps on the edge of a narrow cobbled path, and its ambitious composition makes a comparison between two types of womanhood: the innocent or semi-divine and the erotic or worldly, themes central to this chapter. Pippa is slight and virginal, dressed in what could be a simply draped nun's habit and with her hair loose but pulled back to fully expose her face. She holds one hand protectively at her waist, a barrier between herself and the girls to her right, and this separation is emphasized by the central position of a substantial stone double pillar which supports part of the railings which surround the shallow steps on which the women sprawl. The prostitutes are thus effectively depicted as a semi-independent entity. In her left hand Pippa carries what could be an olive branch and this symbol of reconciliation is echoed in her acknowledging glance which is at once both interested and fearful. The three women are the antithesis of Pippa in their posture, clothing and expression. Blousy and vulgar, they lounge together gossiping about their clients, one literally with her feet and skirt in the gutter. Their poses are exaggeratedly convivial and lack Pippa's serenity. One sits slightly higher than the rest and appears more exuberant; with an expansive gesture she beckons Pippa to join them, her voluptuous figure emphasized by her corseted dress and low neckline. All three sport conspicuous jewellery and have rounder faces with coarser features. Faithful to the poem, the drawing does not allow Pippa more than a sideways look in passing but in placing these opposites together Siddal has shown that neither is exclusive. Each represents an aspect of womanhood and thus an aspect of love, the essence of Dante Rossetti's artistic and poetic philosophy which integrates the two media to celebrate the sensuous and erotic by encouraging the spectator to respond romantically to what they see or imagine in contemplation of the work. Physical, human love had its corollary in the mystical and divine and coexisted in woman; this thesis/antithesis/synthesis model, illustrated by the Siddal's lyrics and embodied in the sonnet form of *The House of Life* sequence by Dante Rossetti, is the focus of this chapter.

The scene has been carefully and delicately rendered with accomplished assurance and close attention to structural detail. There are many vertical lines which show artistic precision whilst empathetically stressing the imprisoning nature of the lives of the three women. Prostitution was a topical theme and an urgent social problem in mid-Victorian Britain and as such it had already been depicted by Holman Hunt in *The Woodman's Daughter* (1851) and *The Awakening Conscience* (1853) when Rossetti began his own oil exploration of the theme, *Found*, a piece that despite intermittent attention between 1854 and 1881 would never be finished.[1] An 1853 preparatory ink drawing is the most complex realization of the idea, in which a drover bringing a calf to market in London abandons his cart to run back to a girl who has recognized him and collapsed to her knees in shame against a churchyard wall. Rossetti's treatment of this fallen woman is both realistic and symbolic. The drover is holding her hands to support and protect her, perhaps from self-harm, but she cannot meet his eye. In the oil version (figure 2) her greenish pallor implies sickness and destitution, and in the drawing her dark cloak contrasts with his white smock. The calf carries religious connotations and is restrained under heavy mesh, just as she is captured by her descent into prostitution. A rose lies

2 Dante Gabriel Rossetti, *Found*, begun 1859, oil on canvas

discarded in the gutter and those on her dress are sullied. In the drawing a gravestone bearing an incomplete inscription on the theme of forgiveness is visible in the churchyard, and railings high on the wall keep the woman away from holy ground. Blackfriars Bridge appears in the background, potentially where she could drown herself. The woman's face is obscured and unattributable in the drawn version but in 1858, having gained a new commission for the work, Rossetti invited Fanny Cornforth, with whom he would have a close professional and personal relationship, to pose for the oil painting, and this later depiction of prostitution is rather different. Whereas in the drawing the woman is thin and collapsing, turning away in shame, in the oil she is plump and healthy, her feathered bonnet indicating a degree of affluence, even glamour. This is a 'swell prostitute' who has chosen the profession and is resisting being pulled away from it.[2] *Found* would bring Rossetti a new muse and an end to his portrayal of frail medieval maidens; perhaps it also brought acknowledgement that prostitution depended on fallen women for it to thrive, one reason for his never completing the work.[3] Cornforth's face appears in a number of Rossetti's depictions of women of beauty, but the fact that she features in this particular piece adds another dimension to its already emotive subject matter. Siddal was not the first Pre-Raphaelite woman artist to attempt a female perspective: Anna Mary Howitt's *Margaret* (1854) and *The Castaway* (1855) were precedents, but it was still an unusual choice of subject even allowing for Siddal having undoubtedly seen prostitutes working in London. Rossetti was keen to show Browning Siddal's 'little design' and later reported to William Allingham that Browning had been 'delighted beyond measure' with it.[4] Thus another relationship was at least temporarily cemented. Siddal sold *Pippa Passes* to Ruskin in 1855, but she also made another two identical copies, perhaps with a view to further sales in the prevailing sociopolitical climate.[5]

Browning's poem is about four concepts of love: carnal, married, filial and divine. In *Pippa Passes* Siddal captures two of these in her opposing depictions of women, whilst showing how the boundary between them is not entirely solid. This dualism is more evident in another, very different work, a set of three rough sketches done to illustrate the Rossetti poem *Sister Helen*, first published in 1854. The sketches were not intended to be a narrative sequence; instead, as in the poems considered below, they depict different but sympathetic reactions to a central affecting dilemma, the passion generated by the potential conflict between earthly and divine love. At the root of Rossetti's poem is a medieval superstition that revenge may be obtained by melting a waxen image of one's enemy, and the narrative of the poem, a duologue between Helen and her younger brother, reveals that she has been deserted by her lover who will now die in pain and fear despite the pleadings of four of his relations who intercede with her via the boy. The scene is a lonely hall with an open fire and a gallery above that looks out on to a wild and windy moor in moonlight, and the drama unfolds through question and answer, reinforced by variations on a repeated refrain that interprets the action. Helen is aware that as she's working with witchcraft, she will be destroyed as she destroys. This adds to the pervading sense of gloom, intensified by economical use of language, as the 'murder' unfolds. Despite the important role of the child in both driving the action and forwarding and symbolizing innocence, it is Helen's voice that dominates, and Siddal's drawings capture this just as they do the historic setting and the conflicting passions of the central character. Helen is consumed with physical love and with Christian certainty that her soul is lost both for taking another's life and for abandoning a dependant, and Siddal makes this clear in all three sketches despite their varying degrees of completeness. The most simplistic (figure 3) shows the boy holding Helen's hands as they clasp the wax image and as he points out of the window. His lips are pursed and he's frowning, but she is impassive and not looking at him, while to her left the fire blazes in the hearth above which hangs a crucifix. The third drawing is a more finished and delicate version of the second, but in both Helen is kneeling in front of a large fireplace dragging at her throat with her hands and with her eyes fixed on a wax doll on the hearth that is beginning to disintegrate in the heat. This could indicate she has pulled the effigy out of the flames as her conscience pricks and that therefore she is in greater emotional turmoil than Rossetti allowed for.[6] This Helen, by virtue of her reconstruction in female hands, has a more complex psychology as she appears to be considering the power she wields over life and death. Her brother is clambering up to a window and gesturing out while turning back to Helen to address her. Her horrified stillness is in stark contrast to his urgency just as the brightness of the flames throws the rest of the scene into sinister shadow. The crucifix has been replaced by an illuminated oval opening above the fireplace that in the final sketch is especially reminiscent of a halo. Helen's posture of pseudo-piety reinforces the interaction and conflict

3 Elizabeth Siddal, *Sister Helen*, 1851, pencil

between passionate earthly love turned to hate, and religious faith both Christian and pagan. This sketch in particular may lead the viewer towards a more sympathetic impression of Helen. As the scene was not taken from a specific line in the poem many readings are possible: perhaps the boy was climbing back into the room not escaping from it; perhaps Helen was choking on tears of repentance, frozen with indecision after the effigy fell out of the fire of its own accord. Whatever, her entire focus is on the wax man, just as previously it was on the living man, before his new bride usurped her place in his affections.[7]

   Siddal's artwork and the poems that inspired or provoked them demonstrate different sets of dualisms, and the contention here is that four of Siddal's poems illustrate the balance between erotic, earthly love, and its religious or spiritual counterpart, and that this same dualism lies at the heart of Dante Rossetti's sonnet-sequence *The House of Life*. If the latter explores the relationship between human and divine love then Rossetti himself is the personification of dualism; both Italian and English, revolutionary and reactionary, painter and poet, fleshly and spiritual, his work blends medievalism with contemporariness, Ruskinian realism with sensory imagination, and regard for the established church with an interest in mesmerism and Swedenborganism. For Rossetti human love had a counterpart in love eternal that did not require specific religious conviction, and this is mirrored in Siddal's poems, arguably the most emotive and emotional of her oeuvre. She uses eroticism to comment on its garnering as a means of control rather than a way of expressing her own sexuality, but alongside this there are strong religious elements in her poems that bring both aspects of love together. Siddal and Rossetti worked at a time of significant scientific challenge to religious conviction, of the emergence of a social conscience and of a shift in attitude to previously accepted rules of sexuality and sexual conduct, so that as well as being a 'dialogue of the mind with itself', as Matthew Arnold argued all poetry ought to be, these poems and sonnets constitute a search for an exploration of love, and also a search for the self.[8] For Siddal and Rossetti this is an integrated process; these poems foreground love, in whatever form, as being essential to life and a means of reaching an understanding of the self. A search for the self therefore pervades Siddal's poetics and is conducted through a dialogue with her texts that both examines and tests belief in something divine beyond the self, and devises mechanisms to cope with loss and failed relationships. This dialogue allows for positive expression and reconciliation of doubt and fear of the future and thus becomes a pathway to self-awareness and self-control, attributes which Siddal also appeared to seek and value in her personal life.

Literary and personal associations

Much of Siddal's biography is conjectural, extrapolated from a very limited and sometimes unreliable primary record and imbued with heady Gothic fascination; as a result few Victorian women have so rich or contentious a historiography.[9] Born in 1829, little is known of her activities until she came to the notice of the Pre-Raphaelites around the end of 1849; thereafter some aspects of her narrative can be fixed within their personal histories. The connection with the Brotherhood began with Walter Deverell, and Siddal did sit for the figure of Viola in his RA submission *Twelfth Night* as well as for an etching for the PRB magazine *The Germ*. However, an obituary published in a local Sheffield newspaper a month after she died in February 1862 points to her initially being introduced to Deverell senior to whom she showed her sketches and drawings in his capacity as principal of the Government School of Design.[10] Interesting as it is to unravel the myths and unsubstantiated stories that cluster around Siddal, the important point here is that this revised account implies she was producing artwork before she became model, muse and pupil of Dante Rossetti, and that he did not beget or discover her talent as official PRB history lays down.[11] Between 1850 and 1852 she sat for Holman Hunt and Millais, and others, but sometime in 1850 she first went to pose for Rossetti and by 1853 was sitting for him exclusively. She was no ordinary model; she came to personify his ideas about the mystery of woman, appearing in his paintings of the Virgin Mary, Delia, Francesca and, above all, Beatrice – a reflection of Rossetti's emotional, literary and artistic relationship with Dante Alighieri. Drawing her unconventional beauty became compulsive and it produced an extended series of works akin to a series of love poems that has no precedent in British art.[12] By 1854 these drawings (for example, figures 4 and 5) increasingly show her as a friend or even a Beloved, intimate portraits as opposed to morally charged or religious tableaux. Changing personal circumstances are visible alongside her always enigmatic, shuttered, strangely unemotional demeanour which was exemplified by her downcast, heavily lidded eyes, pursed mouth and loose curtain of straight hair, all of which place a barrier between subject and viewer.

At the centre of Rossetti's art was the celebration of woman, and through her the power of love. Woman enshrined the mystery of existence, and all his work concerns different aspects of womanhood. In the mid-1850s Siddal encapsulated his ideal of untainted and virginal love, yet by this time she was installed in his home at Chatham Place, possibly accepting his tutelage in payment for her modelling. The exact nature of their personal relationship is impossible to determine, but W. M. Rossetti believed his brother

4 Dante Gabriel Rossetti, *Elizabeth Eleanor Siddal*, 1855, pencil and ink

to have been deeply in love with her, citing their mutual use of pet names as evidence of their easy familiarity.[13] Holidays together followed (though no formal introduction to his mother or sisters), but after the 1857 Exhibition and amid growing speculation about her health, his wavering attention and an unofficial engagement, Siddal disappeared to Sheffield for four months where she attended art school, while Rossetti joined William Morris and Edward Burne-Jones in Oxford to paint Arthurian murals in the debating

5 Dante Gabriel Rossetti, *Portrait of Elizabeth Siddal Reading*, 1854, graphite, pen and ink

chamber of the University Union, an auspicious endeavour as it turned out. A six-month reconciliation followed, but by the following spring Rossetti was alone in London, and his artwork together with his attitude to women changed as Siddal faded from view. For almost two years nothing is known about her, and Fanny Cornforth became her substitute as model, muse, companion and possible mistress. Around Easter 1860 Siddal became seriously ill, perhaps as a result of an overdose of laudanum. Rossetti was alerted and promised marriage if she recovered, the ceremony taking place in May. Their union would only be short lived; a stillborn daughter was delivered a year later and Siddal took a fatal overdose in February 1862. She was 32 years old.

Their relationship appears to have been as complex as their individual personalities: Siddal was his Beatrice but she was also his real-life artistic partner, seen in his 1853 sketch *Rossetti Sitting*

Siddal, Dante Gabriel Rossetti and the duality of love 27

6 Dante Gabriel Rossetti, *Rossetti Sitting to Elizabeth Siddal*, 1853, pen and brown ink

to Elizabeth Siddal (figure 6) leaning attentively towards him over her easel. Her stance indicates she both knows and is learning about him so the balance of power between artist and pupil (and possibly between two lovers) is momentarily disturbed; generally, Rossetti preferred the traditional role as tutor, as Georgiana Burne-Jones recalled: 'When E. S. had achieved something artistic general consensus was that one sees in her black and white design and beautiful little watercolour Gabriel always looking over her shoulder, and sometimes taking her pencil or brush from her hand to complete the thing she has begun.'[14] The connection between Siddal and Rossetti would be posthumous, in both literal and literary senses of the word. On the day of her funeral Rossetti placed in her coffin her Bible, and a small leather notebook containing his manuscript poems and fragments of verse he had been preparing for publication. This appears to have been a spontaneous and unreasonable gesture of guilt and divided loyalties as the poems were not love poems or written to or specifically for her, nor were they a sign of his neglect during her periods of illness.[15] His sacrifice can be seen as crossing the barrier between personal and artistic identity as their relationship was founded on cooperation. Siddal's position as model and muse was made more dignified by it, and her sacrifice of her life and that of her baby has its equal in his action.[16] Whatever his motives, Rossetti apparently had cause to rue his decision as in August 1868 Charles Howell offered to coordinate the exhumation of Siddal's remains so that the notebook could be retrieved and its contents finally put in the public domain. It would eventually be incorporated into *Poems* (1870), a collection of previously printed and now revised poems, plus those from the past buried with Siddal for which he had only imperfect manuscript copies, and fifty sonnets of a sequence to be called *The House of Life*, the full version of which would appear in *Ballads and Sonnets* (1881), the text used in this chapter.

Various reasons have been put forward for why Rossetti chose to embark on a venture that would surely offend Victorian sensibilities, especially after ghoulish tales of Siddal's still-youthful beauty and still-growing luxuriant red-gold hair were circulated. Possibly it was to prove he had outgrown his emotional gesture, and to ask the grave to yield the secrets of her suicide.[17] Perhaps it has more to do with Jane Morris to whom, by the late 1860s, Rossetti was deeply attached and who, like Siddal and Cornforth, exercised great artistic and personal influence over him. This then makes the exhumation stand as a sign of Love's death and rebirth, his adoration of Lizzie transferred to Jane.[18] A rather different slant is put on the event by Rossetti himself who wrote to Swinburne in October: 'No-one as much as herself would have approved of my doing this. Art was the only thing for which she felt seriously. Had it been possible for her I should have found the book on my pillow the night she was buried: and could she have opened the grave no other hand would have been needed.'[19] Presumably, if the book was still reasonably intact it implied Siddal's forgiveness and blessing for the future, but it says much about their relationship that Rossetti considered his place in it to be secondary. Alternatively, the book became a form of Siddal's body and a complex substitute for his own so that retrieval was like throwing himself into the grave in reverse.[20] This creates a bond with Siddal whereby his words and her flesh are transubstantiated, symbolic of High Church thinking. More prosaically, failing eyesight led him to seek an alternative career to painting, although it can be argued that the principal motive lay in Rossetti's fear that the poetry he already had available was too slight for a book, and that he also wanted to keep the reputation as a precocious poet he had cultivated.[21]

The exhumation, which Rossetti didn't attend, took place on 5 October 1869; the notebook was sent for disinfection and then returned to Rossetti for transcription. It was badly water-damaged, and much of the writing obliterated. Pages were stuck together and worm-eaten, and as only three survive it's not possible now to say definitively what poems were interred, or whether any of the fragments found their way into *The House of Life*, but seventeen of the eventual 102 sonnets can be dated to before 1862 so could conceivably have been buried with Siddal. Whether they were, or whether they were written with his love for her in mind is not the issue, what is important is their published association with a woman who evidently inspired Rossetti to begin an exploration of what love, both physical and spiritual, entailed. Rossetti said both the 1870 and 1881 texts were an effort to draw together a 'complete *dramatis personae* of the soul' and the whole piece does appear deliberately clouded, the ambiguities all pivoting around his complex love commitments to Siddal and Jane Morris especially. However personal the work seems, Rossetti insisted on its symbolic and impersonal character, modelling *The House of Life* on Dante's autobiography *La Vita Nuova*, which he'd already translated. The story is outwardly simple: a young man loves and then loses his beloved and then finds love again with a new beloved, so the Rossetti sequence could be referencing either two love affairs or the ideal love that both symbolized. It is misleading to associate Siddal or Morris or different aspects of love with any particular sonnet. Instead, the work's love ideal is a fusion of spirit and flesh, and if they represent anything, the two women signify two different conditions of lost love, one in life and one in death.[22] *The House of Life* is Rossetti's testament to Love, and his guide to its understanding by others. Siddal's life course is naturally important to this process but, more significantly, her poems also point to a similar search for understanding of love in its various potentially conflicting forms, and of herself through its agency. Where and how poets are buried plays a significant role in their textual afterlife.[23] The separation of Siddal's artistic and literary reputation from the image of her undecayed body in the 1980s began the process of its restoration and reassessment.

Several women other than Siddal sat for Rossetti after 1856 and of these Fanny Cornforth and Jane Burden (Morris) are the most noteworthy here as they embody the changing representations of beauty.[24] Cornforth was his principal model in the 1860s, and was his collaborator in some of his most ambitious and successful works, those that celebrate voluptuous beauty and passionate love. Robust and plump (Rossetti nicknamed her 'Elephant') with waves of blonde hair, easy, affectionate and undemanding, she was in many ways the physical antithesis of Siddal and came to Rossetti's notice when Siddal was no longer in London to claim his attention. She represented another type of love; pictures of her concentrate the gaze on her sexuality, not her thoughts or feelings. The ultimate woman of pleasure in his studies of her, Cornforth was both mistress and goddess. Some of the images may seem rather too welcoming, lacking the threatening sexuality of his subsequent work with Jane Morris for example, but sketches of Cornforth in a domestic setting eating, sewing or simply sitting, actually make her alive compared with Morris's static, isolated and aloof demeanour.[25] She was also professionally useful to him – the seduced girl of *Found* blossomed into a full-blown *Bocca Baciata*, and Rossetti's feelings developed into tenderness and duty towards an 'unfortunate'.[26] She became his housekeeper at Cheyne Walk, part of his social if not family circle, and remained associated with him until his death in 1882. She was devastated by his marriage, a fact George Boyce, landscapist and friend of both parties, recorded in his diary.[27] Cornforth may not have known Siddal as the latter was not a constant presence in Rossetti's life in the later 1850s, but historiographically both women have been afforded largely the same treatment. Without Rossetti Cornforth has hitherto had no meaning and his biographers have shaped her image through his works, for just one period of her life and often through a filter of prejudice because she wasn't of his class or intellect.[28] Now, however, the recovery of her rather different 'voice' has begun, illuminating an association between artist and muse based on mutual need and dependence.[29]

Rossetti met Jane Burden while working on the Oxford murals, and her marriage to William Morris two years later allowed an easy friendship to develop between the two couples. After 1868 she became his frequent model and guest and between 1871 and 1874 she, Morris and Rossetti became joint tenants of Kelmscott Manor near Lechlade. Rossetti's passion for her survived several periods of separation yet would always be tempered by the fact of her being married to one of his (one-time) closest friends. If Siddal represented virginal and religious love and Cornforth its physical equivalent then Morris was the synthesis, the ideal union of both elements and an illustration of the thesis/antithesis/synthesis model around which this chapter hangs. Tall, pale, sombre, with a swan neck, a mass of black hair, heavy brows and full lips, Morris had the mystic and enigmatic qualities of Siddal together with the sensuousness of Cornforth, and these merged in the extraordinary series of pictures Rossetti created of the visionary woman in the 1870s such as *Pandora*, *Mariana* and *Astarte Syriaca*, the Syrian Goddess of Love. Morris was a pioneer of art embroidery and Rossetti valued her suggestions about costumes used in his pictures of her. She was thoughtful and well-educated, widely read and able to discuss literature and art with Rossetti as their correspondence reveals.[30] However, the latter discloses nothing of a sexual nature, nor does it contain any evidence of shared trysts at Kelmscott; it actually seems more sensual than erotic, surprisingly mundane at times, symbolic of caring friends not lovers. Other than his mother and sister Christina, Jane Morris was the only female beneficiary of his will, the four chalk drawings to be left to her carefully itemized. Marriage gave Morris an identity but she still recedes behind a series of constructs or familiar tropes of femininity that make her identifiable but still intangible.[31] The same can largely be said of Siddal. The relentless aestheticism of Morris served to seamlessly merge the woman and the icon thanks in part, somewhat ironically, to the success of Rossetti's belief that the individuality of a model should not be subsumed into the artist's imaginative conception but remain identifiable in the final work.[32] Furthermore, Morris became inseparable from the characters she represented, her face deemed to have inexhaustible meaning, the unconventional or androgynous aspects of her appearance being reconciled into a coherent entity.³³ Rossetti's later work depicted her as the melancholic woman with downcast suffering expression, neglected or confined against her will like Proserpine. She was also the doomed Iseult or Guinevere, regal but powerless, spearheading the medieval revival, the ultimate tragic figure set apart from her contemporary context. She was the ethereal beauty Astarte, out of place in mundane surroundings by dint of her exotic ethnicity. Yet beneath all these public faces Morris herself was very modern, socially upwardly mobile and culturally aware, her circulated image making her a perhaps not unwilling celebrity.³⁴ It has been suggested that Morris actually had 'agency' and was not a victim trapped within these pictures. Rather, she was involved in a process of self-formation, the promulgation of her image part of the mid-century movement of art and literature towards a mass audience and away from the domain of the properly informed cognoscenti; Rossetti was complicit in this and Morris was drawn in via her conspicuous presence.³⁵

In his neat tripartite scheme Morris reconciled the opposites existing in Siddal and Cornforth, but in so doing all three women surrendered their identities to become signs of Rossetti's. His paintings stand as material evidence of the phases in his artistic development and whether idealized or realistic such images place the subjects in a power struggle with his ego and with biographers who use them as talismans of his artistic vision.³⁶ Morris was the woman most often caught up in this imbalance of power because she was repeatedly drawn as herself or exaggerated in caricatures, a sort of blank canvas on to which allegorical or historical figures could be inscribed.³⁷ Rossetti was fascinated by portraiture in poetry as well as art; 'The Portrait', Sonnet 10 in *The House of Life*, blends verbal and visual images together while still exploring the tension between the two media. There is no record of which, if either, Siddal preferred or believed more powerful as a means of expression, but Rossetti felt his loyalties were divided. Adept at both disciplines, early on in his career he vacillated between both and eventually chose painting because it would earn him a living, but he never abandoned poetry. Some of his earliest writings were translations of Dante's *La Vita Nuova* and he would have been aware of the controversy in which his father, a Dante scholar, was involved about whether Beatrice had ever been a real person or an allegorical abstraction of Love. He provided an answer in *Beata Beatrix* (1863–70), a study of Dante's Beloved at the moment of her death. In using Siddal posthumously as model for Beatrice, Rossetti, who had a keen interest in spiritualism, made a memorial to his Beloved whilst keeping her alive; at the same time, he used art to venture beyond the literary images handed down by Dante over which he had no control. In his early drawing *Dante Drawing an Angel on the First Anniversary of the Death of Beatrice* the poet wakens from a deep trance to find friends examining his picture, the idea of being both artist and poet physically encapsulated in Dante's sleep-state.[38]

Beatrice, the personification of a love that never dies but lives on in poetry and art, can be seen in the multiple images Rossetti made of Siddal. Real or not, Dante's Beatrice was not only his muse but also an idealized portrayal of love that goes beyond the purely physical to provide heavenly guidance and sanctuary. He gave her life-service in the belief that the capacity to love was an index of spiritual nobility, a sentiment perfectly in tune with the moralistic elements of nineteenth-century British society. Beatrice, the perfect unattainable woman, fits very well into the Victorian ideal of womanhood in which middle-class women especially were worshipped from afar and remained untainted by sexuality. Glorification of the female form was a central tenet of Pre-Raphaelitism and in this context Beatrice becomes an image dependent on Rossetti, but also the embodiment of his 'intelligence in love' and used as a way to reveal his understanding, thoughts and philosophies.[39] Siddal fulfilled the same role, and whereas it is important to avoid taking purely biographical readings from his work, Rossetti gave literal form to Beatrice by placing Siddal centre stage in a number of illustrations of the Beatrice narrative so that she came to personify both ideal love and its loss.

Siddal must surely have been aware of this conflation. In 1852, early in their relationship, she appears as an onlooker in *Beatrice Meeting Dante at the Marriage Feast, Denies him her Salutation*, prominent in cool green and blue, proud and withdrawn but in close proximity to the figure of Dante. There is great intensity in their shared gaze and upright posture, the bride and groom themselves relegated to the hazy margin of the picture; deliberately or otherwise Rossetti has identified Siddal with the love Dante had for Beatrice. In the same year he completed *Giotto Painting the Portrait of Dante*, and in it the latter is part of a group supposedly working together whilst his attention is actually firmly on the women walking below; Beatrice/Siddal is easily recognizable among them with her red hair and down-cast eyes. The watercolour *Dante Drawing an Angel on the First Anniversary of the Death of Beatrice* (1853) has Siddal again at its centre as Dante's future wife Gemma Donati, and three years later Rossetti executed *Dante's Dream at the time of Beatrice's Death*, which shows Love leading Dante to Beatrice's corpse as he leans in to kiss her farewell. When this was reworked in 1871 Beatrice was modelled by Jane Morris, but even before Siddal died in 1862 the latter had become Rossetti's new Beatrice, in unfinished cupboard panels entitled *Dantis Amor*; the relationships in the real triptych were apparently beginning to shift. *Beata Beatrix* is the idealization of the death of two women; the face and hair belong to Siddal but the pose is that of Beatrice at the end of *La Vita Nuova*. In each of its six versions there is the same necrophilial longing despite the implied predominance of sacred love over the purely physical.

The identity of Dante's Beatrice is unknown and she exists largely through him. Siddal has a meagre primary record so she been recognized largely by association with those artists she sat for, but she appears to have shunned any limelight this may have given her. The few personal accounts of her that survive speak of her cultivation of a mask of untouchability, of her being aloof and removed from those around her which gave a sense of her being merely an observer, a ghostly presence in a scene. All this could afford Siddal a 'Beatrice persona', but her poems and artwork tell a different story. Far from wanting adoration on a pedestal Siddal sought artistic independence from both Rossetti and John Ruskin, as the next chapter explains. Her art may illustrate macabre tales of tragic love in which her female characters die young but the latter are valiant and resourceful, politically focused and engaged in gender discourse, visible not for their beauty but for their strength of character, women who are making choices for themselves. The speakers in her poems are introspective and often obsessed with death, but they can also be secretive, bitter, ironic, mistrusting, railing against men who have betrayed the trust placed in them. Siddal may well have been aware of the persona imposed on her but that perspective isn't carried through into what she produced.

The House of Life celebrates the sacred relationship between Lover and Beloved in language that is often evasive and which defies meaning, so that first and foremost it creates generalized visual images of female beauty akin to the many representations of Siddal, Cornforth, Morris and others who become 'real' presences in the poem. There is nothing to attribute individual sonnets to any one woman even if there is differentiation between love in its various forms. Given the sensational narratives bound up in its emergence it is hard not to personalize the sequence; the intention, however, is through it to explore the duality and significance of love as professed by Rossetti and echoed by Siddal's poems, not mine it for any specific reference to Siddal in particular. The complexities of its evolution are unimportant here; suffice to say that the 102 sonnets of the 1881 edition are not in chronological order of writing so cannot be related to particular events or people and should not be used to imply emotional change in the poet over time.[40] The sonnets selected have been chosen on the basis of their visionary language, images of water and fire and metaphors of music, magnetism and dreams, and to avoid the sense of loss that for whatever reason pervades the later stages of the sequence.

Concepts of beauty

An obsession with the nature of femininity and womanhood pervades Pre-Raphaelite painting and indeed the term is now synonymous with a specific feminine appearance: long loose (often red) hair, large soulful eyes, elongated skewed neck, full fleshy lips, and bodies draped in unstructured clothing as befitting a classical or medieval backdrop. This conception was revolutionary and needs to be set in context, a period of rapidly shifting mores and morals in which traditional ideology was challenged and reworked. In Pre-Raphaelite art opposing but complementary images of female sexuality and sanctity reflect differing types of women and the changing relationships between the sexes that in part define the Victorian age as a whole. The nineteenth century was an extraordinary period of socio-economic revolution that altered patterns of work and family life and shifted attitudes towards women who were themselves beginning to explore expanded roles. This cultural climate encouraged varied perceptions of women that both drove and reflected the philosophy of the Brotherhood. Their women were virgins and fallen angels, witches and stunners, reflections of a predominantly middle-class society in which females could be put on a pedestal but also (not always metaphorically) imprisoned and subjugated. These talismanic images were symbols of eroticism, of male desire, rather than depictions of women that most would recognize and it is this objectification that Siddal rejects in 'The Lust of the Eyes'. The Pre-Raphaelites idolized women and worshipped their beauty, and with the advent of cheaper printing and the burgeoning number of public art galleries representing mid-century civic pride, their paintings and drawings facilitated female deification and the establishment of a so-called 'religion of beauty', with Rossetti as its high priest. In this complex sexual relationship, the male is enslaved by womanly beauty but the woman only exerts this power because he is looking at her. The picture is therefore a comment about visual beauty as well as exemplifying the visually beautiful.

Rossetti's pictures of women immortalize more than their appearance. Excellence, love, sensuality, and their power over men are all enshrined in his work, but it is the sheer physicality of his images that creates their impact. This is partly the result of new techniques developed in the 1860s whereby narrative or dramatic incident is avoided and replaced by a concentration on beautiful paint handling, especially of flesh. Small brushstrokes or stippling and purity of colour typical of early Pre-Raphaelite work were abandoned in favour of layered, deeply lustrous hues that allowed the blending of multiple nuances of tone. Rossetti copied rapid flesh painting from the Venetian Old Masters like Titian and echoed the flesh tints in hair, robes and backgrounds. Like theirs, his portraits are half-length and draw attention to areas of sensuously exposed flesh around the shoulders. There are fewer specific textual references and this allows the woman's eyes to begin to tell their own tales even when the face is otherwise expressionless. The viewer is immediately drawn to interact with the subject even though her distracted gaze is frustratingly not focused upon them. The richly envisioned and often symbolic details of these paintings give them a powerfully close proximity. There is a sense that the viewer is being touched emotionally, bewitched even, and that barriers are somehow being broken down.[41]

Definitions of beauty necessarily vary, and some contemporary critics failed to appreciate the magnetic appeal of such works. In May 1879 the *Illustrated London News*, referring to Burne-Jones, remarked that 'this supersensuousness was derived from Mr Dante Rossetti's queer idea of womankind – with hollow cheeks and square jawbones, necks like swans with goitre ... lips ... "stung", therefore swollen, with kisses'.[42] Placed within the wider contemporary debate about the distinction between 'legitimate' culture and pornography, between the nude as art or object of erotic arousal, this judgement is interesting. Obscenity laws had been operating since 1824, but the Obscene Publications Act of 1859 was the first to deal with pictorial and literary pornography. It would remain effective for the next one hundred years, and the prudery it encouraged provided a thin veneer of hypocrisy under which was a seething underworld of sexual activity of every variety, including prostitution. As if to emphasize the double standard, it was considered admissible to draw and sell images of classical nudes, which could account for the popularity of studies of Venus, the beautiful Grecian form rather than the immoral pagan character, undertaken by two artistic circles associated with the Pre-Raphaelites in the 1860s.[43] These were distinguished on the basis of flesh painting; the Holland Park circle favoured the use of just one other colour as per classical tradition, but the Cheyne Walk circle of which Rossetti was a part called for flesh to be strictly and specifically true in its rendering. This group venerated colour as a sensual element and risked affronting those who saw the latter as defining fleshliness of body as opposed to the female soul, an inward sign of her beauty according to Rossetti.[44] He actually did very few even partial nudes; beauty for him encompassed not just the female face and form but the textiles with which it could be draped, however suggestive or insubstantial that drapery was. For Rossetti, face and form had a central place and profound symbolic significance, suggestive of great value. If the mouth was the most sensuous part of the face the eyes were the most spiritual, filled with infinite and perfect love that elevated the woman to something divine.[45] This went beyond cultural-historical interests to the inspiration that comes from a beloved woman; the face held an occult message, and even averted eyes could hint at mysteries therein. This could explain his tendency to focus on bodies which are elusive, ghostly or inaccessible, and to show them mediated through mirrors, corpses or shadows.[46] Siddal is a case in point.

However, it is also true that Rossetti made some of his painted women immediate and tactile, and this offended some Victorians. He intended to represent extremes of love and beauty, complex subjects, as Swinburne explained in article notes for a Royal Academy exhibition in 1868: 'Beauty may be strange, quaint, terrible, may play with pain as with pleasure, handle a horror till she leave it a delight; she forsakes not such among her servants as Webster or Goya'.[47] Rossetti can surely be implicated here, for he was not idealizing physical beauty but confronting it at its most intense, which led some, including Ruskin before 1858, to conclude that such close observance of female physicality was unnatural, irreligious and bordering on eroticism.[48] Victorian sexuality and obsession with birth and fertility, never freely discussed but always there in scientific and medical argument, is now known to have been a much more dominant discourse than previously thought, but it still needs to be placed alongside the repression that stifled desire and its expression.[49] Paradoxically, this merely generated yet more ferment which produced a whole host of binaries that clustered around the quarrel between those who would control sex in bed and in print and those who would allow it freedom. A new concern with respectability developed with the emergence of an enlarged middle class, evangelical tendencies and the attack on working-class libertinism and profligacy. This Puritan re-awakening produced calls for emotional restraint in public and a limit to sex within the bounds of marriage, but it was answered in the arts by graphic exploration of adultery, prostitution, same-sex love, and a particular fascination with love and sex after death. In this context Siddal's exhumation takes on a different meaning, paving the way for heavenly reunion and passion. Dead women become alluring objects of desire, Rossetti's *Beata Beatrix* being a prime example. Aestheticized representations such as this took away sexual agency but still confused the viewer and further stimulated the controversy about the boundary between art and voyeurism.[50]

Rossetti envisioned women in several ways, and individual works could contain opposite types. He used them to personify ideal love, female excellence, sensuality and beauty, and the power of woman over man, and put in this order his many drawings and paintings show a development in his philosophy and creative thinking. *Ecce Ancilla Domini!/The Annunciation* (1849–50) uses traditional iconography to create a modern image at a time when literal interpretation of the Bible was being questioned in some circles. The Virgin is seen crouching against a wall on a simple bed, being presented with a lily by the Angel Gabriel. The room is cell-like and ascetic, with minimum detail, to focus attention on her response. Devout Christina Rossetti was used as model and William Michael was Gabriel. Three lilies embroidered on a pennant are echoed in the real flowers the angel carries, one of which is angled at her womb, possibly to suggest conception.[51] Mary is stunned and pensive, recoiling from sexual advance, and barely woken from her dream. She is girlish and entirely human, not splendid or enthroned, her halo the only sign of divinity. She is diminutive compared with the elevated Gabriel, but still dominant. The simple colour scheme uses bold primaries sparsely: red for the Passion, royal blue in the wall hangings to signify her status as Queen of Heaven, gold, and white for purity. The overall whiteness of the composition evinces a strange, almost empty feel and it is this rather than the humble setting that challenges the viewer. The picture was widely criticized at the time, paradoxically, for its mundanity and its imputations of Catholicism, hence the adoption of its English title.

The emotion lacking in *Ecce Ancilla Domini!* is clearly apparent in *Beata Beatrix* (1864). This representation of ideal love (figure 7), a conflation of Beatrice and Siddal, blends the physical with the religious and is more interpretation than illustration. The scene is muted, dimly lit and ethereal, a visionary portrait of Beatrice in a trance or sudden spiritual transformation. She sees heaven even with her eyes closed in a moment of religious or sexual ecstasy, and there are many symbolic references. The bird is a messenger of death carrying a poppy (Siddal died from an overdose of an opiate)

7 Dante Gabriel Rossetti, *Beata Beatrix*, c.1863–68, oil on canvas

to drop into her open hands; there is a number nine on the illuminated sundial and Dante died at nine on the ninth of June 1290. The figure of Love, startlingly clad in red, carries a lamp with a dying flame; Beatrice is dying as time runs out. She has a slightly open mouth as she takes her last breath and a column of gold light pours

8 Elizabeth Siddal, *Self Portrait*, 1853–54, oil on canvas

down to envelop her head. Whether Beatrice or Siddal, this figure is venerated and mystical, already remote and other-worldly but still generating warmth, very different from the Siddal in *Self Portrait* (1853–54) (figure 8). This was her only venture into oil on canvas and is starkly direct, unglamorous and untouchable. Her eyes are challenging but veiled and heavily lidded, the hair pulled back uncompromisingly from her face. Beatrice is blind but sees a vision of something divine while being watched over by Love and Dante whereas Siddal is unflinching and unemotional, all-seeing without giving herself away. This self-portrait gives a rare opportunity to appreciate how women imagined themselves whilst being the objects of male desire.

Bocca Baciata (1859) is a very different proposition. The first done using the new techniques of flesh painting, it is a small but striking bust-length picture of a voluptuous, glowing, physical woman with Cornforth as model, richly decorated with flowers and jewels. There is no implied narrative or moral commentary, although the prominent apple could signify Eve. Its textual reference is simply a quotation from Boccaccio: 'A kissed mouth loses no savour, but rather renews itself like the moon.' The face tantalizes and excites, the hands are slightly extended towards the viewer as they play with a lock of hair, and the gown is unfastened to give a glimpse of chemise. Colours are deep and vibrant and the flesh has a rustic, healthy sheen. Cornforth also modelled for Lady Lilith (1867), the original femme fatale, the embodiment of the struggle between two aspects of womanhood: beauty and devilry. Here she is a menacing figure and the work contains what may be read as references to Siddal and her death, extending its dualist inspiration; candles are snuffed out and a red silken cord on the wrist is echoed in a large red poppy, reminiscent of opium. Hebrew mythology has Lilith as the murderer of children and Siddal reputedly miscarried as a result of laudanum. Thus, Siddal is not only the bride of death in Beata Beatrix but, at a time when use of birth control was widely considered to be defying God's will, also a child-killing demon. Put very simplistically, Siddal the addict had aborted their child, and Rossetti was venting his anger towards his late wife.[52]

Astarte Syriaca (1877) (figure 9) moves the physicality of Bocca Baciata and Lady Lilith into a new direction and represents the power of a beautiful woman to enslave a man. The female figure is seen almost in entirety, tightly encased in a frame that makes it appear yet more powerful and intimidating. The rich colours of Bocca Baciata are replaced by a more subdued green/blue/grey palette and the paint finish is more matt and crumbly, which helps to achieve a sense of masculinity within an obviously feminine form in which the eyes and lips are deliberately over-emphasized. The face is extraordinary and memorable but not coarse or crude, the treatment dramatic but finely judged and three-dimensional.[53] The mood of the picture is threatening and quite malign. The two

Siddal, Dante Gabriel Rossetti and the duality of love 43

9 Dante Gabriel Rossetti, *Astarte Syriaca*, 1877, oil on canvas

messengers carrying torches behind the central figure are silhouetted against a setting sun and a rising moon, but elsewhere their loose dark green garments merge into the sombre background from which the ancient goddess appears to be striding towards the viewer.

There is no equivalent to these powerful and deeply emotive images of women in Siddal's artistic catalogue. Few of her pictures focus on a sole figure, and almost all of them have an implied narrative, usually with a textual reference. She may interpret such a reference in a unique or obscure way but she rarely embarks on a purely imaginative drawing. Interestingly, the one exception to this is *Lovers Listening to Music* (1854) (figure 10), a pen and ink composition very similar in technique to *Pippa Passes*. A man and a woman sit physically entwined on a bench listening to music played by two dark-skinned women. The child standing close to them could be Cupid; its expression is certainly detached and soulful

10 Elizabeth Siddal, *Lovers Listening to Music*, 1854, pen and brown ink

and it appears to go unnoticed by all other characters. Compared with a painting such as *Clerk Saunders*, for example, this depiction of love is far more natural and uncontrived. The main protagonists are similar in appearance to Siddal and Rossetti and W. M. Rossetti believed its inspiration was not literary but a cliff walk near Hastings the two were fond of.[54] If true, this could be Siddal's only truly imaginative piece. None of her women are shown because they are beautiful; they are there because, literally or figuratively, they illustrate a moment of crisis or great emotion. Their faces are a canvas on which the latter can be drawn, and Siddal often does this in very few strokes. She appears not to be confident with anatomical detail so bodies are stiff and completely covered, and quite androgynous in form. Few men appear in her art, and female gender is mainly differentiated via clothes and hair. *Lovers Listening to Music* and *Pippa Passes* are the exceptions, having a greater degree of characterization in all their figures and a diversification in the female form that suggests the power of female sexual attraction, even beauty, over men.

Physical and erotic love in Rossetti's poetry

In his poems Rossetti explores love in various forms: religious, filial, chivalric and platonic, as well as physical and erotic. The principal concern in *The House of Life* will be with the interwoven strands of physical and religious love, but the sequence as a whole also embraces love as an over-arching concept. Siddal does not engage with chivalric or platonic love; her poems make no allowance for relationships devoid of sexual attraction and desire. The friendship she had with Swinburne for example has no match in her writing and, with the exception of various sketches of the Madonna and Child, all her artwork refers in some way to close, even passionate sexual relationships even if they no longer exist in earthly form. Siddal's poems can be sexually ambivalent but even in their condensed form their fervour is clear, especially when sexual love is reworked as the longing for divine love. However, unlike *Pippa Passes*, none of her poems comment specifically on contemporary concerns about women and sex, sexuality or marriage and even in this drawing her opinion is given in the context of a very different situation, one lacking the economic and moral pressures of a rapidly changing and complex industrial society. It is left to the viewer to decide to what extent Siddal empathizes with the prostitutes; Pippa is not shunning them as she walks past, but neither is she addressing them, in condescension or out of simple charity.

In the mid-nineteenth century prostitution was a question of social purity not just respectability. It was tackled by reformers like Dickens and William Gladstone who aimed to limit its public appearance and bring sex workers back to other employment. They advocated medicals for prostitutes to prevent the spread of disease, and believed prostitution was a given, to be channelled and controlled. Taking a very different approach were the moralists, whose voice in the end prevailed. They organized mass movements, which included women, to put their agenda ahead of the socio-political one, to condemn not to regulate the practice. Men were encouraged to refrain from fornication and to limit sex to marriage, and women were led to believe they were so free from desire that they could largely be celibate unless it was for the purposes of procreation or pleasing their husband. This perplexed, skewed thinking about sexuality informed poetry and art so that, for example, the subjects of Rossetti's sensual portraits in oil and poetry became more warm and desirous when placed out of reach.[55] In *Aurora Leigh* Marian Erle regains social acceptability along with respectable family life after her seduction and descent into (albeit enforced) prostitution, and in 'A Castaway' (1870) by Augusta Webster an upper-class prostitute expresses sympathy for the suffering of poorer streetworkers. Rossetti empathizes with a 'fallen woman' in *Jenny* which according to his brother was the most important poem exhumed in 1869 for which he had no complete copy 'already in his hands, or indeed any example at all'.[56] This is a dramatic monologue by a studious man on whose knee the eponymous woman has fallen asleep, a rambling meditation on her physical charms as well as his varying attitudes towards her and her 'profession' in general. Jenny is depicted as a besmirched but still desirable beauty who deserves a moment's rest from the men who have made her a whore and from the women who combine to pass judgement on her without knowing her particular circumstances. *Jenny* is a cipher for a social problem, not just a depiction of one individual. On this occasion she is allowed to sleep all night but she still gets paid. The narrator puts a cushion under her head and coins into her golden hair as he leaves, aware that despite his brief empathetic attachment to this woman he has entered as expected into her commercial world, one he can afford to slip away from when she cannot.

The House of Life as published in 1881 consists of 102 Petrarchan sonnets plus an introductory sonnet, and is a perplexing mix of love, mysticism, Dante-esque love, exultation, natural phenomena, deep despair and autobiography. It is divided into two parts, 'Youth and Change' and 'Change and Fate' and whereas groups of sonnets adhering to one theme tend to be grouped together, in the second part there are 'rogues' that are miscellaneous and individual. There are many eccentric rhymes and obscure phraseology abounds, and the sequence is deliberately obfuscated. It is Rossetti's most profound experience, an accumulation of his deepest personal emotions and aspiration, and if only earthly love is identified within it then it tells of feelings for one woman replaced by those for another, misery before mutual admission of love, loneliness and remorse after the first love dies, new passion then its decline once unreciprocated. However, if read as an autobiography of thoughts and moods then it becomes a developing commentary on his life and a retrospective of what he would have liked it to be.[57] Love is the centre of secular human life and the arts that shape and communicate it, but secular love cannot exist without the divine that elevates and sanctifies it, so religious love plays a more dominant role in this interpretation. 'Youth and Change' focuses on the love found in the ideal Beloved, its manifestations and its permanence and employs rich mythological and religious imagery. The speaker wonders how his Beloved feels about him and how he can be worthy of her, but gradually his contentment fades and there emerges a latent but inherent fear that love may die, a dreadful prospect as without love life is worthless, so is like death. The possibility of love being able to conquer death and survive earthly decay becomes a preoccupation. Part II is more reflective of the experiences of love and begins to accept grief as a form of inspiration. The search for love, hope and beauty is still evident but there is now also a concern for the poet's immortal soul, possibly in preparation for Rossetti's own death. The development of this philosophy occupies *The House of Life* in its entirety but it has a parallel in microcosm in individual Siddal poems, especially where they end in an acceptance of death as an answer to grief, or a yearning for religious rather than sexual ecstasy. Siddal has the ability to condense conflicting emotions into a very few lines, so that love can be erotic, isolating, savoured and regretted, almost simultaneously.

Rossetti offers himself as a poet of heterosexual fascination, mixing sonnets about two women, Siddal and Morris, but he is also making it clear that it is his consciousness, not just a relationship, that he wants love to build, because love engenders self-awareness, so attuned is it to personal thoughts and associations.[58] This has to be a symbiotic process, and indeed in the opening sonnets mature sexual love is shown as a reciprocal event. Absolute communicative responsiveness is found in sight, sound and touch in a shared language of physical intimacy which renders even articulate speech unnecessary. Sonnet 15 'The Birth-Bond' personifies love as the most perfect contact with another human, the epitome of kindred spirituality in which language interchange becomes a melody, something all lyric poetry should aspire to.[59] Love is an all-embracing concept that manifests itself in a new symbol that combines three constituents identified as Christ, The Romantic Lover and Dante. Christ is a sign for love with humanity, the Romantic Lover is an emblem with potential for transcendence, and Dante a motif for Love personified.[60] Rossetti's love exists in the speaker's Beloved and appears in their love for one another. It is pure because it contains an element of divinity, making its sexual expression pure also. Indeed, Christianity is implicit in the whole sequence and Revelation takes place through the rebirth that is death. How the reader reacts to any of the constituents depends on their own perspective, but it avoids blasphemy, because it directly asks for 'Inclusiveness'. This is a Rossettian concept that meant openness to differences of belief and interpretation in the self and in the poetic text, very important in *The House of Life* because it clears the way for more open-ended or acceptable readings.[61] In opening up a contemporary context for more liberal discourse Rossetti was broadening the definition of love to include aspects that would provoke public controversy. It is perhaps not surprising then that following the attack made by Robert Buchanan on the so-called 'Fleshly School of Poetry', in the later sonnets love also takes on the mantle of loss, disillusionment and despair, a connection frequently made in Siddal's poems.[62] The fifty-three sonnets written after 1872 lack the moments of great joy and positive images of love that typify those included in *Poems*. There are fewer questions and more statements, biblical references and pronouncements. The 1881 version claims to be complete but this is still very open to conjecture because of its rejection of linearity and the unknown relationships of individual sonnets with the whole sequence. Rossetti gives no guide so the reader decides the role and place of each one and can take them out at random or for a purpose.[63] Self-determination, permission to isolate or extract individual sonnets from the sequence, is part of 'Inclusiveness' but it has an additional benefit; it facilitates their reading alongside Siddal's poems that were never intended to be part of a unified whole.

Sexuality is all-pervasive in Rossetti's poems, a primal force and an integral aspect of the human self that is essentially good. In art it is exemplified in *The Blessed Damozel*, dead but still 'fleshly' in form and desires. This concept of sexuality is multi-faceted, encompassing the ideal and the actual, the moral and the malign, the secret and the public. It emanates not just from his experience and emotion, because Rossetti wants to make readers reflect on their own sexuality and face up to their own sexual needs.[64] Neither is it 'hidden' in historic figures; divergent and contradictory attitudes to sexuality are shown through different types of woman, meaning that a man can be drawn to the bodily comforts of one while searching for another of beautiful soul who will offer salvation. This in turn questions whether consummation of true love can ever be sinful. The act of physical love is being defended, not denied, preserving its righteousness rather than its innocence.[65] Sexuality is the centre of identity and central to the discovery of selfhood. Although in *The House of Life* it has a manifestly heterosexual orientation this is not essential if the concept of 'Inclusiveness' is upheld. Rossetti also articulates it publicly, and in the Victorian context this appeared non-human and therefore deeply disturbing.

Religious love

Victorians looked to religion and science for opinions on sexuality and as the moralist language of religion permeated all aspects of society repressive attitudes to fornication were readily found in the Bible. Conversely, they also asked for religious authority to adopt a more liberal position; the Brownings, for example, had a loving, sexual marriage within a general Christian context. Rossetti's poems work in between, bringing together carnal desires and religious language and iconography in a way that typifies the post-Darwinian period of philosophical re-alignment. *The Origin of Species* was published in 1859 and almost overnight contributed to an erosion of faith which in turn ushered in a new age where it was no longer possible to dissent and not threaten the superstructure. This is analogous with a new philosophy in art whereby ambitious and selfish individualism was justified and innovation was advantageous. Victorian histories of art were therefore written as a progressive sequence in which stronger or more original artists supplanted the weaker or obsolete.[66] Not everything in the arts was so cut-throat however; *The House of Life* is arguably free from any predatory cruel understanding of sexuality because Rossetti's lovers are fighting the same battle for social and sexual equality. There is no social history in the sequence as their world is too internal; its preoccupation is with survival in the face of death, and the survival of identity amid upheaval and change.[67] This reading of the sonnets allows them to sit comfortably in a shifting cultural context, and it suggests parallels with Siddal's poems that are similarly devoid of socio-historic orientation but still press for the recognition of a new identity or autonomy in the face of loss or bewildering transformation.

In this period of unprecedented questioning of established norms, the concept of 'Inclusiveness' had appeal. It begins in the eponymous Sonnet 63 of *The House of Life* which expounds a vision in which no one view of the world can claim primacy and one thing has different faces for different people according to different conditions. The sonnet implies acceptance of a state of fluidity in which it is important to address different perspectives and to try to comprehend possibilities even if they are alien and disturbing, an ethic and a method Rossetti embraces.[68] As such 'Inclusiveness' can be seen as an extrapolation of 'negative capability', whereby uncertainty was perceived as a positive attribute. This suggests that any image, either visual or verbal, can be capable of evoking a series of significances depending on the life experience of the individual, and this could be the key to reading Siddal's seemingly over-simplistic poems; their meaning may not be as important as the responses they draw out, especially when sudden intense feelings of anger or desperation illuminate the text. Rossetti realizes that what he writes will resonate differently with different people; he simply asks that readers reflect on their own beliefs and accept the fact that his poems may present other readings to other people. Such a process allows contradiction and fusion which is positive in the search for self-knowledge.[69]

During the 1840s a debate about religious observation broke out in Britain, which would act as a backdrop to the scientific challenges posed by theories of evolution and natural selection. The Anglican Church was unsettled by competing Evangelical, Tractarian and broad church factions, and was facing an external assault from revived Catholicism and non-conformism. Although the arguments were rooted in doctrine they were felt in material culture and the paraphernalia of worship, such as vestments and church architecture. Protestant artists were tasked with reviving religious art without falling back on idealizing Catholic conventions and emphasizing moral subjects as key agents of spiritual regeneration. The Pre-Raphaelite response was to combine the iconographic language of Renaissance Christian painting with didactic qualities, a decidedly artistic rather than a devout strategy but one which would encourage the audience to accept the new empirical Pre-Raphaelite methodology and acute observation of nature along with more familiar codes.[70] Personal religious affiliations were varied: James Collinson was a practising Roman Catholic, Millais an Anglican, Brown a Broad Church supporter of Christian Socialism, Hunt a religious intellectual who espoused all three sets of beliefs and argued for the harmonization of science and scripture. Rossetti was much more of an agnostic, with an interest in spiritualism despite his High Church family background. Regardless of individual creed the Pre-Raphaelites put Christ at the top of their List of 'Immortals', but most names on the list are secular, an indication that human endeavour is considered more worthy of worship.[71]

From the 1820s onwards the Bible began to be seen as much poetry or myth, part of the literature of the world, as a record of Divinity. Christ's holiness and sanctity were being undermined by a recognition of him as an inspirational orator and a man, to the extent that biographies of Jesus appeared accompanied by calls for the scriptures to be read as a document. to be questioned, taking into account their fallible and fragmentary sourcing. Ruskin is quoted as saying that Rossetti believed the Old and New Testaments, along with *Vita Nuova* and Malory's *Morte d'Arthur* were the greatest poems he knew – another indication of his complex, indefinite beliefs.[72] As a child he attended church with his mother whose background was Evangelical, but he stopped this practice at 14 when he went to art school. His father was a Catholic politically opposed to the papacy so neither son was pressed to go for confirmation; William Michael subsequently rejected all revealed religion completely. When Anglo-Catholic fervour swept the parish where the family worshipped and it became a Tractarian conversion centre, spearheading a new religion of asceticism, self-sacrifice and repentance, all the Rossetti women espoused it with ardour, Maria becoming an Anglican Sister. Christina's faith was the strongest force in her life and hundreds of devotional poems bear witness to its depth. Earthly love could not compete and in her writing Rossetti envisions herself as the wife of Christ, albeit in a marriage where sexual union is replaced by the divine. A woman needed to be patient and passive, until Christ called her into an ideal relationship, a union of souls in which physical desire is transferred into fervent spiritual aspiration. Despite the Christian association there is overt eroticism in descriptions of this union. In 'The heart knoweth its own bitterness' (1857) the language of scripture refers repeatedly to the human body and physical experience and the longing for Christ takes on a decidedly worldly edge.[73] As a wife a woman could not give her undivided attention to Christ, so solitariness was therefore central to Rossetti and her poetic identity, a feminist revision of cultural expectations of a woman at this time. Rossetti elevated unattached women from being unfortunate spinsters to privileged individuals, a premise that lies at the heart of 'Repining' (1847) in which the heroine finally sees that whereas a future in company can be very bleak, alone she can control her experiences without potentially destructive attachment.[74] Hemans, Greenwell and Ingelow also wrote of their desire to fuse human and divine love, but there were anxieties; religious and sexual love inspired similarly deep emotional responses and implied a patriarchy that was being increasingly challenged. Rossetti and Barrett Browning faced a dichotomy when the soul is represented as female and Christ is a maternal, caring figure yet all still readily submit to God the Father, and organized religion sanctions the acceptance of the secondary nature of the female position.[75]

Rossetti was not drawn to Tractarianism, but neither was he an atheist; his brother agreed that he was not a strict doctrinal Christian but, like Dante, he 'had an earnest reverence for a Christian ideal and a delight in Christian legend and symbol'.[76] In 1881 Rossetti reportedly asked for absolution whilst in a deep depression and failing health. This seeking of religious solace rather mystified his brother who believed him totally sceptical about many alleged facts and averse to formulaic dogmas or discussion of them, even if he had a deep reverence for the person of Christ, albeit alongside a fascination for 'the marvellous and the supernatural'.[77] In a letter to William Allingham in 1856 Rossetti refers to spiritualism at the Howitt household being 'in the ascendant', a 'modified form' of his own thinking about it.[78] W. M. Rossetti commented that he was aware of his scorn about spiritualism at that time but that 'in later years (beginning, say in 1864) he believed in it not a little'.[79] This would tally with reports of several séances attended by both men between 1865 and 1870, at one of which Dante Rossetti apparently called up Siddal's spirit by table-turning.[80] Rather conveniently perhaps, Cornforth became a medium in 1865, conducting a session the following year at which Siddal apparently reassured Rossetti she was at peace, approved of his art, was his constant companion and happy to give her blessing to his relationship with Fanny.[81] Henry Treffry Dunn, Rossetti's studio and household assistant, said his employer had an interest in spiritualism and mesmerism, attributed to early influences from his father when he was working on alchemy, freemasonry and Swedenborganism.[82]

In the nineteenth century mesmeric power was also known as magnetism, a forerunner of hypnosis, and séances were held in which eye-to-eye gaze induced a coma or trance during which the mesmerist speaks the subject's thoughts. Such events were also considered medically therapeutic as pain relief, and Rossetti attended one in August 1854 to have a formal magnetic cure to help insomnia and pain in the limbs. This neatly fits the Rossettian idea of woman as a magnetic force drawing in the poet/artist so he can depict her.[83] Rossetti's interest in Swedenborg again appears quite pertinent. In a letter to Jane Morris he refers to Sonnet 58 which opens with the lines: 'If to grow old in heaven, is to grow young / (As the seer saw and said)'. The seer was Swedenborg, and 'the saying a very fine one'.[84] Swedenborg believed God was not an ethereal spirit but Divine Man, and that sexual love led to and was essential for Divine Love, sentiments that are likely to have chimed with Rossetti's own. In the absence of religious faith love was the substitute that lay the ground for what he artistically and poetically rendered. Love informs all and is beyond the poet's self; without love his artistry is 'soulless self-reflections of man's skill', as Sonnet 74 has it. Love, reflected in and from the eyes of the poet/self enables the soul, which is revealed through both the poet/artist and their subject. Artist and subject are therefore indistinguishable, making Siddal more than her physical self; she is the 'meaning' of the many drawings Rossetti undertook of her.[85] He imagined Siddal waiting for him in heaven where lovers could be reunited. Earthly love was just a premonition of sexual ecstasy there and love with God would supersede married love, the theme of Siddal's 'Early Death' and 'Lord May I Come'.

Predictably, little is known about Siddal's religious faith, but some deductions can be made. The Sheffield obituary refers to her father having been for many years leading singer of Congregational churches in Sheffield and London, so by inference she was brought up in a non-conformist environment.[86] She also produced a series of religious sketches that may have been intended as a sequence for the life of Christ in keeping with the mood of Anglo-Catholic revival in the 1850s. Only two of the proposed watercolour series were completed: *The Virgin and Child with Angel* (*c.*1855–57) in which the angel holding a musical instrument stands to the right of a seated Virgin who is looking out from the stable to the landscape beyond, and an unusual *Madonna and Child* (figure 11) showing Christ as an infant with startling red hair and dark purplish garments standing on his mother's knees and gesturing outwards from a gloomy room to a verdant garden. These pictures do not prove Siddal was a religious believer (Rossetti was undertaking a similar project at the same time), rather they indicate a commitment to the religious themes that were an important element of Pre-Raphaelite art at this stage in its development. The subjects may also have been chosen to appeal to Ruskin who in 1855 bought Siddal's entire output. As W. M. Rossetti put it: 'I never perceived her to have any religion; but a perusal of some of her few poems may fairly lead to the inference that she was not wanting in a devotional habit of feeling'.[87] Siddal keeps religious references largely ambiguous, private and self-centred; belief provides hope that the next life will be better than the current bleak and demoralizing existence. This contrasts sharply with Hemans who used her obvious Christian faith for political purposes, to validate the role of women, and women poets in particular. Her later poems move her poetics on from the affectional poetry that reflected the mild piety of a lady of her class to accommodate a new specific vocation in which she adopts prophetic qualities usually ascribed to male Romantics, giving her a new feminine calling. 'A Poet's Dying Hymn' (1834) says the poet is called by God and therefore has a divine warrant. Religion gives transcendence to domestic subjects such as the suffering of women both in public and private, or being a Protestant in the reign of Queen Mary ('The English Martyrs') or dealing with family illness ('Flowers and Music in a Room of Sickness'). The identification of poetry with Christ's suffering elevated it beyond mere self-display and focused attention on female characters in New and Old Testaments. In her *Fifteen Female Characters of Scripture* sonnet sequence (1833) most portrayals are of pious domestic martyrs like Martha and Mary, sisters of Lazarus, but Hemans balances this with Mary Magdalene, the sexually powerful repentant sinner, a character closer to Siddal's portraits of flawed, albeit unidentifiable and non-religious women.[88]

11 Elizabeth Siddal, *Madonna and Child (The Nativity)*, date unknown, watercolour

The Victorian sonnet sequence

Very few major poets in Britain have not attempted sonnets, the form offering precision, balance and flexibility. Narrativizing sonnets in particular, especially those about love, have a strong pedigree that has flourished at different times whilst falling out of fashion at others, so *The House of Life* can be seen as constituting part of a varying tradition whilst making a decisive individual contribution to sonnet development. Victorian artists constructed an ideal version of womanhood to involve sensation and an appetite for the fleshly alongside purity, and this ethical dilemma had a parallel in poetry. The pull between sensual and ideal occupied Victorian poetry of love and marriage, and the sonnet sequence permitted writers to enter into the debate with extended narrative and more drama. Each sonnet was perfect in itself, but as 'sonnet-stanzas' they were mingled together to allow an over-arching theme or narrative to unfold.[89] Nineteenth-century female sonneteers were drawn to the form and exploited it to give themselves a unique poetic and political voice and, at the same time, made a distinct contribution to its development. From 1818 Hemans translated a number of sonnets by earlier European poets including six on the theme of Italian nationalism and patriotism in 1821. She later returned to the genre, publishing several sequences, most notably *Fifteen Female Characters of Scripture* (1833) which depicted biblical women such as Ruth and Mary Magdalene in conflicted circumstances or suffering. Sonnet writing was still a gendered process especially when writing about desire, but as Petrarchanism was the language of desire and it carried literary authority it was seen as a way of making respectable the claim of women to public admission of sexual feelings, and poetic recognition.[90] Elizabeth Barrett Browning and Christina Rossetti were among a number of women poets who wrote about and with desiring voices by cloaking them with Christian spirituality so that in their hands the sonnet became a legitimate vehicle for self-expression, especially when the poet was skilled at hiding or putting on a mask of disguise. The sonnet was particularly suited to this because its restricted form and economical language allows the omission of salient details. Likewise, imagery and metaphor are used in this type of lyric to put over complex emotional messages, and these puzzling references are not easily decoded by the reader.[91]

Elizabeth Barrett Browning's *Sonnets from the Portuguese* (published 1850) was one of the first love-sequences. It also completes itself and is one of the few to end happily so is part of an ongoing process of innovation in form and content. The deliberately misleading title veils poems of an intensely personal nature, written before her marriage in 1846. They were not intended for publication, an interesting parallel with Siddal, and Barrett Browning's letters reveal she also hid other poems in her childhood crib to keep the occupation secret.[92] The title is a form of disguise, a purloining of a traditional literary form to make the female voice and desiring self more intense and muscular. The forty-four poems form a narrative, a development of the speaker's perception of the relationship with her Beloved, and they contain multiple metaphors for love and her experience of it. She initially believes herself unworthy of his love but nursed by its health-giving properties she seeks and gains the perfect partnership based on physical and spiritual equality. The apparent inevitability of the equation of perfection with marriage has led critics to question whether *Sonnets from the Portuguese* was a stereotypical chronicle of growth towards acceptance of a conventional relationship, or a female poet's pioneering struggle to find not only a poetic voice but public acceptance of her right to an autonomous sexual persona.[93] On balance, the conquering power of love brings both surrender and liberation in these poems, an indication that the sequence is not the inaugurator of a new tradition but a memorable moment in a developing process whereby the sonnet increasingly affords the female poet a specific, significant and compelling voice.

Christina Rossetti adopted a very different stance in *Mona Innominata* (1881), in which she argues for the expressive rights of unmarried women in poetry, that is, the ability to express sexuality and the freedom to be undignified if feminine sexuality needs it.[94] The female object of this sequence speaks back to her idealizing male lover, so has her own voice as both subject and object. She is no longer, like Beatrice or Petrarch's Laura, someone eulogized from a distance, or after death. This inverts power relations between

Lover and Beloved, and calls for the equality if not supremacy of the female voice, so it is interesting Rossetti does this in Petrarchan form. In fact, Rossetti stresses the precedent by having fourteen stanzas broken into an 'octave' and a 'sestet', but at a point where promises to love unstintingly are broken by a recognition that her lover's poetics is outstripping hers, despite her greater skill as a writer. The sonnet-lady is a poet, to give her the necessary voice, but, in another bit of irony, at the end she is doomed to be elderly and alone because as the 'I' of a Petrarchan sonnet her Beloved is unattainable.[95] Self-determination is upheld however; the speaker chooses to surrender her Beloved to God's love and to immerse herself in the same, working on the belief that human love is mutable and transient and therefore inferior, a suggestion familiar in *The House of Life*.

Quite different again from *Sonnets from the Portuguese* and *Mona Innominata* is Augusta Webster's *Mother and Daughter* sequence, published posthumously in 1895. It is a unique portrayal of maternal same-sex heterosexual love written by a dying Webster intent on giving to her daughter tangible evidence of love that would outlive her. This love supersedes that between man and woman, even in dreams and after death, something Christina Rossetti, who dedicated all her poems to her mother, would surely have agreed with. The bond is strongest in childhood, and as the child grows the mother fears loss of the relationship, the most dynamic a woman can experience, but she goes on to rationalize her concerns and recognize that mother and child make each other whole, beyond fear of mortality and dissolution. This image of perfect unity connects with the traditional materiality of the sonnet, showing how Webster allied the organic force of the form with a changed content to produce a new configuration that repudiated the sonnet's association with death and parting.[96]

The taking of sonnets out of a sequence so they may be regarded as individually beautiful achieved new heights under Dante Rossetti. At the same time, he constructed revolving themes and patterns of symbolism between one sonnet or group and another which gave a sense of unity without the need for a narrative thread. In short, he re-fashioned the Petrarchan sonnet for contemporary England, making *The House of Life* an essential and unavoidable point of reference for lyric and introspective poetry for forty years.[97] He was drawn to the sonnet-sequence for a number of reasons. Nineteenth-century sonnets were preoccupied with religious belief and doubt, sexuality and gender, national allegiance and imperial mission, all features of Victorian identity, so by extrapolation this means that collectively sonnet sequences are about developing a poetry of self-hood, a concept Rossetti initiated as a means of exploring his own identity in a fluctuating context.[98] Sonnet writing brought art and poetry together in a way that was philosophically important to the visionary imagination, and this in turn affected Rossetti's relationship with the reader because condensed imagery and rhetorical questioning enabled the debate essential in the reader's search for the self. The sonnet sequence was open-ended, multi-faceted and fluid, allowing it to be reordered and adapted, which encouraged introspection and self-analysis. Similarly, a cryptic, ambiguous or enigmatic text need reveal little of the poet whilst drawing the reader into exploration of a contentious theme, in this case the dual centrality accorded to sexual love and religion.[99]

Siddal will always be personally associated with *The House of Life* because of the history of its compilation and publication and because its sonnets are in part inspired by her and the impact of her particular kind of physical beauty. The sequence makes equal two different types of love and this mirrors the dualistic thinking evident in her poems, facilitating their comparison with Rossetti's much longer work. As well as Barrett Browning Siddal is likely to have been at least generally aware of the prevalence of nineteenth-century female sonnet-writers. A number, some anonymous, are referred to by critics in the 1820s and a minority carved out a name for themselves: Mary Tighe, Mary Bryan, Caroline Norton and Hemans were all given the title 'poetess' as a sign of authority and respectability in a male literary world.[100] Siddal did not become part of this specific process, and indeed may have chosen to deliberately reject sonnet traditions in that 'The Lust of the Eyes', in which she speaks as a man whose aesthetic adoration of female beauty is at the expense of a woman's inner being, can be read as satirizing them. However, several of her poems do contend that physical, human love coexists with mystic and divine love in the human psyche, and that a search for love is a search for an understanding of the self.

Images of love in the poems of Siddal and Rossetti

The four Siddal poems to be read here are ostensibly quite different from each other in form and content. The most simplistic is 'Early Death' (1862) which consists of just three iambic quatrains with an abcb rhyming scheme. Apparently slight and unsophisticated, it conforms to a standard Victorian idea that grief can be assuaged by meeting with the dead in heaven. 'A Silent Wood' (1857) again has three quatrains, but the addition of a separate rhyming couplet at the end makes it seem almost sonnet-like in structure. There is no division into octave and sestet and the thought process is continuous, without the change of direction often seen in the sonnets of *The House of Life*, but the couplet does introduce a variation of rhythm and pace that together create a definite sense of conclusion often absent in Siddal's work. This is a much more enigmatic piece, full of gloomy regret for a relationship that has been lost or broken down. 'The Lust of the Eyes' (undated) has been mentioned earlier because as an examination of hypocrisy it is the exact opposite of the image of worshipful beauty promulgated by Rossetti. More complex in theme and in format, its predicable iambic metre is disguised by prose-like linguistic flow which sharpens the bitterness of its attack on the aesthetic adoration of women. This piece reads more like narrative than lyric verse, and it has a trick in its tail, a sudden injection of sentiment that cries with feeling, making this (along with 'Love and Hate') the least constrained of Siddal's poems. 'Lord May I Come?' (early 1862) is one of her most sophisticated; it reads like a devotional incantation but is a begging for death rather than a hymn of praise. All seven verses end in similar prayer-like phrases, but are of varying length: five, three, three, three, five, three, seven lines long, respectively. Furthermore, each verse has a different pattern so that they are held together not by rhythm but by rhyme. Despite its somewhat random appearance there is structural balance and the poem does have thematic development, soulless existence on earth giving way to anticipation of eternal joy in heaven. All these poems interweave threads of divine and human love, but individually they balance these components differently; as the speakers try to make sense of the emotional dilemmas confronting them, their responses register varying degrees of hope of salvation, both temporal and spiritual.

The fourteen sonnets extracted from *The House of Life* were chosen because they each encapsulate and compare the two aspects of love – human and divine – weaving the strands together in one piece to show the extent of their interdependence. They are a synechdochal and ekphrastic representation of Rossetti's adoration of female beauty, but they also acknowledge that beauty extends to the mind and that the effect of this on the lover is transformative. They were also chosen because they open up the possibility of a dialogue with Siddal's texts that address the same dualism and the associated problem of balancing two theoretically opposing needs, for human and spiritual comfort and support. Their solutions are different: Rossetti's adherence to a worshipful cult of feminine beauty is in itself an illuminating compromise, but it makes Siddal's centred and self-determining response that much more esoteric and challenging. Rossetti recognizes the importance of physical and emotional communion with another, but Siddal rejects this in favour of self-reliance which indicates not only a desire for individualism but the extent to which she was moving away from the Victorian middle-class female stereotype. Her poems are very austere compared with Rossetti's richly textured sonnets but despite the lack of obvious parity they can be profitably read alongside the latter because they approach the same dichotomy, and through this process of mutual exchange new light can be thrown on disguised meaning and the measure of philosophical difference marked.

Just as in Siddal's poems, expositions of love in Rossetti's sonnets are diverse. The introductory poem 'A Sonnet is a Moment's Monument' is ostensibly a definition of this poetic form, but in likening the sonnet to a double-faced coin it opens the way for several dualisms: loss and presence, what lasts and what should die, a single glorious moment of passion as opposed to an eternity of bliss for the soul. Rossetti teases the reader with conflicting images of devotion, making the meaning of this sonnet one of the most difficult to deduce. 'Love Enthroned' (1) describes love as a supreme secret, inextricable from beauty, its visible sign, and better than Truth, Hope, Fame, Youth, even life itself.[101] 'Heart's

Hope' (5) sees love as a mingling of the physical, the spiritual and the divine; through which all things can be understood and known. 'The Kiss' (6) is a very literal description of sexuality, a validation of sexual love by reference to religion endowing one single physical act with the power to unite body and soul. 'Nuptial Sleep' (6a) follows 'The Kiss', and shows lovers in sexual exhaustion, taking pride and satisfaction in the enjoyment of sex before falling into a deep and dreamless sleep watched over by spirits. 'Love's Lovers' (8) contrasts the frivolity of some women's love with that of a Beloved whose love is pure and immortalizing. This and Sonnet 18, 'Genius in Beauty', are the antithesis of Siddal's 'The Lust of the Eyes'. In 'Passion and Worship' (9) the Lady enjoys fleshly passion but recognizes that when desire dies love still holds sway in its spiritual form. 'The Portrait' (10) is an ekphrastic poem in which a picture immortalizes beauty and worships it, creating a perpetual shrine to the soul. This very personal exposition has echoes of *Beata Beatrix*, Rossetti's posthumous monument to Siddal. In 'The Birth-Bond' (15) Love and its Beloved share a kindred spirituality closer than that found in any other relationship, a union that is perhaps even pre-natal. 'Genius in Beauty' (18) celebrates the richness of beauty and its imperishability in one woman whose appearance will survive the destruction of time and change. As poetry is linked with beauty in this sonnet, Rossetti is also commenting on the immortality of the Poet. 'Love-Sweetness' (21) itemizes the attributes of a beautiful woman in the octave, but in the sestet claims that these amount to nothing without true spirituality of the soul. As in several of these sonnets, reciprocal love is equated to the kindred spirit meaning perfection is found in a combination of physical and divine passion. 'Heart's Compass' (27) has a much more spiritual timbre, the Beloved representing the soul of all whoever lived and died, making this Rossetti's meditation on love in all its infinite range. 'Her Gifts' (31) is the only sonnet in this collection that is not subdivided into octave and sestet. Full of different incidents, it glories in a woman's physical and intellectual attraction whilst still saying her soul outshines everything. 'The Dark Glass' (34) looks at love in an abstract way then personifies it in both human terms and as a supreme God, meaning this sonnet is the most overtly mystic or religious. The speaker is in awe of such a manifestation of love, saying his place in the world is, by comparison, a very insignificant one.

Siddal depicts love metaphorically in two distinct ways, as an illusion and as a journey. In 'Early Death' it is earthly love that is illusory; it opens in sorrowful consolation as the speaker (notably ungendered) begs their young lover not to grieve with 'bitter tears' as life 'passes fast' (1–2) and they are destined for heaven where only real love exists: 'But true, love, seek me in the throng / Of spirits floating past, / And I will take thee by the hands / And know thee mine at last' (9–12). They have been chosen by love to join those who have loved before them, and the poem is imbued with a sense of acceptance that heavenly love is to be eagerly anticipated, not feared: the speaker asks their lover to 'sit down meekly at my side' (5) as they wait for their untimely demise. 'Silent Wood' is a poem of introspective questioning; the speaker is sitting in a place of shadow and gloom and where 'grey owls flit' (6) trying to recapture a time of happiness when she and her lover were there under different circumstances: 'Can God bring back the day when we two stood / Beneath the clinging trees in that dark wood?' (13–14). She is aware something precious has been lost, her virginity as well as her relationship, and that even her memories are proving difficult to hold on to. She begs that she 'may not faint or die or swoon' (8) because she needs to keep remembering her anguish, implying that whatever has caused her to be alone was her fault.

'The Lust of the Eyes' treats the illusory theme differently by creating a double-bind: it is the woman's physical beauty that will fade but the (presumably) male speaker is rejoicing at the prospect because the lady has already destroyed the love that existed between them:

> I care not where be my Lady's soul
>   Though I worship before her smile:
> I care not where be my Lady's goal
>   When her beauty shall lose its wile.
>
> Low sit I down at my Lady's feet
>   Gazing through her wild eyes
> Smiling to think how my love will fleet
>   When their starlike beauty dies. (1–8)

The Lady has played her lover for a fool but he is internalizing his anger, instead keeping up a pretence of adoration while secretly willing the power that beguiled another to desert her and leave her loveless. Human love, based on transient ephemeral attributes is exposed as a sham, and not the path to divine union that 'Early Death' prophecies. That earthly love is an illusion is also clear in 'Lord May I Come?', but Siddal takes this a stage further here by questioning the presence of divine love too:

> How is it in the unknown land?
> Do the dead wander hand in hand?
>   God, give me trust in thee.
>
> Do we clasp dead hands and quiver
> With an endless joy for ever?
> Do tall white angels gaze and wend
> Along the banks where lilies bend?
> Lord, we know not how this may be:
> Good Lord we put out faith in Thee-
>   Oh God, remember me. (20–9)

The speaker has found little contentment in temporal relationships: 'Hollow hearts are ever near me, / Soulless eyes have ceased to cheer me: / Lord may I come to thee?' (6–8). She has been betrayed or deserted and longs for something better, but appears also to doubt her faith in spiritual companionship as the poem ends. Rossetti doesn't speak of love as an illusion; on the contrary it is physically and spiritually real and vibrant, but in 'Nuptial Sleep' the lovers are deserted by their dreams as they sink into post-coital slumber: 'Sleep sank them lower than the tide of dreams, / And their dreams watched them sink and slid away' (9–10). The sense of escape and complete freedom after the intensity of sexual closeness is palpable, and for that brief interlude even love appears distant and intangible.

'Lord May I Come?' and 'A Silent Wood' make the clearest statements that the search for and experience of erotic and religious love can be seen as a journey, and one fraught with uncertainty and loneliness. In 'Lord May I Come?' this is literal: wherever her 'footsteps come and go', 'Life is a stony way of woe' (3–4). Later, she implores God to lift her 'from life's stony way' (11) and wonders whether even the dead are unable to rest in one place (21 and 25–6). There is emotional movement throughout the poem as stages in her narrative unfold: the inability to appreciate the most basic of earthly pleasure, life, youth, the warmth of the sun (9), then the longing for 'holy death' (13) amid the sorrow and despair of bereavement (12), and finally the recognition of the need to find a substitute for human comfort. The journey can therefore also be transformative just as love is shown to be in the majority of the poems under consideration here, but unlike Siddal, for Rossetti the process is a positive experience because love, in whatever form, brings enlightenment and richness. In the sestet of 'The Kiss', for example, Rossetti describes how that one simple action can change attitudes and physical responses to a woman from the human to something divine:

> I was a child beneath her touch, – a man
> When breast to breast we clung, even I and she, –
> A spirit when her spirit looked through me, –
> A god when all our life-breath met to fan
> Our life-blood, till love's emulous ardours ran,
> Fire within fire, desire in deity. (9–14)

As an aside, these lines amply demonstrate Rossetti's ability to paint a picture that the reader assimilates even before becoming aware of the language he has used to create it, a case of the whole being much greater than the sum of the component parts, but magnified by the transference from one medium to another. *The House of Life* sonnets contain many such instances where linguistic complexity ceases to be problematic when supplanted by visual images so that words are rendered temporarily unnecessary. For Siddal, certainly in 'The Lust of the Eyes' and 'A Silent Wood', the speakers have seemingly been irrevocably changed into something alien by the experience of love. 'A Silent Wood' makes the journey analogy central to the narrative, the speaker moving into this claustrophobic and unknown place as the poem begins. The reader follows her progress to its very heart amid 'the darkest shadow' (5) where she sits, 'Gazing through the gloom like one / Whose life and hopes are also done' (9–10). She has made this journey before, but not alone, the 'clinging trees' (14) echoing the way she and her lover once clung together. Her journey now is a deliberate attempt to recapture the past by retracing physical and emotional footsteps in order to rationalize the loss of religious faith implied in the last two lines.

By contrast, 'The Lust of the Eyes' explores the mental journey of a speaker experiencing conflicting emotions. The poem begins with anger expressed through bitter sarcasm and sly wit, but in verse 3 the mood changes:[102] 'I care not if my Lady pray / To our Father which art in Heaven / But for joy my heart's quick pulses play / For to me her love is given' (9–12). The speaker initially dismisses the possibility of God forgiving his faithless lover or listening to her plea for eternal youth, but then, recalling his physical response to the gift of her love, he appears to relent as the last verse indicates: 'Then who shall close my Lady's eyes / And who shall fold her hands? / Will any hearken if she cries / Up to unknown lands?' (13–16). He is asking who will care for her when her beauty is gone, and who will lay her out when death claims her once she is rejected in favour of another more attractive woman, but it's how the words are grasped that captures the interest. This could be a flicker of genuine concern for the Lady's welfare that echoes the remembered sentiment of the preceding verse, or it could be an escalation of the irony inherent in the earlier parts of the poem in which a man is prepared to abandon a woman before she inevitably loses her looks, despite her feelings for him. Either way the poem takes an unexpected turn at this point, and if the second reading is adopted then the speaker clearly has disregard for both her mortal and spiritual self. Such 'Godless hedonism' goes against male and female contemporary poetic expectation but shows real insight on Siddal's part.[103] There is no uncertainty in 'Early Death'; this journey will end in reunion in heaven because the speaker is certain that the 'solemn peace of holy death' (7) will come quickly to her loved one after her demise. There is a sense of cyclical completeness also in the structure of this poem, as the first and last verses are similar in wording and sentiment: God's love in all its glory will surpass any that has been experienced even during a lengthy span on earth.

In each of Siddal's poems there is a clear sense that the speaker is searching for an identity, a new persona, in the wake of emotional trauma. This mirrors the differing degrees of doubt the poems exhibit through rhetorical questions or statements of intent. If they are read autobiographically then they are an indication of the importance Siddal placed on independence or autonomy within a relationship, either human or religious. 'The Lust of the Eyes' argues for a woman to be seen as more than just an object of desire regardless of her age or appearance; 'A Silent Wood' could be a plea for toleration of female sexual freedom; 'Lord May I Come?' queries a woman's place within a wider social context, perhaps a reflection of evolving attitudes towards literate women in the mid-nineteenth century as much as Siddal's fluctuating and at times tumultuous personal circumstances. The poems offer some clues here; Siddal almost always uses the present tense which gives the impression she is relaying her thoughts as they occur, and this creates a sense of urgency especially when combined with the use of the imperative as in 'Early Death'. She also literally freezes the action in 'A Silent Wood' where she is tautologically 'frozen like a thing in stone' (11), and in 'Lord May I Come?' where the speaker likens her life to a lily held in a frozen rill (16). In doing this she appears to be taking stock, evaluating her responses to bewildering change enveloping her. Rossetti also uses a motif of suspended animation; when the portrait is completed in the eponymous sonnet for example, 'Lo! It is done' (9) marks the point at which the speaker draws breath to admire his creation, but Rossetti does this to capture a specific moment in time rather than allow a period of constraint or holding back of emotion as Siddal does. In general, Siddal's poems have to date been seen as more reactive than proactive, but if read as a search for the self this position is reversed and Rossetti principally uses *The House of Life* to facilitate something similar.

Rossetti sees love as a form of eternity already attained rather than a journey towards its understanding as Siddal does, but quite what his eternity consists of can be difficult to grasp. The introductory sonnet speaks of a memorial from the eternity of the soul to a 'dead deathless hour', an intriguing play on words that combines the passing of time with time that never actually moves. There is a similar dichotomy in the illustration Rossetti made to accompany the sonnet; the winged woman holds an hour-glass in her left hand yet the double coin pictured bottom left has a representation of a snake enclosing an alpha and an omega, all signs of eternity. 'Love Enthroned' is a little less obscure; the sonnet literally and figuratively elevates Love above many things man finds beautiful and in doing so gives it a stasis that not even the merest breeze can trouble: 'Love's throne was not with these; but far above / All passionate wind of welcome and farewell / He sat in breathless bowers they dream not of;' (9–11). In 'Heart's Hope' the sestet is again used to graphically reinforce a visual message of love's cyclical permanence, and the first line neatly draws body and soul and God's love together:

> Yea, in God's name, and Love's and thine, would I
> Draw from one loving heart such evidence
> As to all hearts all things shall signify;
> Tender as dawn's first hill-fire, and intense
> As instantaneous penetrating sense,
> In Spring's birth hour, of other Springs gone by. (9–14)

'Genius in Beauty' and 'The Portrait' envisage love in the form of beauty and immortalize it. They capture the moment as the introductory sonnet does, yet in 'The Portrait' especially this is also a process of de-animation. The lady's face has become her 'shrine' (12) implying she is dead, existing now frozen for the future rather than living for the present in an alternative eternity. If this is the case then love has moved into a purely spiritual state, which in turn endows the poet/artist with great power. 'Heart's Compass' makes the connection between love and beauty even more explicit. The woman is a 'breathless wonder' (3), whose lips and eyes are the embodiment of beauty and purity. All this is then likened to Love who is conqueror of doubt, 'the gathering clouds of Night's ambiguous art' (11), and the personification of 'some heavenly solstice hushed and halcyon' (4). Rossetti makes Love's/Beauty's eyes 'the sun-gate of the soul' (6), moving this sonnet away from 'The Portrait' and 'Genius in Beauty' that celebrate beauty simply for its own sake, and towards the appreciation of female intellectual worth found in 'Her Gifts'. These four sonnets can therefore be read as part of a dialogue with 'The Lust of the Eyes' which exposes the potential shallowness of poems that appear to undervalue the wider nature of womanhood. 'Love-Sweetness' and 'The Dark Glass' explore further the concept of the personification of the soul. In the former the soul is referred to as 'the confident heart's still fervour'

(11), one's innermost being that even when still and silent still pulsates with the very essence of life, and which makes sweeter even the sweetest joy of physical love: 'The confident heart's still fervour; the swift beat / And soft subsidence of the spirit's wing, / Then when it feels, in cloud-girt wayfaring, / The breath of kindred plumes against its feet' (11–14). The soul doesn't have to mean something holy, but these lines equate the soul, the heart of being, with angels, or kindred spirits at least, and this gives the poem an air of personified religiosity. 'The Dark Glass', another visually striking piece, takes this motif a stage further and makes Love himself human, the lord of all who gifts understanding of the innermost secrets of life through the eyes of a woman worshipped by a man. Personified thus, Love becomes a tangible entity whose all-embracing power can be both nurturing and awe-inspiring:

> And shall my sense pierce love, – the last relay
> And ultimate post of eternity?
>
> Lo! What am I to Love, the Lord of all?
> One murmuring shell he gathers from the sand, –
> One little heart-flame sheltered in his hand.
> Yet through thine eyes he grants me clearest call
> And veriest touch of powers primordial
> That any hour-girt life may understand. (7–14)

As in 'Love-Sweetness', the unknowable is made known through the knowable, just as spiritual love is only known via the physical, which is why Rossetti generally devotes the octave of a sonnet to the adoration of female physical beauty, leaving the sestet to honour the spiritual and mystic aspects of her love. In keeping the two aspects separate he stresses the dualism but also posits the idea of the soul as the Self, the very heart of character and being, a concept Siddal touches on in 'Early Death' where as a spirit the speaker reaches emotional and physical fulfilment (9–12).

Both Siddal and Rossetti depict love as a metaphorical rebirth. 'Lord May I Come?' anticipates this in its longing to escape a temporal existence full of woe, and 'Early Death' is certain it will happen, making its tone more optimistic as a result. Although the speaker in 'A Silent Wood' doesn't want to die she knows her 'life and hopes are also done' (10) and wants to return to a previous existence. 'Nuptial Sleep' makes the analogy very clear in the sestet; whilst asleep after their transformative sexual experience the lovers are in the womb from which they will emerge with new identities. Each Beloved becomes a new creation, but as partners they also become a third, a fulfilment of visionary longing greeting a new world full of wonder found through love:[104] 'Slowly their souls swam up again through gleams / Of watered light and dull drowned waifs of day; / Till from some wonder of new woods and streams / He woke, and wondered more: for there she lay' (11–14). 'The Birth-Bond' is more abstract in its treatment but it still carries the same message, that lovers/kindred spirits will be born again together even if they originally knew each other before time began, the same comforting scenario Siddal envisioned in 'Early Death'. This sonnet is more discursive than most, musing about the closeness of some siblings that enables them to read each other's thoughts. The speaker goes on to speculate whether, because he and his Beloved have this same unbreakable bond, it must mean they were themselves related in a past life but have been reborn to recognize each other as partners in a new and very different relationship: 'Oh born with me somewhere that men forget / And though in years of sight and sound unmet, / Known for my soul's birth-partner well enough!' (12–14). The language of 'The Birth-Bond' can be equated to melody, so perfect is the lyric poetry it forms, and although Siddal doesn't use this metaphor at all, Rossetti describes love, both sexual and religious, in musical terms in six of these sonnets.[105] 'The Kiss' speaks of a woman's lips playing those of her lover as Orpheus would have loved to play his lute (5–8), and in 'Love's Lovers' it is claimed some women copy the silvery tones of Cupid's lute to draw attention to themselves (4–5). 'Passion and Worship' is structured around musical instruments that stand for sexual passion and spiritual worship, and musical terminology is ingeniously drawn into the language throughout. In 'Heart's Compass' the Beloved's lips are 'music's visible tone' (5), a form of the ekphrasis in 'The Portrait'.

As has already become apparent, most of these sonnets are woven around dualisms or opposites, or the congress of two elements; that between art and poetry, and music and poetry, are prime examples. The 'double work of art' is a central tenet in the understanding of

Rossetti's poetics, where a picture is followed by a poem, usually a sonnet or a pair of sonnets that comment or elaborate on it. This is readily demonstrated by the introductory sonnet to *The House of Life* where textual and visual elements are inseparably bound together in a piece that celebrates a series of opposites. Rossetti was very influenced by William Blake in this, but unlike Blake Rossetti keeps the two works apart by making each present a unique view of an ideal seen through a different form. The double-work can still be a 'moment's monument' and a prized entity in itself, as well as a recognition of body and soul and human love and God's love in unity, but these components are always appreciably separate and individually cherished.[106] As a metaphor for Rossetti's vision of love as a congress of elements of the human and the divine that are both separate and yet symbiotically unified, the double-work thus defined has much merit.

The sonnets of *The House of Life* are often poems of two halves that deliberately draw opposites together to highlight the dichotomy of individuality and partnership. The opening sonnet defines the sonnet itself in two ways, in octave and sestet, and in doing so contrasts love and death, eternity and ephemerality, day and night, things gained and lost, memorial and portent. Similarly, 'Love Enthroned' lists in the octave all those things that are less important than love, before in the sestet weaving the positives, Truth, Love, Hope, Fame, Youth and Life, which together create one composite and aspirational vision from which only Past, Oblivion and Death are omitted. 'Love's Lovers' dismisses those women 'who kissed [Love's] wings which brought him yesterday / And thank his wings today that he is flown' (7–8), a neat summary of their fickleness. Rossetti compares this with the behaviour of 'my Lady [who] only loves the heart of Love' (9) and for whom Love has 'a bower of unimagined flower and tree' (11) as her reward. The neatest and most memorable division occurs in 'Her Gifts'; having eulogized the simplicity, glance, pallor, heart, mouth, hair, neck, hands and feet of the perfect woman the poem ends with a perfectly succinct couplet: 'These are her gifts, as tongue may tell them o'er. / Breathe low her name, my soul; for that means more' (13–14). The Lady may have different attitudes and expressions but nothing expresses her better than her own name which is uniquely hers and worthy of no other, and therefore cannot be spoken. Like her soul it outshines everything else so must be kept silent, but even thus it reminds the reader that the congress of human and divine love is the most powerful metaphorical union in *The House of Life* sonnets. Siddal's 'Early Death' and 'Lord May I come?' celebrate it, 'A Silent Wood' looks to it for salvation, and even 'The Lust of the Eyes' in all its cynicism has to acknowledge its influence.

The emerging balance or compromise

A reader of *The House of Life* may well find their initial perception of individual sonnets is visual, a reflection perhaps of the difficulties encountered in unravelling complex and at times opaque language that only reluctantly yields its meaning even when read aloud. Rossetti creates vibrant and memorable images of religious and sexual love that draw the reader into the text and encourage its dissection. The visual exposition may be triggered by one isolated phrase in a largely conceptual poem but it will be enough to dramatically illuminate its argument, as in 'The Birth-Bond' where the kindred siblings are said to have 'silent speech' (7), which instantly makes their love visible and tangible. In the introductory sonnet the catalyst comes at the beginning of the sestet; likening the sonnet to a coin, even without the accompanying illustration, brings all the dualities listed in the octave into focus and allows the reader to acknowledge the fact that one perfect entity can be made up of opposing constituent parts. The octave of 'The Dark Glass' attempts to explain conceptually what love feels like, something that blinds and deafens (6) and can reach the very limit of eternity (8), but it is only in the personified image of Love cradling and sheltering even his lowliest subject (10–11) that the reader comes to appreciate its all-embracing essence. 'The Portrait' makes the process explicit and literal: 'Oh Love, let this lady's picture glow / Under my hand to praise her name, and show / Even of her inner self the perfect whole' (2–4). In this ekphrastic poem the reader might expect a lengthy description of the lady's physical attraction, but only throat, mouth and eyes are mentioned in a succinct comment that immediately captures her facial beauty as well as the infinite capacity of her soul: 'Lo! It is done. Above the long lithe throat / The mouth's mould testifies of voice and kiss, / The shadowed eyes remember and foresee' (9–11). The portrait becomes a sonnet which becomes a picture again, a cyclical movement rather like the two faces of the coin that when spun become one integrated whole. Siddal's poems generally do not have this painterly effect because their ostensibly plain language makes them more readily accessible, she uses adjectives selectively, and she places less emphasis on colour and sharply rendered detail. With a couple of exceptions her poems are very short, making every word significant especially when they are repeated; the reader tends therefore to focus on specific monochrome images rather than assimilate an entire tableau. However, in more abstract poems like 'A Silent Wood' she does create a visual atmosphere that enables the reader to identify with the predicament of the speaker, who sits isolated among semi-human trees that act as sentinels, an enclosing barrier to communication that possesses ghostly voices (3) of its own: 'In thy darkest shadow let me sit / When the grey owls about me flit (5–6) ... Frozen like a thing in stone / I sit in thy shadow – but not alone' (11–12). Why the speaker is alone is initially unimportant, it's the fact that she is that encourages the reader into the poem.

'A Silent Wood' hints at an unseen or supernatural presence which can be interpreted as the mystical experience of sexuality or a sense that the soul is inseparable from the human body. This woman is apart from society because of a clandestine love-affair and is haunted by its memory, capable of no emotion beyond regret and guilt, her constant companions. Interestingly, despite this she is not asking for absolution; instead, she wants the relationship to be reinstated. Sexual, not religious love is to be her redemption, even if she is asking God to facilitate it, as the last two lines of the poem indicate. In complete contrast, 'Early Death' is built around the premise that heavenly spirits, although unseen, are credible and substantial enough to make a relationship ethereal as well as physical. In 'Lord May I Come?' the dead still have life despite being 'lost' (18) to those remaining on earth.[107] Siddal illustrates this graphically, comparing the coldness of what remains of her physical heart with the warmth that currently eludes her:

> My outward flesh feels sad and still
> Like lilies in a frozen rill;
> I am gazing upwards to the sun,
> Lord, Lord, remembering my lost one.
>   Oh Lord, remember me! (15–19)

The sun represents the comfort of heaven and there is an earlier mention of 'summer weather' (9) in this poem, but these are rare occurrences. Love for Siddal is usually cold, as in 'A Silent Wood', or colourless as in 'Early Death', or white as in 'Lord May I Come?' where lilies and angels stand by frozen water. Passion, however much yearned for, is made pale, uninviting and something to be avoided. Not giving in to emotion makes retention of control and the pursuit of the autonomous self easier. Even in 'The Lust of the Eyes' anger is guarded and calculating; only the Lady's 'wild eyes' (6) convey a definite sense of unguarded feeling. In comparison, Rossetti equates passion with fire; in 'Heart's Compass' it burns as 'the sun-gate to the soul' and within the all-knowing eyes of the Beloved (6–7) and in 'Passion and Worship' sexual love is represented by a 'flame-winged' figure (1). 'Smouldering senses in death's sick delay' (1) and 'seizure of malign vicissitude' (2) are robbed of their power by a kiss that makes fire burn within fire (14) in 'The Kiss', yet such intense emotion is also 'Tender as dawn's first hillfire' (12) in 'Heart's Hope', a sonnet that makes the birth of passion synonymous with the cleansing brightness of the young sun.

Religious images abound in 'Early Death', 'The Lust of the Eyes' and 'Lord May I Come?', all of which stress the presence of divine love alongside the sexual. 'Early Death' describes the gates of heaven opening wide (2) to accommodate the 'throng of heavenly spirits' (9–10), and the 'solemn peace of holy death' (an expression also used in 'Lord May I Come?') coming quickly to the lover left behind. The use of the archaic 'thee' adds specific Christian emphasis as it also does in 'Lord May I Come?' The word 'Lord' occurs nine times in the latter poem alone, 'Father' and 'God' appearing elsewhere. The final two verses have a rather more esoteric image of the afterlife than the ghostly procession presented in 'Early Death'; tall white angels are the heavenly equivalent of lilies that grow by the same river on earth, a sign that the two worlds are interrelated.

Strangely, the clearest iconography comes in 'The Lust of the Eyes'; the speaker 'worships before [his lady's] smile (2) and sits low at her feet, gazing up in pseudo honour (5–6). He refers to her reciting the Lord's Prayer before painting a verbal picture of the Lady prepared for burial with hands folded across her chest (13–14). All this is said ironically but the depiction is strongly medieval and clerical. Worship is stated or implied in almost every one of Rossetti's sonnets as their very nature makes likely, but religious references of any specific persuasion are less conspicuous. Cupid appears in 'Heart's Compass', where he has decidedly Christian overtones, and in 'Love's Lovers' and 'Love Enthroned'. There are winged figures with plumed feet that could be angels at the end of 'Love-Sweetness', and again in the first line of 'Passion and Worship' in which a 'white-winged harp player' symbolizes the purity of spiritual adoration. The only specific biblical analogy, and one that suits the Victorian context, is taken from the Old Testament: the parting of the Red Sea is used in 'Heart's Hope' to convey the extent to which the speaker is prepared to explore the meaning and understanding of Love: 'By what word's power, the key of paths untrod, / Shall I the difficult deeps of Love explore, / Till parted waves of Song yield up the shore / Even as that sea which Israel crossed dryshod? (1–4). The word 'deep' is interesting here since it has two inferences; love is an ocean, and it is as difficult to fathom. The speaker is not just searching for the key to a manifest destiny, communion with his Beloved, he also searching for a lost poetics, and this bestows on this sonnet an air of self-discovery.

One might expect, given his reputation as a fleshly poet, that there would be more references to the body in *The House of Life* than there are in Siddal's poems, but this is not the case. Conversely, there are unexpected references to the body and its sexual power in her poems, which on first reading appear to concentrate more on depictions of mental anguish than physicality. Hands are held out as a gesture of welcome in 'Early Death' (11) and they again provide comfort in 'Lord May I Come? (21, 23); in 'The Lust of the Eyes they are folded as a symbol of death. Eyes are 'soulless' (7) as well as 'loved' (12) in 'Lord May I Come?', so as in 'The Lust of the Eyes' they are the seat of some emotion. Only the heart is mentioned in 'A Silent Wood'; 'filled with misery' (2), it neatly encapsulates the being of the speaker and contrasts vividly with that 'filled with all life sown and mown' (8) in 'Heart's Compass' and that 'enthralled' in 'Her Gifts'. There is a degree of coded eroticism in Siddal's poems, although in 'The Lust of the Eyes' it largely rests in the title. In 'A Silent Wood' both ferns (4) and trees (14) cling suggestively, and in 'Lord May I Come?' the speaker asks whether in the unknown land dead hands clasp and quiver with endless joy (23–4), giving the clearest indication that sexual love does not have to cease with death. This poem is full of anticipation and repeatedly asks for permission to proceed further along the road to divine love, so could be read as a coded desire for coition. The same sense of congress is apparent in 'Early Death'; the woman is a protagonist, seeking and claiming her relationship, and in a neat inversion it is her male partner who is 'meek' (5), a sign that self-determination is considered desirable. 'Lord May I Come?' stresses autonomy, the emerging self seen in the questions posed about the future and the need for divine not human security to safeguard it.

When *The House of Life* was first published in 1870 'Nuptial Sleep' was singled out for its perverse eroticism, yet it is not the only sonnet to sanctify a sexual relationship. In an echo of Rossetti's pictures of women in which they are clothed and only half seen, the beauty of the female body is almost exclusively represented in sensual descriptions of the face, the mouth especially, which inject elements of eroticism that are just as powerful as the depiction of sexual intercourse in 'Nuptial Sleep'. In 'Her Gifts' the woman has 'a mouth whose passionate forms imply / All music and all silence held thereby' (6–7), conjuring up an image of mystic capability as well as sexual allure. Four sonnets concentrate on the kiss bestowed by such a mouth, and here Rossetti draws physicality and emotion together in memorable fashion. 'Love-Sweetness' describes an encounter that begins quite chastely but which becomes increasingly passionate:

> Sweet dimness of her loosened hair's downfall
> About thy face; her sweet hands round thy head
> In gracious fostering union garlanded:
> Her tremulous smiles; her glances' sweet recall
> Of love: her murmuring sighs memorial:

Her mouth's culled sweetness by thy kisses shed
On cheeks and neck and eyelids, and so led
Back to her mouth which answers for all:— (1–8)

In 'Love's Lovers' the kiss is given power to award eternal life: 'There kneels he now, and all-anhungered of / Thine eyes grey-lit in shadowing hair above, / Seals with thy mouth his immortality' (12–14). 'The Kiss' itself tells how: 'For lo! even now my lady's lips did play / With these my lips such consonant interlude / As laurelled Orpheus longed for when he wooed / The half-drawn hungering face with that last lay' (5–8). It then goes on to relish the empowering impact of such communion. 'Nuptial Sleep' begins where 'The Kiss' ends, and by repeating the 's' provides the most sensually sibilant description of love making:[108]

At length their long kiss severed, with sweet smart:
And as the last slow sudden drops are shed
From sparkling eaves when all the storm has fled,
So singly flagged the pulses of each heart.
Their bosoms sundered, with the opening start
Of married flowers to either side outspread
From the knit stem; yet still their mouths, burnt red,
Fawned on each other where they lay apart. (1–8)

The poem is explicit in its description of ejaculation and the impact this has on the body, but it is the picture of the lovers 'fawning' over each other, reluctant to tear sore lips apart, that is the most prevailing.

Rossetti draws on a language of desire and adoration that renders sensuous the most prosaic commodity. Water is a loud tumultuous sea of blinding spray when compared to the power of unknown, mystic love in 'The Dark Glass' (5–6). It is 'wan' (12) and trembling in the moonlight of a grove that represents death that cannot separate the lovers in 'Passion and Worship', and it is the amniotic fluid in 'Nuptial Sleep' that filters and reflects light with a gleam of its own (13–16). It is thus almost personified, touched by divine hand whilst still commonplace. Love and female beauty, its earthly representative, is worshipped in sumptuous hymns of praise and elevated to sacred status, very different from the precision and clarity that typify Siddal's verse. In her work description is merely suggested, lending it an ethereal or spectral quality that hints at detachment and a searching for independence. Her language of desire is not celebratory, but instead dominated by regret, fear, uncertainty and suffering. Her female protagonists are generally alone, complaining of unrequited love, beseeching an absent lover to stay or return, or begging a divine equivalent to offer solace. The partnerships so celebrated in Rossetti's sonnets are absent here, meaning that Siddal's women have to be self-reliant and make individual choices. They are seeking the relationships Rossetti's lovers already have and are revelling in, and this process of exploration is reflected in the anger and pain, and the occasional joy, evident in these pieces. Rossetti's sonnets have an outward air of certainty and confidence that is lacking in Siddal's poems, but they are still very open to interpretation as their language is often secret and enigmatic and difficult to fathom. Sentences are truncated and word ordering inverted to achieve the designated rhyming pattern and syllabic structure. Opposites are deliberately put together and archaic word-forms used, so that when unexpected references are then added to the mix precise meaning can seem frustratingly unattainable even when the general drift is understood, as in 'Genius in Beauty':

> Beauty like hers is genius. Not the call
> Of Homer's or of Dante's heart sublime, –
> Not Michael's hand furrowing the zones of time, –
> Is more with compassed mysteries musical:
> Nay, Not in Spring's Summer's sweet footfall
> More gathered gifts exuberant Life bequeaths
> Than doth this sovereign face, whose love-spell breathes
> Even from its shadowed contour on the wall.
>
> As many men are poets in their youth,
> But for one sweet-strung soul the wires prolong
> Even through all change the indomitable song:
> So in likewise the envenomed years, whose tooth
> Rends shallower grace with ruin void of ruth,
> Upon this beauty's power shall wreak no wrong.

Siddal's poems appear predictable, repetitive and even child-like in their simplicity, but this is deceptive. In 'Lord May I Come?' the verses are quite independent of each other and could be re-assembled in a different order and still achieve the same effect. This apparent lack of development is explained by the fragmentary nature of the original manuscripts from which editors have had to work, but it compounds the elusiveness of her poetry whilst leaving open the possibility of multiple readings. These poems and sonnets therefore set an interpretative challenge, but the responses this generates are more important than the establishment of definitive meaning because through questioning the reader is able to formulate opinion, a step towards knowledge of the self. Siddal and Rossetti establish a dialogue with the reader, adding voices to those speaking in the poems: the dead lover, the Beloved, the narrator, Love himself, or God. Collectively these voices are seeking a synthesis, a balance between the influence and importance of religious and human love.

The sonnets of *The House of Life* make plain that Rossetti believed human and divine love was inseparable, and that to worship a woman's physical beauty was to appreciate the true worth of her soul, the key to immortality. Beauty is the manifestation of the soul, the essence of being and the personification of an omnipotent God who represents all love, both spiritual and temporal. Rossetti's women therefore have to be seen as objects of desire as much as deities, worshipped but not worshippers, a reflection of his skill as poet/artist and an extension of his narcissism.[109] Yet this is not the whole picture; these sonnets also speak of how men are empowered or diminished by female beauty and worth, and 'Love-Sweetness' and 'Nuptial Sleep' make plain that enjoyment of sexual love has to be mutual for it to become the pathway to the sacred love that Rossetti establishes as a goal. Balancing the need for aesthetic and sexual fulfilment with the primordial need for some form of religious faith emerges in the development of self-awareness, the acquisition of the confidence to explore theories and influences outside experience and express them without losing sight of individuality, in other words, to welcome inclusivity as an opportunity to formulate a personal creed. *The House of Life* is preoccupied with unsettling questions of sexual identity and religious belief, but Rossetti is not didactic; instead, the sequence is an enabling tool that holds a mirror up to the reader so they may adopt or reject elements as they wish. As a result, the emerging self is not Rossetti or any one individual but a reflection of the poet and all his readers.[110] Rossetti encourages debate and challenge by posing questions to force readers to subconsciously query the personal relevance of the sonnets, and the extent to which they are modified by them.[111] He gets the readers to explore themselves, giving them fragments to investigate, concentrating on sexual love and their own mortality and faith because he believed these things were the fundamentals of human existence.[112] Rossetti was addressing the meaning of life and death in a destabilized world but his answer does not lie within traditional Christian doctrine. He doesn't ask the reader to suspend disbelief and doesn't want to disrupt their faith, but his sonnets do ask that they be open to the experience of life to keep alive that faith, and with it their awareness of the power of love.

Siddal's poems place divine love above the human and question the attention paid to physical beauty as opposed to the soul or conscience. Religious love is shown as being more reliable and more fulfilling than sexual love which is often associated with betrayal or disappointment. There is little confidence in human relationships, but crucially, neither is there a guarantee of religious love. It is likely that if Siddal had a faith it would have been Christian, and there is nothing to indicate in these poems that she had embraced secular religion as envisaged by Rossetti; however, sexual desire is frequently couched in religious terms so the textual evidence may not be so far apart. Divine love appears not to engender the exultation so apparent in Rossetti's sonnets, and there is a certain reservation, even in 'Early Death', the most obvious declaration of faith in its security. These poems, like much of Siddal's oeuvre, constitute a poetic of withholding and of introspective soul-searching which indicates here that Siddal placed more value on the self than on God or man. She searches for the self by questioning the role and purpose of human and religious relationships, but unlike Rossetti she holds up no template for others to copy, neither does she engage in dialogue with a third party. Her dialogue is with herself, in poems arguably written to facilitate the formation of thought intended to remain private, their purpose being to express personal frustration or explore ideas that might lead to independence of thought or self-reliance. Siddal's speakers are aware of the contradictions and dualisms inherent in their arguments and they attempt to rationalize them. They cannot abandon their belief in a loving God, yet there is insufficient proof of His existence. They long for a sexual relationship yet experience tells them that human love brings disenchantment; female beauty is a magnet for men who are quick to adore, but beauty is transient and does not imply any form of eternity. Rossetti's lovers see a seamless integration of different aspects of love, but Siddal's women know this not to be the case, as indicated by the rhetorical questions that persist even into the conclusions of three of these poems.

Debate with the self is empowering nonetheless, even when consciousness is explored under some obvious duress, and out of it comes some resolution. Religious love, a more autonomous entity than that promulgated by Rossetti, is given precedence, but whether it will prove emancipatory or imprisoning is left to the reader to deduce. In the Preface to the 1853 edition of *Poems* Matthew Arnold expressed regret at the tendency of modern poets to indulge in 'too much mental anguish unrelieved by incident or hope', and urged them to avoid subjects that were 'allegories of one's own mind'.[113] Siddal and Rossetti independently engage in such a dialogue of the mind with itself and acquire self-knowledge in the process. It is important to remember, though, that Siddal wrote in private of feelings about sex and religion at a time when such subjects were shrouded in secrecy, in a voice not intended to be heard, and this presents those wishing to place her poems in the public domain with an ethical dilemma.

Notes

1 Rossetti wrote a dramatic monologue on the subject of prostitution, *Jenny*, begun in 1847 and published in 1870.
2 Kirsty Stonell Walker, *Stunner: The Fall and Rise of Fanny Cornforth* (spacecreate.com, 2006), pp. 42–5.
3 *Ibid.*, p. 45.
4 Jan Marsh, *Elizabeth Siddal. Pre-Raphaelite Artist 1829–1862* (Sheffield: Ruskin Gallery, 1991), p. 47.
5 Jan Marsh and Pamela Gerrish Nunn, *Pre-Raphaelite Women Artists* (London: Thames & Hudson Ltd, 1998), p. 115.

6. Beverly Taylor, 'Beatrix/Creatrix: Elizabeth Siddal as Muse and Creator', *The Journal of Pre-Raphaelite Studies*, Vol. 4 (Spring 1995), 29–50, p. 34.
7. Jill R. Ehnenn, '"Strong Traivelling": Re-visions of Women's Subjectivity and Female Labor in the Ballad-work of Elizabeth Siddal', *Victorian Poetry*, Vol. 52, No. 2 (Summer 2014), 251–76, p. 265.
8. Matthew Arnold, *Poems 1840–1866*, ed. R. A. Scott-James (London: J. M. Dent and Co., 1908), p. 3.
9. Marsh, *Legend* comprises a very comprehensive exposition.
10. *Ibid.*, p. 156.
11. William Michael Rossetti, 'Dante Rossetti and Elizabeth Siddall', *Burlington Magazine*, No. 1 (May 1903), 273–95, p. 277.
12. Julian Treuherz, Elizabeth Prettejohn and Edwin Becker, *Dante Gabriel Rossetti* (London: Thames & Hudson, 2003), p. 37.
13. W. M. Rossetti, *Burlington*, p. 276.
14. Georgiana Burne-Jones, *Memorials of Edward Burne-Jones*, 2 vols (London: Macmillan and Co. Ltd, 1904), Vol. 1, p. 266.
15. Jan Marsh, *Dante Gabriel Rossetti. Painter and Poet* (London: Phoenix paperback edition, 2005), p. 244.
16. Samantha Matthews, *Poetical Remains. Poets' Graves, Bodies and Books in the Nineteenth Century* (Oxford: Oxford University Press, 2004), p. 21.
17. Rosalie Grylls, *Portrait of Rossetti* (Carbondale, IL: Illinois University Press, 1964), p. 130.
18. Jan Marsh, *Pre-Raphaelite Sisterhood* (London: Quartet Books, 1985), pp. 259–60.
19. Dante Gabriel Rossetti, *Letters*, 4 vols, eds Oswald Doughty and John Robert Wahl (Oxford: Clarendon Press, 1965–67), Vol. 2, p. 761.
20. Lindsay Smith, *Pre-Raphaelitism: Poetry and Painting* (Tavistock, Devon: Northcote House Publishers Ltd, 2013), pp. 30–3.
21. Walker, *Stunner*, p. 103 and Rossetti, *Variorum Edition*, p. 227.
22. Dante Gabriel Rossetti, *Collected Poetry and Prose*, ed., Jerome McGann (New Haven and London: Yale University Press, 2003), pp. 386–7.
23. Matthews, *Poetical Remains*, p. 115.
24. Ellen Smith, Maria Spartali, Annie Miller and Alexa Wilding also posed for him as professional models. It was a general PR principle not to have models who sat for art students as they tended to carry an air of impropriety, so known associates were often asked as they maintained spiritual and physical contact with the artists.
25. Walker, *Stunner*, p. 181.

26 Grylls, *Portrait of Rossetti*, p. 114. This emanates from the belief that if the Establishment accepted double standards of sexual ethics (several accounts record Cornforth as having been a prostitute) then anti-Establishment figures like Rossetti believed himself to be should rescue the unfortunate products of these and make allowances for them. The 'Dear Elephant' letters quoted here give a good indication of his feelings for her.
27 Marsh, *Pre-Raphaelite Sisterhood*, pp. 185–6.
28 Walker, *Stunner*, p. 183.
29 See Walker's biography.
30 Dante Gabriel Rossetti, *Correspondence with Jane Morris*, ed. John Bryson in association with Janet Crump Troxell (Oxford: Clarendon Press, 1976). Rossetti speaks of his painting and poetry (new stanzas for *Sister Helen*, No. 83, pp. 124–5, and progress of *The House of Life* Nos 122, 124 and 125, pp. 165–8, and its publication, No. 136, p. 178) and a wide range of contemporary literature, which implies their relationship was at least part built on intellect.
31 Wendy Parkins, *Jane Morris: The Burden of History* (Edinburgh: Edinburgh University Press, 2013), p. xi.
32 *Ibid.*, p. 113.
33 *Ibid.*, p. 114.
34 *Ibid.*, p. 136.
35 *Ibid.*, pp. 124–5.
36 Elizabeth Prettejohn, *Rossetti and His Circle* (London: Tate Gallery Publishing, 1997), p. 9.
37 Colin Cruise, *Pre-Raphaelite Drawing* (London: Thames & Hudson Ltd, 2011), p. 97.
38 Colin Cruise, 'Pre-Raphaelite Drawing', in Elizabeth Prettejohn, ed., *The Cambridge Companion to the Pre-Raphaelites* (Cambridge: Cambridge University Press, 2012), pp. 47–61, p. 51.
39 Jerome McGann, *Dante Gabriel Rossetti and the Game That Must be Lost* (New Haven and London: Yale University Press, 2000), p. 36.
40 Rossetti, *Variorum Edition* deals with the evolution and structure of the poem comprehensively.
41 Treuherz, Prettejohn and Becker, *Dante Gabriel Rossetti*, p. 56.
42 Alison Smith, *The Victorian Nude. Sexuality, Morality and Art* (Manchester and New York: Manchester University Press, 1996), p. 180. 'Supersensuousness' was a derogatory term applied to those of the ultra-sensual school and implied sexual deviancy, morbid introspection, effeminacy and androgeny.

43 *Ibid.*, p. 117 quotes the critic A. H. Wall redefining the significance of Venus in society and modern art in 1864.
44 *Ibid.*, p. 26.
45 Catherine Maxwell, *Second Sight. The Visionary Imagination in late Victorian Literature* (Manchester and New York: Manchester University press, 2008), p. 6.
46 *Ibid.*, p. 7.
47 Treuherz, Prettejohn and Becker, *Dante Gabriel Rossetti*, p. 78. The notes were jointly written with W. M. Rossetti.
48 *Ibid.*, p. 76.
49 See Michel Foucault, *The History of Sexuality*, 3 vols (New York: Vintage Press, 1990), Introduction to Vol. 1.
50 John Maynard, 'Sexuality and Love', in Richard Cronin, Alison Chapman and Antony H. Harrison, eds, *Companion to Victorian Poetry* (Oxford: Blackwell Publishers Ltd, 2007), pp. 543–65 explores these socio-political issues in the light of more modern sexual theory.
51 Tim Barringer, Jason Rosenfeld and Alison Smith, eds, *The Pre-Raphaelites. Victorian Avant-Garde* (London: Tate Publishing, 2012), p. 120.
52 Walker, *Stunner*, p. 80.
53 Treuherz, Prettejohn and Becker, *Dante Gabriel Rossetti*, pp. 93 and 96.
54 Marsh, *Sheffield*, p. 45.
55 Maynard, 'Sexuality and Love', pp. 551–2.
56 William Michael Rossetti, *His Family Letters with a Memoir*, 2 vols (London: Ellis and Elvey, 1895), Vol. 1, p. 274.
57 Elizabeth Helsinger, *Poetry and the Pre-Raphaelite Arts. Dante Gabriel Rossetti and William Morris* (New Haven and London: Yale University Press), p. 223.
58 Maynard, *Sexuality and Love*, p. 554.
59 Helsinger, *Poetry and the Pre-Raphaelite Arts*, p. 224.
60 John Holmes, *Dante Gabriel Rossetti and the Late Victorian Sonnet Sequence* (Aldershot, Hampshire: Ashgate Publishing Ltd, 2005), p. 16.
61 *Ibid.*, p. 15.
62 Marsh, *Dante Gabriel Rossetti*. pp. 431–7 dissects the arguments of Buchanan, Rossetti and the periodicals that subsequently became involved.
63 Holmes, *Late Victorian Sonnet Sequence*, pp. 21–3.
64 *Ibid.*, pp. 66–7.
65 David Sonstroem, *Rossetti and the Fair Lady* (Middletown, CT: Wesleyan University Press, 1970), p. 104.

66 Marsh, *Dante Gabriel Rossetti*, p. 212.
67 Armstrong, *Victorian Poetry*, p. 456.
68 Holmes, *Late Victorian Sonnet Sequence*, p. 15.
69 *Ibid.*, pp. 15–18. Holmes identifies four devices used to create this inclusive approach to meaning, symbolism, multiple voices, asking questions and using the image of the reader to reflect back the mind of the poet. Siddal also uses some of these techniques.
70 Barringer, Rosenfeld and Smith, eds, *Victorian Avant-Garde*, pp. 114–15.
71 Michaela Giebelhausen, 'The Religious and Intellectual Background', in Prettejohn, ed., *Cambridge Companion to the Pre-Raphaelites*, pp. 62–75, p. 67.
72 *Ibid.*, p. 72.
73 Burlinson, *Christina Rossetti*, p. 59.
74 *Ibid.*, pp. 63–5.
75 Dorothy Mermin, *Elizabeth Barrett Browning. The Origins of a New Poetry* (Chicago and London: The University of Chicago Press, 1989), pp. 70–1.
76 W. M. Rossetti, *Family Letters with a Memoir*, Vol. I, p. 408.
77 *Ibid.*, p. 380.
78 Dante Gabriel Rossetti, *The Letters to William Allingham*, ed, George Birkbeck Hill (London: T. Fisher Unwin, 1897), Letter XXXII, p. 195.
79 *Ibid.*, p. 204 editorial comment.
80 W. M. Rossetti, *Family Letters with a Memoir*, Vol. I, p. 255.
81 Walker, *Stunner*, pp. 95–8 describes two such sessions and investigates claims of Cornforth's 'gift'.
82 Maxwell, *Second Sight*, pp. 25–6.
83 *Ibid.*, p. 55 Maxwell also quotes Edmund Gosse, William Sharp, Thomas Hall Caine, Theodore Watts-Dunton and Sidney Colvin who variously testify to Rossetti's personal magnetism: his powerful, compelling, wilful character, irresistible charm over the young, and his sonorous, hypnotic voice.
84 D. G. Rossetti, *Rossetti and Morris. Their Correspondence*, No. 124, pp. 167–8. Rossetti used Swedenborg in his Dante studies and Dr Garth Wilkinson who attended Siddal in 1854 was a well-known follower.
85 Lawrence J. Starzyk, 'Elizabeth Siddal and the "Soulless Self-Reflections of Man's Skill"', *The Journal of Pre-Raphaelite Studies*, Vol. 16 (Fall 2007), 8–26, p. 10.
86 Marsh, *Legend*, p. 157.
87 W. M. Rossetti, *Burlington*, p. 274.

88 Julie Melnyk, 'Hemans's Later Poetry: Religion and the Vatic Poet', in Nanora Sweet and Julie Melnyk, eds, *Felicia Hemans: Reimagining Poetry in the Nineteenth Century* (Basingstoke: Palgrave, 2001), pp. 74–85.
89 Matthew Campbell, 'The Victorian Sonnet', in A. D. Cousins and Peter Howarth, eds, *The Cambridge Companion to the Sonnet* (Cambridge: Cambridge University Press, 2011), pp. 204–4, p. 205.
90 Natasha Distiller, *Desire and Gender in the Sonnet Tradition* (Basingstoke, Hampshire: Palgrave Macmillan, 2008), p. 99.
91 Amy Christine Billone, *Little Songs: Women, Silence and the Nineteenth Century Sonnet* (Columbus: Ohio State University, 2007), p. 7.
92 Marianne van Remoortel, *Lives of the Sonnet, 1787–1895. Genre, Gender and Criticism* (Farnham, Surrey: Ashgate Publishing Ltd, 2011), p. 111.
93 *Ibid.*, pp. 89–113 looks at both sides of the argument in the light of Barrett Browning's life-history.
94 Armstrong, *Victorian Poetry*, p. 334.
95 Distiller, *Desire and Gender*, p. 124.
96 Alison Chapman, 'Sonnet and Sonnet Sequence', in Cronin, Chapman and Harrison, eds, *A Companion to Victorian Poetry* (Oxford: Blackwell Publishers Ltd, 2007), pp. 99–114, p. 111.
97 Holmes, *The Late Victorian Sonnet Sequence*, p. 4.
98 *Ibid.*, pp. vii–viii.
99 *Ibid.*, p. 3.
100 Van Remoortel, *Lives of the Sonnet*, p. 98.
101 The bracketed numbers are those given in the sonnets in the final 1881 version of the sequence as published in Ballads and Sonnets. 'Nuptial Sleep' (6a) was included in the 1870 edition but omitted in 1881 following criticism of its alleged eroticism.
102 The W. M. Rossetti transcript of Siddal's incomplete manuscript has the following wording which is also used by Lewis and Lasner, but the Marsh *Sheffield* edition has a different second couplet: 'Then carry me through the dim twilight / And hide me among the graves.' There seems little logic or rhyming continuity in the placement of these lines which also appear at the conclusion to 'At Last'.
103 Hassett, 'Elizabeth Siddal's Poetry', p. 462.
104 Maxwell, *Second Sight*, pp. 49–50.
105 Helsinger, *Poetry and the Pre-Raphaelite Arts*, p. 224.
106 Jerome McGann, 'The Poetry of Dante Gabriel Rossetti (1828–82), in *The Cambridge* Companion to the Pre-Raphaelites, pp. 89–102, pp. 96–9.

107 As this poem can be dated to early 1862 this could be a reference to Siddal's stillborn daughter.
108 D. M. R. Bentley, '"Bocca mi Baciò": The Love Kiss in the Works of Dante Gabriel Rossetti', in *The Journal of Pre-Raphaelite Studies*, Vol 16 (Spring 2007), 31–44, p. 38.
109 Maxwell, *Second Sight*, p. 41 suggests this is why images of water are so prevalent in Rossetti's poems.
110 Holmes, *The Late Victorian Sonnet Sequence*, p. 7.
111 *Ibid.*, p. 24.
112 *Ibid.*, p. 25.
113 Arnold, *Poems 1840–1866*, pp. 5, 10.

2

Siddal, Swinburne and the ballad tradition

Clerk Saunders

Siddal's watercolour *Clerk Saunders* (figure 12) was shown at the Pre-Raphaelite salon at Russell Place in 1857 and was also included in the British Art exhibition sent to the United States that same year, from where it was purchased by Charles Eliot Norton of Harvard University. Considered one of her finest works, this intensely emotive piece was one of several that took their subject from Walter Scott's three-volume *Minstrelsy of the Scottish Border* (1802–03) and depicts May Margaret kneeling on her bed as the ghost of her murdered lover Saunders enters through a wall. Scott's poem, itself derived from an earlier version published in 1776 by David Herd, tells how Saunders persuades his lover to deceive her family and spend a night with him. He pays with his life at the hands of her seven brothers and Margaret awakes to find a corpse by her side. Refusing earthly comfort and eager for answers to her questions about the afterlife, she welcomes Saunders's spirit to give him a last token of her affection. This cannot be physical; instead, as he finally departs, she passes him a glass wand and promises never to love another as passionately.

Like Siddal, Swinburne found fascination in the popular ballad and earmarked George Ritchie Kinloch's fragmentary version of this same poem for inclusion in an (unfinished) anthology in preparation between 1859 and 1861. Given their closeness after her marriage to D. G. Rossetti in 1860 it is possible Swinburne was familiar with Siddal's three preparatory sketches if not the finished article, yet these two works differ substantially in content.[1] The poem

12 Elizabeth Siddal, *Clerk Saunders*, 1857, watercolour

narrates events surrounding Saunders's murder; Siddal's interpretation focuses on the aftermath, in particular on the presentation of the crystal wand kissed by the heroine as a pledge of her troth, an episode taken from verses which only appear in Scott's edit of the original song. Swinburne, presumably familiar with the latter, chose to ignore it in this early example of his editing technique.

Their divergent approaches here are interesting, and brought into sharp focus by the shared subject. Swinburne maintains a poetic tradition that is linked inextricably to his Northumbrian roots: border dialect is preserved, the narration is terse, and there is little preamble to the bloody deed even if, in the last verse, Margaret's father does acknowledge his sons' fatal error when it becomes apparent that Saunders was not the lowly individual he was assumed to be. Of the fourteen stanzas transcribed all but four are quatrains of four iambic beats per line and an abcb rhyming pattern which propels the story on with limited emotional involvement required from the reader. The anomalies are sometimes unavoidable because Kinloch indicates that lines are missing. For example, Swinburne creates a six-line second stanza by combining verses 2 and (an incomplete) 3 from Kinloch. More interestingly, Swinburne's fourth and fifth stanzas, in which Saunders suggests ways of circumventing the ban on his physical presence in Margaret's chamber, are an amalgamation of four from Kinloch. The two sections run thus, beginning with Kinloch's version that parallels Saunders' instructions and Margaret's specific obedience:

5. 'Ye'll tak a lang claith in your hand,
    Ye'll haud it up afore your een,
That ye may swear, and save your aith,
    That ye saw na Sandy sin yestreen.

6. 'And ye'll tak me in your arms twa,
    Ye'll carry me into your bed,
That ye may swear, and save your aith,
    That in your bour-floor I never daed.'

7. She's taen a lang claith in her hand,
    She's hauden't up afore her een,
That she might swear, and save her aith,
    That she saw na Sandy sin yestreen.

> 8. She has taen him in her arms twa,
>   And carried him into her bed,
> That she might swear, and save her aith,
>   That on her bour-floor he never gaed.[2]

Swinburne reworks this version by truncating the repetition which was a feature of oral tradition and yet could be considered in print to be delaying the narrative. This hints at an adaptive technique to be developed in later ballads:

> Ye'll tak a lang claith in your hand,
>   Ye'll haud it up afore your een
> And ye'll tak me in your arms twa,
>   Ye'll carry me into your bed
> That in your bower floor I ne'er gaed.
>
> She's tane a lang claith in her hand,
>   She's hauden't up afore her een
> That she might swear, and save her aith
>   That she saw na Sandy sin yestreen.[3] (14–23)

Structural changes apart, crucially, the archaic language has been almost entirely preserved. In contrast, Siddal captures one lyric moment from a longer episode yet she also manages to supply a context and a note of subjectivity that the ballad omits. The bed in the dark chamber is rumpled, evidence of its recent occupation, her prayer book is closed upon its desk, her faith being no longer of use; the sands of the prominent hour-glass have run out as the breaking dawn heralds her final moments with her lover. Through the window, deep-set to emphasize the sense of separation, can be seen a verdant landscape and the tightly packed roofs of a town that constitutes reality. There is a direct intensity to the gaze between the two characters, yet she cannot touch this ghost; the wand acts as their medium as he extends empty arms towards her. Margaret's red hair, an obvious link to Siddal, suggests further identification between painter and subject. Siddal, who avoided physical communication with all but a few, has arguably composed a 'ballad' about herself.[4] Pre-Raphaelite artistic influence can be seen in the rich green and cobalt hues of the clothing and draperies, the medievalism of the setting and Margaret's long loose hair, but Siddal's colour and figure work is strongly individual and as such it contrasts markedly with a literary counterpart that Swinburne felt was important to conserve in its antique form.

Siddal's portrayal of the relationship between Margaret and Saunders illustrates a moment of mediated communication. Death has physically separated the two lovers in Siddal's painting, so they can no longer speak. Their communication has become figurative, finding a new more powerful voice whose 'text' is the wand passed between them. In her ballads, death and the necessity for tactile physicality will be similarly transcended, making genderless communication possible. Communication, or more accurately its absence, is central to the narrative of each of Siddal's ballad fragments. In her hands the ballad (traditionally a mode of oral communication) metaphorically explores the failure of communication, the inability of women to express themselves, especially to men, whilst still paying homage to the antique ballad format. The message of the ballad text, like the wand of the painting, links speaker and audience, who otherwise would not be able to hear each other. 'Clerk Saunders' therefore, in both its incarnations, serves as an illustration of a wider thesis, that Siddal and Swinburne, starting from a shared set of generic influences adapted or extended the ballad tradition for their own purposes. For Swinburne the ballad was a living current of historical inspiration that for forty years informed a novel and some of his poems; for Siddal, if only for a fraction of that time, it was the basis of a fair proportion of her art and her poetry and it moved her work into spheres that are unexpected and unconventional. She experimented with a ballad format in ways that became increasingly lyrical, and created a double meaning within a deceptively simple structure.

Siddal and Swinburne

The relationship between Siddal and Swinburne came about because of her marriage to Rossetti to whom the student Swinburne was introduced in September 1857 whilst, along with certain other members of the PRB, he was painting Arthurian murals in the Oxford Union. The two men established a friendship that would survive Siddal's death; as a widower Rossetti invited Swinburne to share rooms with him at Cheyne Walk in Chelsea, an arrangement that would last a further ten, rather fitful, years. From the autumn of 1860 Swinburne was a constant visitor to the marital household in Chatham Place and was regularly included in their social activities. He dined out with them the night before Siddal died of a laudanum overdose on 11 February 1862 (incidentally seeing nothing unusual in her behaviour) and as a result had to give a statement to the coroner two days later. The following month he spoke rather obliquely of these events in a letter to his mother, actually the earliest of only five such documents in publication which refer to a woman whose friendship he obviously valued:

> I would rather not write yet about what has happened – I suppose none of the papers gave a full report, so that you do not know I was almost the last person who saw her (except her husband and a servant) and had to give evidence at the inquest. Happily there was no difficulty in proving that illness had quite deranged her mind, so that the worst chance of all was escaped ... I am only glad to have been able to keep him company and be of a little use during these weeks.[5]

The verdict of accidental death thus saved the family from the stigma of suicide, apparently Swinburne's immediate concern. Thirty years later he would be far more effusive in his description of Siddal's qualities, but regardless of this his biographers have still tended to trivialize the relationship, devoting little time to her. Their red hair, regarded as unlucky in the mid-century, set them apart, as did their 'inexperience, restlessness, waywardness and playful absurdity', a belittling portrait that was mirrored elsewhere.[6] The same tendency is found among Siddal commentators, even the most recent.[7] Swinburne has been dismissed as a diversion for Siddal, one who could read to her, keep her company and make her laugh, not an intellectual meeting of minds but a companionship that arose out of shared misfortune, and one given approval by her husband so he could paint another 'delectable model' behind closed doors.[8] Others have given the relationship more credit, but Swinburne is not seen as central to the narrative, a champion of her memory rather than being a particularly close friend.[9]

Siddal was not Swinburne's only female idol. He was especially close to his favourite sister Edith who died of consumption in 1863 nineteen months after Siddal, who interestingly looked very like her, sharing the same red hair, elongated neck, prominent nose and heavy-lidded eyes. From 1854 until her death in 1866 Swinburne was under the unofficial patronage of Lady Pauline Trevelyan whose estate at Wallington in Northumberland had become an important cultural centre. He was also romantically attached to his cousin Mary Gordon but in general he was not successful in such relationships, and devotion since childhood to Gordon coupled with his masochistic tendencies put a conventional marriage beyond him.[10] A special fascination however was reserved for women as poets, and Swinburne himself wrote several poems honouring Sappho.[11] He elevated this mortal woman into an immortal goddess whilst still allowing her to retain 'sisterly' qualities that make her a kindred spirit with whom he could easily identify.[12] This fusion of male and female minds would facilitate the writing of poetry that was perfect, and this again suggests a parallel with Siddal's work. Sappho the mortal is transformed in death, losing her body and thereafter existing only as fragments of poetry. These can be continually reconfigured and their meaning reinterpreted, a process enabled by their brevity and disassociation.

Swinburne could not have thought of Siddal as a reincarnation of his Sapphic muse while she was alive as he appears not to have known of her poetry until well after she died. Similarly, whereas it cannot be said with certainty that Siddal was aware of Sappho or identified with her, there is evidence to make it a likelihood. Sappho was a very powerful muse, fascinating because of her association with a love so intense its loss led to a literal leap into the unknown. There may never have been a real Sappho but she exists because she is the embodiment of suffering in love and her poet descendants animate her by repeatedly re-envisioning her death. She was considered the pinnacle of female poetic achievement but very little of her reputation was based on her poetry as few Victorian women could read Greek, so it is her legend that predominates. She seemed to match what women should write about and what the female situation was, one of constantly repeated loss. Intense emotion epitomized women's lyric poetry, and their responses centre around the moment she sings her farewell song and leaps into the sea; the woman poet as art object in a moment of abandonment taking a leap of faith and leaving only a text behind.[13] Sappho dies and becomes that text, which appealed to nineteenth-century women poets when permission to write was not always granted. Penning Sappho's last words they gave themselves that permission even if they are then killing her to assure their own literary survival.[14]

L. E. L., Hemans, Barrett Browning, Christina Rossetti and Caroline Norton were all drawn to Sappho's fragments in gestures of absorption and imitation, beginning what would be a long tradition of appropriating her poetry and her persona to explore the issues and anxieties behind female creativity and erotic experience.[15] 'Sappho' (1822) by L. E. L. uses a mixture of tenses to show Sappho is dead but still alive, remembered for posterity, and in 'An Indian Woman's Death Song' (1828) Hemans writes of how a deserted wife canoes herself and her children over a cataract on the Mississippi, a poem Yopi Prins places in the Sapphic tradition.[16] Rossetti uses a counter-factual approach in 'What Sappho would have said had her leap cured instead of killing her' (1848); a tongue-in-cheek poem that gives the dead speaker back her voice only for her to find her 'cure' robs her of her very selfhood. She needs pain to exist at all, a sentiment that would surely have chimed with many nineteenth-century women. In 'A Vision of Poets' (1844) Barrett Browning went further, positing Sappho as the inspiration for all women who subsequently wrote or relived her leap.

This pervasive Sapphic culture is assimilated into Siddal's poems, their critical reception and her biographical treatments. Sappho and Siddal share themes of loss, longing, desire, pain, love, ecstasy, exile, banishment, absence and bereavement. They speak of the empty persona that is there purely for the reflection of that pain, using inward-looking, often suicidal, lyrics and mixed tenses that point to a constantly repeated and miserable present as well as a preordained future. Their voices come from beyond the grave to emphasize the cyclical nature of existence. The recovery of a 'lost' poet like Siddal is predicated on their having been forgotten, and she is a fragmentary, ghost-like figure with a fractured afterlife that can resurface in various guises depending on the cultural context. Much of her back-story has been mythologized, speculation surrounding her relationships and infamous death the attraction, not her poems, a situation also shared with L. E. L. More positively however, as with Sappho the Siddal fragments have gained an independent afterlife enabling their critical reception and assimilation into a literary canon, and Swinburne's devotion to Sappho allows Siddal's work to be considered in a new light. Separate verses that can be reassembled to present further readings, and brevity that masks a deeper philosophical meaning link it to the Sapphic corpus. Siddal's ballads show little interest in the physical body except its sensory capabilities. She then comes to represent communication that has no boundaries or limits, the very thing she recognizes as lacking for women in mid-Victorian society. Swinburne's poetess does not conform to the Victorian ideals of marriage, motherhood and domesticity. She will suffer, be the epitome of tragic and glamorous love, but in tackling taboo subjects like female sexuality and independence her enhanced alienation has the potential to create a new poetry, beyond anything mainstream and conventional.[17] Siddal and her work as poet and artist can be made to fit these models and Swinburne appears to recognize the fact in letters exchanged with W. M. Rossetti towards the end of the century.[18]

Swinburne's first reference to Siddal comes in a letter to the editor of *The Academy* in December 1892 in which he defends her reputation against phrases written about her in William Bell Scott's *Autobiographical Notes*:

> It is impossible that even the reptile rancour, the omnivorous malignity of Iago himself could have dreamed of trying to cast a slur on the memory of that incomparable lady [...] To one at least who knew her better than most of her husband's friends, the memory of all her matchless charms of mind and person – her matchless grace, loveliness, courage, endurance, wit, humour, heroism and sweetness – is too dear to be profaned by any attempt at expression. The vilest of the vile could not have dreamed of trying 'to cast a slur on her memory'.[19]

A similar sentiment but minus the scathing anger pervades the correspondence with W. M. Rossetti, spread over a nine-year period during which the latter published various volumes of family papers and reminiscences. Swinburne had been asked for contributions to the first of these, *Dante Gabriel Rossetti. His Family Letters with a Memoir*, and upon receipt of his copies, included the following in his letter of congratulation to the author. Two features are most telling, the lack of superficial intimacy, and the acknowledgement of her intelligence as reader and critic:

> It would have given me great pleasure if you had asked me a word or two more about dear Lizzie. (Though we did not call each other by our Christian names, I hope I may now speak of her as a sister). Except Lady Trevelyan, I never knew so brilliant and appreciative a woman – so quick to see and so keen to enjoy that rare and delightful fusion of wit, humour, character-painting and dramatic poetry – poetry subdued for dramatic effect – which is only less wonderful and delightful than the very highest works of genius. I used to come to read to her sometimes [...] and I shall never forget her delight in Fletcher's magnificent comedy 'The Spanish Curate' [...] I can hear her laughter to this day [...] she thought it 'better than Shakespeare' and though I could not allow that, I do think it better than anything except Shakespeare's best.[...] I won't enlarge on the deeper and sadder side of my brotherly affection for her, but I shall always be sorrowfully glad and proud to remember her regard for me ... She was a wonderful as well as a most lovable creature.[20]

The reference to Siddal's love of dramatic performance is also interesting because it goes against the popular conception of her as a withdrawn observer. It also calls into question the purely autobiographical nature of her poetry, which can at first reading appear to be purely a commentary on a sad and unfulfilled life. Three years later Rossetti published *Ruskin: Rossetti: Pre-Raphaelitism. Papers 1854–62* and Swinburne wrote to him in mild rebuke:

> I cannot thank you enough for the gift of your beautiful volume. You know how exceptionally interesting to me is everything that concerns 'Lizzie', and you will not take it amiss if I say that I am a little disappointed to find you have made no use of the recollections I sent you, and which you said you meant to utilize in any future edition of your Memoir. Her unique and indescribable personal charm is no doubt reflected to considerable extent in this book for all who have eyes to see anything; but I did hope, as I had hoped for years, that you would find occasion to put on record my evidence to the fact that her sense of humour, her fine appreciation and exquisite relish of poetic

comedy and dramatic invention or satire, could not be surpassed, and would have sufficed to confute the charge that *no* woman can enjoy the finest effects or creations of satiric humour [...] as thoroughly and heartily as men do. I don't at all mean that I think *most* women can.[21]

Her love of theatre is reiterated here, but there is an implied guilt or hesitancy in Swinburne's use of Siddal's diminutive fore-name when it is placed in inverted commas. Post-mortem Siddal is treated with greater familiarity and therefore acquires a different persona, but this shift in the relationship does not affect Swinburne's opinion of her intellectual worth. He credits Siddal with a higher degree of literary appreciation than most of his contemporaries would have been prepared to do. The matter was settled in 1903 with the issue of an article in the *Burlington Magazine* and with *Some Reminiscences of William Michael Rossetti* in 1906. Whatever the relationship with Siddal the years had not dimmed its impact: 'I could not write all at once to acknowledge the arrival of your splendid present: there was simply too much to thank you for [...] only I will gratefully say [...] how I sincerely I thank you for printing at length my little reminiscence of your sister-in-law. I did want to see that in print.'[22] The *Burlington* piece itself carries the most pertinent Swinburne testimonial, W. M. Rossetti prefacing his generalized reference to fifteen of her poems thus:

> Mr Swinburne expressed the quality of her verse with equal intuition and precision. 'Watts (Theodore Watts-Dunton) greatly admires her poem "A Year and a Day", which is as new to me as to him. I need not add that I agree with him. There is the same note of originality in discipleship which distinguishes her work in art – Gabriel's influence and example not more perceptible than her own independence and freshness of inspiration.'[23]

Swinburne recognizes the dichotomy in Siddal's poetry, 'A Year and a Day' being a good example of how a traditional form can be acknowledged but taken in a new direction. Its ballad narrative is replaced with a conversation with the self, a musing on detachment from physical surroundings that has arisen from the ending of a relationship. It is alive with references to communication, physical, figurative and spiritual, but their precise nature is uncertain, which stresses the effect of their failure. Swinburne's opinion is undated but as his earliest documented meeting with Watts-Dunton was in 1872 the implication is that not even he saw any of Siddal's manuscripts while she was alive. This is his only known reference to them despite their all having been published by his close friend W. M. Rossetti between 1895 and 1906, the period covered by the letters quoted.

Swinburne's ballads and their critical reception

Siddal and Swinburne are at first glance unlikely poetic associates yet there is a powerful similarity in their work in the ballad tradition. Despite the fact that the variety and extent of their respective outputs are vastly different, they share certain important facets, common interests in medievalism, tragic/romantic themes, and the work of Walter Scott, a source Swinburne relied upon in compiling his aborted anthology.[24] Published in 1866, *Poems and Ballads* included three Swinburne medieval or Chaucerian imitative pieces: 'A Christmas Carol', 'The Masque of Queen Bersabe' and 'St Dorothy'.[25] Similar echoes are found in Siddal's poetry: 'True Love' is addressed to the dead Earl Richard whose lover keeps a vigil by his white stone effigy; the sarcastic tone of 'The Lust of the Eyes' is enhanced by the repetition of 'My Lady' amid the courtly language; and 'At Last' consists largely of a list of archaic funeral practices and instructions. Swinburne ballads almost always depict domestic tragedy rather than political or topical issues, and every one of Siddal's sixteen poems deals with romantic loss in one form or another. Siddal had volumes three and four of Scott's *Minstrelsy of the Scottish Border* and inscribed both with her name.[26] In volume three pencil marks on the contents page against seventeen titles suggest she intended to illustrate these border ballads and it is known that in 1854 she and D. G. Rossetti planned to collaborate on an illustrated edition of old Scottish ballads.[27]

When *Poems and Ballads* was published it was immediately greeted with a storm of protest. Regarded collectively as outrageous, blasphemous and immoral, the sixty-two poems included five ballads at the end of the volume which became overshadowed by the infamous remainder, and this is reflected in the contemporary

Siddal, Swinburne and the ballad tradition 101

critical reaction. John Morley writing in the *Saturday Review* on 4 August 1866 was one of several to deny any literary or linguistic merit to the work, maintaining furthermore, 'There are not twenty stanzas in the whole book which have the faintest tincture of soberness.'[28] Robert Buchanan in the *Athenaeum* was similarly scathing, saying that in total the poems were actually:

> too juvenile and unreal (to be of immoral influence) [...] The strong pulse of true passion beats in not one of them. They are unclean, with little power; and mere uncleanness repulses. Gross insincerity in dealing with simple subjects, and rank ravings on serious themes, makes one suspicious of a writer's qualities in all things, and a very little examination enables us to perceive that these poems are essentially imitative.[29]

There is a certain irony here as what Buchanan intended as criticism Swinburne would have welcomed. *Poems and Ballads* included deliberate imitations of not only Scottish and English ballads and medieval verse but French and Italian lyrics and dramatic writings of classical antiquity. Swinburne was proud when he managed to pass off one of his own ballads as the real article when he read it aloud at the family home in Northumberland.[30] He had great faith in the ballad institution because of the community cohesion it brought about through its ability to link successive generations of oral tradition. This chain of communication was socially important because it maintained a focus on the culture of working people, vital for one who held republican sympathies. Ironically, the ballads Swinburne set out to conserve keep the social status quo in their emphasis on class structure and gender inequality. The ballad tradition is essentially masculine and in writing his own versions Swinburne largely follows it, subverting the form to comment on the failure of women to express themselves, Siddal acknowledges this and laments the lack of a dominant female voice. Buchanan made no specific mention of the five ballads but an anonymous critic in the *London Review* did make a brief comment in a piece which otherwise adopts a derogatory tone:

> 'Anactoria' and 'Dolores' in particular [...] are especially horrible [...] impossible to see why they should have been written. (but) [...] In some of the poems, 'The King's Daughter', 'After Death', 'May

Janet', 'The Bloody Son' and 'The Sea Swallows' – Mr Swinburne has imitated with singular felicity the manner and phraseology of the old ballad-writers.[31]

Only W. M. Rossetti in *Swinburne's Poems and Ballads* (1866) made any further reference to the above titles, and even he was dismissive of their significance. He argues that out of 'four main currents of influence and feeling', the poems that are 'Assimilative or Reproductive in Form' are the least important. The 'Passionately Sensuous', the 'Classic or Antique' and the 'Religiously Mutinous' are considered more significant.[32] He refers to a quintet of ballads (unidentified, unlike other imitative poems mentioned in his essay), 'carefully balanced in shade, but mainly conforming to the old ballads of North Britain [...] exceedingly fine, startlingly similar to original models yet very definitely Swinburne's own'.[33] Ignored by contemporary reviewers because they were archaic and uncontroversial, these ballads continue to receive scant attention.

Swinburne's ballads may have been overlooked but they are in fact part of an ongoing tradition that gained respectability in the early eighteenth century as poets began creating literary ballads, finding stimulus among the traditional folk songs or ballad poems of the English-Scottish border in particular. Both traditional and literary ballads have certain characteristics: an abrupt beginning, simple language, a repeated refrain, a story told swiftly through dialogue and action that allows dramatic oral communication, an often tragic theme which deals with a single dramatic episode, unsentimental treatment, minimal detail of surroundings or character, and an impersonal narrator who does not voice an opinion. Broadsides, which developed as an urban sub-culture of the traditional folk ballad, show interesting variations to this model. Written by professional authors and journalists and focusing on topical issues, they attempted to tell a whole story with accompanying detail and some moralizing. This is not to imply that any of these types was prescriptive or stagnant, as all were adapted and imitated. Neither was the term 'balladeer' considered derogatory; medieval folk ballads played a vital part in maintaining the customs of illiterate or semi-literate societies, their stories evolving with each generation of singers. William Morris called literary ballads 'the finest poems of our language' and Swinburne as ballad-writer 'among the most precious treasures of our own or any language', ballad imitations by 'cultivated' poets clearly evincing the highest expression of praise.[34]

Swinburne's ballads have been divided into three types: those he edited, such as 'Clerk Saunders', those that were deliberate imitations of existing examples, and those that had a philosophical component.[35] The imitative ballads attempt to recreate the antique form in which personal and modern elements occasionally intrude. Comment by the speaker is minimal but can be used to interrupt the narrative to pass a contemporary judgement, making a nineteenth-century presence felt among ancient, almost buried, legend. The philosophical ballads shift the balance between ancient and modern by introducing a greater degree of personal opinion or moralistic lecturing. Ballad techniques, such as 'the undersong of balladry', the fatal and tragic themes which hold such gruesome fascination, are still upheld, but the focus is not the climax of the narrative or even the narrative itself.[36] It is instead the symbolic point reached through passages of lyric description after which, for example, the speaker pronounces on the fate of mankind in general. Imitative ballads may end briefly with a moral judgement, an opinion about the awfulness of a crime or the severity of the punishment enacted, but philosophical ballads look more into the nature of suffering, or the relationship between man and the power of the natural world, or between this world and the next. It is at this point that the form becomes more experimental, the way made clear for the poet to use the traditional format for personal expression. This way the ballad maintains its poetic and historic presence while continuing to evolve, and the balladeer will have fulfilled a duty to both the past and the future.

Ballad influence comes out in many ways and has inspired very different imitative results so that a literary ballad may have a ballad-like plot couched in highly literary language, or a very thin plot but with a ballad ring.[37] There are elements of both in Siddal's ballads and they do have the required storylines, even if the latter are more fragmentary and implicit than those found in Swinburne's work. Similarly, oral transmission becomes conceptualized, not important per se but vital to the double readings her texts provide. In the ballad tradition authors needed to show they were familiar with the efforts of their precursors, thus nineteenth-century literary balladeers sourced their work from anthologies put together from the mid-eighteenth century onwards, to create their own amalgamated versions or completely new pieces in ballad style. These anthologies, notably by Percy (1765), Herd (1776), Scott (1802), Jamieson (1806), Buchan (1826), Motherwell and Kinloch (both 1827) individually provided commonality and continuity, but were in turn collated into one scholarly publication edited by Francis Child. The eight-volume *English and Scottish Popular Ballads* first appeared in 1857–58; and in all likelihood Swinburne used the second edition of 1861 when working on his own aborted anthology.[38] Child printed, without alteration, several versions of the same poem and coupled these with extensive notes which a student of the form, like Swinburne, would have found invaluable.

Hemans too was familiar with Percy and Scott and had an extensive similar library. *A Selection of Welsh Melodies* (1822) and folk song imitations like the four 'Songs of the Cid' (1823) about the eleventh-century Spanish Christian leader have ballad influences, as have a number of lyrics that show extension or development of the form. 'The Landing of the Pilgrim Fathers in New England' (1825) carries a prominent message of heroic religious freedom but there is no extended narrative or decisive iambic beat. 'Night Blowing Flowers' (1817) has a conventional pattern of rhyme and rhythm that is easy to narrate but gives right of reply to those blooms in the last three verses. 'Casabianca' (1826) is about the heroism of a French boy during the Battle of the Nile who cannot leave his post because his father, who alone can give permission, is dead. Hemans uses an ostensibly simple piece to make the reader confront the victim status of children, the way war impacts on family values, and the relative unimportance of fame and glory. Landon used traditional ballad form to expose the evils of the factory system and child slavery that enabled it in 'The Factory' (1838). There is very little narrative, the impact of the poem coming from the contrast between an idyllic childhood and one ruled by the mill bell, but the insistent iambic beat replicates the movement of the machines and shows how simple structure and overt sentimentality can enforce a memorably pertinent message.

Christina Rossetti included a cluster of ballads in *Goblin Market and Other Poems* (1862); 'Love from the North, 'Cousin Kate', 'Noble Sisters', 'Maude Clare' and 'Sister Maude' all indicate her love of traditional themes, but relationships between two women and the crises that result are added. Past history is played down so the reader isn't told why Maude Clare attends the wedding of her rival Nell, or why the latter vows to stand by her faithless lover, or why in 'Sister Maude' the eponymous women betrays her sibling. The significance of the present predominates, allowing the reader to empathize even with a transgressive woman. 'Noble Sisters' is a conversation piece in which two very different attitudes to a lover's promise emerge. It has a bitter sting in the tail as in 'Sister Maude' and 'Cousin Kate' and Rossetti draws attention to each with a structural or rhythmic change, a technique Siddal also uses. Jealousy and revenge draw these ballads together, the defiant speakers not the most beautiful or high class. 'Sister Maude' is the most vitriolic and is reminiscent of Siddal's 'Love and Hate' and 'The Passing of Love' in its direct bitterness. (These two poems are discussed in the next chapter in a feminist context and Rossetti's five ballads also fit neatly into that extended debate). Convention and disobedience sit side by side and this can be extrapolated to suggest Rossetti deliberately made a naive form more demanding by allowing it to hide multiple secrets and that, paradoxically, as a naturally self-revealing writer she found a way of holding something back while again showing how adaptable ballad form could be.[39]

Medieval and contemporary meet again in the ballads of Barrett Browning but critics are divided over the extent to which they were challenging and progressive, or nostalgic escapism. They are tragic narratives that appeal to the conscience of the reader but they move away from the *Minstrelsy* pattern when gender difference is highlighted or the poem has specific purpose, like 'A Song for the Ragged Schools of London' (1854), written to raise funds for a refuge for destitute women set up by her sister. The majority were written between 1836 and 1844 after which she left Wimpole Street and embraced a more modern world view.[40] 'Lady Geraldine's Courtship' (1844), in which Bertram the poor poet writes to a friend about his love for the lady of the manor, exemplifies the contrasting critical analysis. It has been seen as a critique of the Victorian idea of progress that balances loss of moral fibre with increased equality of class and gender, a representation of Barrett Browning's changing ideas about poetry and poetics that adheres to tradition but also reflects issues confronting society, such as female ownership of property.[41] On the other hand, it is judged mere uncensored fantasy, an entertaining story used to carry a passionate message in a permissible way. It depicts two supposedly equal figures but whereas Geraldine is assertive Bertram swoons like a woman in a reversal of stereotypes that renders the poem a less than satisfactory modification; it may be a repudiation of the Victorian ideal of womanliness but the clash between old style and new substance doesn't go far enough.[42] Others argue that it breaks new ground by using an archaic tale subliminally to expose contemporary inequality.[43] To whatever degree, a retrogressive, sentimental genre is undermined to expose the inherent paradox in, and complexity of, ballad form, and the same can be said of the ballad interpretations Siddal produced. Some Barrett Browning ballads also offer moral choices; in 'Bertha in the Lane' a dying sister decides to admit she gave up her lover when she found out he loved Bertha better. Resentment and guilt abound and the poem is full of conflicting impulses, but it is its form that is interesting because it has been considered a ballad in the guise of a dramatic monologue, a cross-over Siddal adopts in 'A Year and a Day' and 'Speechless'.[44]

The Pre-Raphaelites, with their love of medievalism and willingness to experiment, played a specific part in the ballad tradition.[45] When eighteenth-century poets began to imitate the ancient ballads it was broadsides they copied but later two literary forms emerged, the sentimental broadsides continuing alongside a revival of the old folk equivalent championed by the Pre-Raphaelites. Both Siddal and Swinburne found that the ballad genre lent itself to the process of experimentation. Siddal exploited this opportunity more than Swinburne but even at its most lyrical her work retains the rhythmic and rhyming patterns of the traditional format. The uncomplicated structure and the sparseness of language, which create a mood of separation or distance, emphasize the metaphorical absence of verbal communication. For Swinburne the interest lay more in location and tradition. His love of the Borders was lifelong. His paternal family had lived at Capheaton Hall near

Cambo since the seventeenth century, and his grandfather John Edward Swinburne was a prominent local politician and literary figure whose wife was related to the dukes of Northumberland, as was Swinburne's mother who was the Duke's niece. (The wife of Swinburne's mentor in later life, Clara Watts-Dunton, was herself born near Capheaton and she remembered Border ballads often being discussed at The Pines when Swinburne lived there.)[46] Swinburne, imbued with pride in his ancestry and the romance of the past, called himself a Borderer or Northcountryman. The area was rich in ancient balladry which he liked to hear sung as a child, and he liked ballads because he could connect them with the elements, great natural forces such as tempests, waves, light and fire which he linked to 'elements' in human nature, whether violent or pathetic.[47] This same sense of escape from physical and social confines is found in the scabrous themes his ballads exploit: bloodiness, cruelty, sexuality and the erotic. Swinburne's admiration for the fixed poetic form has already been noted; in exploring this love for imitation further Swinburne would have been enticed by the communal effort involved in building something bigger than the sum of its parts and beyond the sum of all its revisions: 'To imitate a ballad would be to recapitulate in a single act an entire history of poetic transmission', the work of many poets merging into one in a pure pastiche.[48]

Swinburne's love of ballads is first seen in the 1861 unfinished edition, which consists of twenty-six completed versions of popular ballads and some preliminary drafts. These were done by collating versions published in earlier collections; some of the resulting poems are direct copies but most are intricate reworkings that use multiple references and include his interpolations. Crucially, the manuscript shows what sources were used and why, allowing Swinburne's technique and reasoning as a young editor to be examined. This is important because it formed part of his training as a ballad author, the close study of old poems leading to an intimate acquaintance with their rhythms, phraseology and spirit.[49] Swinburne was writing ballads at the same time as he was editing the old versions, so he is likely to have used the same methodology, the same traditional devices, on each project, making the annotated manuscript of further interest. Like his predecessors, when editing he appears to have selected stanzas from one source, isolating lines or phrases from another, altering the language throughout. He used a total of eight sources (relying on three) to produce complex constructions that always incorporate at least two. He included his own lines or stanzas in fourteen of the finished products to increase the impact of the macabre or pitiful but did not make these plain, so they only emerge with detailed analysis. The manuscript was not actually published until 1925 when it formed the first section of *Ballads of the English Border* by *Algernon Charles Swinburne*, edited by William MacInnes. The other two parts purport to be Swinburne's 'imitative' and 'modern' ballads but these divisions are meaningless, and unfortunately for the Swinburne scholar the whole volume carries misreadings, omissions, inaccurate transcriptions and punctuation on almost every page, both in the text and in the poet's notes.[50] He wrote around thirty literary ballads, fifteen of which were published in his lifetime. Apart from the five in *Poems and Ballads*, another eight appear in *Poems and Ballads Third Series* (1889), and several are duplicated in his second novel *Lesbia Brandon*, but not all critics have been convinced that they all really belong to the genre.[51] Along with those selected for his anthology, most of them lean towards stories of domestic tragedy. As in other nineteenth-century ballads the stories are of unhappy love affairs ending in violent death, meddling parents who thwart the course of true love, the abandoning of virtuous ladies, the revenge of the more spirited of the latter, and the reappearance of rejected lovers as ghosts.[52] Murder, infanticide, drowning, burning, hanging, suicide, rape, incest and illegitimacy all feature specifically in Swinburne's work.

Siddal's entire output numbers merely around half of just Swinburne's literary ballad collection alone. There are manuscripts for fifteen poems and a few fragments and most are very short and difficult to categorize, self-expressive certainly, but also drawing on literary tradition, especially the Romantic ballad and the elegiac lyric. Five poems show a connection between Siddal's work and the ballad tradition.[53] 'He and She and Angels Three' (1857) is the most slight, three quatrains with largely trochaic rhythm that speaks of heavenly reunion for one torn from her lover. 'At Last' (1861 and initialled E. E. S.) is the most traditional. The eight iambic quatrains relay a dying woman's instructions to her mother for the conduct of her burial and the future care of her son. 'True Love' (1854) is also quite traditional but there is an increased personal element. Dactylic rhythm and brevity of language are used over the five stanzas in which Earl Richard's lover promises to maintain a vigil over his grave. 'Speechless' (1854) has a more lyric feel, with its four quatrains of varying rhythm and greater use of symbolism. Here, a lover has returned too late to rescue the speaker from ignominy. 'A Year and A Day' (1857) the poem so admired by Watts-Dunton, is a solo lyric and barely a ballad in the accepted sense. Its structure is much more complex; the seven iambic sestets begin simply enough with a predictable rhyming pattern and they hint at the story of a tragic relationship, but they become laden with symbolic imagery as the poem develops.

Six of Swinburne's ballads can be dated to between 1859 and 1866, roughly the period when Siddal was writing. All are considerably longer than anything Siddal produced and all but one have four-line stanzas that chiefly have iambic rhythm and an abcb or abab rhyming pattern. Four are from *Poems and Ballads First Series* (1866): 'The Sea-Swallows', an imitative ballad constructed around a dialogue between parent and child that reveals a macabre situation; 'May Janet', which has a rare happy ending; 'The King's Daughter', which deals with incest and through its symbolic use of nature has a philosophical tone; and 'After Death' (originally published in 1862), a much more experimental work with cryptic couplets that reveals the conversation between a dead man and the boards of his coffin. 'Duriesdyke' (1859), is arguably the best early ballad imitation and narrates the ultimately tragic romance between two lovers against the background of the sea. Finally, 'The Worm of Spindlestonheugh' is a rare excursion for Swinburne into the supernatural and therefore included here on this basis. As in 'Duriesdyke', Northumbrian dialect is preserved, unlike the four previous examples. It tells of the mistreatment of a young maiden at the hands of her evil stepmother, who turns her into a hideous creature fit only to live among swine. Published posthumously (1917), its date of writing is unknown, but both MacInnes and Gosse (admittedly sources to be consulted with caution) list it as an early imitation.[54]

There is a degree of commonality in the sourcing of these ballads but as expected Swinburne is more heavily aware of literary precedent, Child being the preferred anthology. 'May Janet' has a series of statements that narrate the travels of the two lovers as they purchase items for a bridal wardrobe: 'The first/second etc. town they came to'. This is a commonplace which also occurs in 'Johnie Scot' and 'The Fause Lover'.[55] 'The King's Daughter' has a similar incremental device to that found in 'Burd Helen', describing the occupations of the young women, and 'The King's Dochter Jean' also deals with the central issue of incest.[56] 'After Death' is compared with the spirit of two further ballads, 'The Twa Corbies' and the 'Lyke-Wake Dirge',[57] while 'The Worm of Spindlestonheugh' is shown to resemble 'Kemp Owyn', 'Allison Gross' and 'The Laidly Worm and the Machrel of the Sea', all of which deal with the metamorphosis of an enchanted woman into an obscene creature.[58] The question and answer technique found in 'The Sea-Swallows' is similar to that used in the popular ballads 'Edward, Edward' and 'Lord Randal'.[59] Some of these older versions appear in Scott's *Minstrelsy*, a source Siddal may have used for poetic as well as artistic inspiration. 'At Last' has a number of motifs found generally in minstrelsy ballads: imminent death, burial preparations and family bonds extending to three generations for example.[60] 'True Love' is directed to Earl Richard; four ballads bear that name in Child's anthology, including a version by Scott, and 'Speechless' may be seen to parallel 'The Gay Goss-Hawk', even if Siddal refused to allow her speaker to be rescued by her lover's touch as in the Scott rendition.[61]

The fractured female voice and barriers to communication

Aside from instances of shared origin or practice, Siddal's ballad texts carry independent meaning as metaphors for the fractured female voice. Her naive poetic form and economy and sparseness of language invite a simple reading, but this same simplicity can also be seen as a comment on female restraint in which lack of structural or linguistic embellishment becomes a metaphor for the withholding of expressive speech. In outline, she takes the ballad, which relies on its ability to be easily transmitted orally, and subverts it to include an ironic message, that the very art of communication is flawed and that there is in women an inability to express the emotion that is essentially feminine. She redefines the ballad, giving it an individual and plaintive form by using it as an inversion of the poetics of expression; the brevity of her condensed language then becomes the means of reinforcing the theory. There is no evidence in her texts to suppose that Siddal had intrinsic interest in the ballad because of its historic importance. The reverse would appear to be more accurate considering how little she adhered to the established formulae. Where she does use a traditional form she uses rhetorical questions which interrogate this from within. The ballad therefore becomes a medium through which Siddal could explore the inability of women to speak, although the greatest irony is apparent in her failure to publish. The political and social comment she was making therefore remained 'unspoken' and secret. Women are unable to speak, of failed relationships with men for example, despite being cast as natural sympathizers and emotional givers, and this comes out in her references to the voice and the ear and its capabilities.

Siddal was not alone in addressing the issue of silence. Working against a culture that deemed it unseemly for women to talk too much or that appeared unconcerned about why women were silent, individual women poets adopted different approaches.[62] Hemans gave *The Forest Sanctuary* (1825) a male narrator, who 'sees' indirectly via three female characters who all die but survive as voices through martyrdom, the focus being the importance of remembering the power of voices and the hazards and temptations of silence.[63] Paradoxes abound: male and female voices inspire yet both are silent when attempting to voice personal suffering; voices are implicit in memories which can be both reassuring and disturbing; silence implies lack of humanity yet is also considered a duty and a virtue.[64] L. E. L. looked at the difference between the published face and the private mask, at how a poet defends herself against sentimentality by using frivolity to protect a vulnerable spirit and keep secrets.[65] There is an autobiographical tone to 'Night at Sea' (1838) as Landon journeyed to Africa after her wedding. Nothing is specific, but a sense of tragedy and loneliness pervades each verse, the marriage already regretted. Most end with a variant of 'Do you think of me, as I think of you?', a trope that reinforces the sentiment and is used by Siddal in 'Lord May I Come?' Both poems encapsulate a sense of longing for another time, but whereas Siddal anticipates her heavenly future Landon finds far greater comfort in her past, and only the present is described in any detail. Barrett Browning, whose elegy for L. E. L. opens with a reiteration of that plaintive question in 'Night at Sea', adopted an overly political stance when exploring the idea that even muted voices can be heard effectively and responded to once in print. 'The Cry of the Children' (1843) and 'A Curse for a Nation' (1856) give a voice to a child, factory workers and American slaves, respectively. By implication, a published poet (and of course Siddal initially was not) is vital to society because they can speak allegorically to control opposition, especially if the poem carries multiple meanings.

Christina Rossetti also wrote an elegy to Landon in which L. E. L. herself speaks of the mask of gaiety she dons to hide her loneliness and isolation. A repeated phrase, 'My heart is breaking for a little love', emphasizes another dualism that pitches inward silence against the possibility of finding a voice elsewhere, and the same possibility comes in *Goblin Market*. The sisters are rendered mute because their mouths are full of fruit (Laura) or clawed at by its sellers (Lizzie) but their speech is replaced by silent laughter. Lizzie runs home to help Laura with the antidote to the toxic fruit she's been beguiled into eating knowing the goblins have been defeated by closed mouths, the girls' laughter even more unexpected because poetry is a hearable art.[66] Fascination with the unsaid also emerges from 'The Queen of Hearts' (1866) in which a clever player always wins the said card. Her method remains a secret as she only utters one line but the poem goes beyond a mere game to look at the power of secrets in a sexual relationship. Rossetti regularly keeps the reader guessing so their responses are never definitive and always subjective. She employs carefully controlled ambiguity to encourage individual interpretations of her texts, and manipulation of secrecy is fundamental to this.[67] The reason for this may not be a personal liking for mystery so much as a desire to follow the tenets of Tractarianism with its doctrine of reserve, a means of revealing the greatness of God's creation without flattery. This could enable a devotional poet like Rossetti to have a relationship with God and still to explore the paradoxes and contradictions that emerge from the clash of earthly and spiritual worlds.[68]

Siddal is concerned with barriers to essential expression in four of her ballads; where there is effective communication between parties (and she indicates that for women this can often be with the self) it actually emphasizes the presence of these barriers elsewhere in the texts. Death, absence and parting are cited as limits or boundaries to shared experience, but Siddal does offer certain solutions to the central dilemma; death is not always an insurmountable barrier and mediated communication can exist beyond it. The artistic narrative of *Clerk Saunders* can therefore be seen to have parallels in her poems. The *Minstrelsy* ballads provided inspiration for Siddal's exploration of aphonia in both her drawings and poems, withheld speech and muteness coming to represent what the 'speakers' do not or cannot say. Often this is a conscious choice, a display of defiance or assertive reticence that not only reinforces the lack of oral association between the sexes or generations, but empowers the female protagonist. An example of this ekphrasis appears in the pencil sketch *The Gay Goshawk* (1854), in which Siddal illustrates the moment at which a cruel stepmother orders her husband to drop burning lead on to the bosom of the heroine to test the efficacy of a sleeping-draught taken to feign death. A similar ploy is inferred in the ballad poem 'True Love'. A moment of triumphant resistance is created in both that makes Siddal a skilful poet even when she is working as a visual artist.

The flawed or stunted nature of communication between men and women is the dominant feature of Siddal's ballad poems and this is apparent in images of often forcible parting as well as muteness. In 'He and She and Angels Three', 'ruthless hands', possibly parental, have torn the woman from her lover who then has to appeal to Christ as advocate as earthly voices cannot or will not intercede for her. 'True Love' is more ambiguous, as it is not clear why the speaker is being made to leave her lover's graveside; a husband, another lover, even death itself are all implicated: 'Soon I must leave thee / This sweet summer tide; / That other is waiting / To claim his pale bride' (9–12). Some external factor threatens to interrupt a dialogue which is already struggling to cross the barrier of the dusty grave evoked in the first verse. 'A Year and A Day' creates a mood of regretful reminiscence, the speaker unable to make verbal or physical contact with the one she has lost. She exists in a state of reverie, partly longing for death while not quite abandoning hope that the old relationship might be re-established. 'Speechless' (also known as 'Fragment of a Ballad') illustrates Siddal's contention in every stanza and is therefore worth quoting in full. The speaker cannot remember or properly hear her lover's words; neither, as victim of her own emotions, can she respond to him. Even his physical presence, arriving too late to rescue her, is insufficient to prevent the sense of excruciation evident in the last line:

> Many a mile over land and sea
> Unsummoned my love returned to me;
> I remember not the words he said
> But only the trees moaning overhead.
>
> And he came ready to take and bear
> The cross I had carried for many a year,
> But words came slowly one by one
> From frozen lips shut still and dumb.
>
> How sounded my words so still and slow
> To the great strong heart that loved me so,
> Who came to save me from pain and wrong
> And to comfort me with his arms so strong?
>
> I felt the wind strike chill and cold
> And vapours rise from the red-brown mould;
> I felt the spell that held my breath
> Bending me down to a living death.

This poem also has a fractured form which acts as supplementary commentary on the main theme. The narrative is incomplete and lacks a back-story; the first two lines especially serve to heighten the sense of drama latent in the text. All her ballads begin mid-story, leaving the reader to make assumptions about why the speaker is in her particular predicament, and therefore engage with her. Similarly, these poems do not have the resolution found in traditional ballads; 'A Year and A Day', 'True Love' and 'Speechless' all end with the speaker being only half-alive, and in a transient place. The absence of a preamble is an essential ballad ingredient, and the same sense of being pitched straight into the narrative occurs in some of Swinburne's work but Siddal's poetry takes this to an extreme and strips out the narrative altogether. Whereas 'May Janet' and 'The King's Daughter' carry a more complete storyline, 'After Death', the Swinburne ballad that is arguably his most experimental, is the closest to Siddal's format in this respect. It plunges into the curses being uttered by the occupant of the coffin with just one couplet presented as intriguing introduction:

> The four boards of the coffin lid
> Heard all the dead man did.
>
> The first curse was in his mouth,
> Made of grave's mould and deadly drouth.
>
> The next curse was in his head,
> Made of God's work discomfited. (1–6)

The relationships between the man and those whose behaviour has caused such vitriolic anger are only revealed by implication, and it is left to the boards, having gleefully reported that the latter are surviving very well without their tormentor, to deliver the final retort which dispatches him to hell: 'The dead man answered thus: "What good gift shall God give us?" / The boards answered him anon: / "Flesh to feed hell's worm upon"' (47–50). Swinburne thus achieves the resolution that Siddal avoids; the fate of the man is known and this is echoed in the stylistic symmetry of the poem, the coffin boards being both cryptic exposition and coda.

'Speechless' can be used to show that attempting to maintain the social position imposed on them by men has rendered women mute. Bourgeois femininity is a social and psychological condition manifest in pleasant appearance, a deferential manner, self-sacrifice and silence; maintaining it was the job of a middle-class woman and Siddal explores this in her poems and paintings.[69] The Victorian woman should be orientated towards the happiness of her man, and Siddal's figures repeatedly depict strained and exhausted females which can be read as meaning the lived female body under such constraint will suffer physical and emotional distress. There is no dialogue in 'Speechless' so the focus is on the female narrator as she hints at subversive behaviour, suicidal thoughts, a sexual history, and a long absent lover received back but not in the expected welcoming way because she's too exhausted to be so. There are no curses or words of vengeance, in fact her breath is held, making her speech-less. Repeated use of the letter 'm': many a mile, moaning, unsummoned, dumb, makes the poem sound dreary and lacking in excitement or complaint.[70] Ballads are palimpsetic, using the same poetic canvas many times over after the original has been erased, which permits multiple interpretations and the scope to modify form and metre while presenting an idealized version of the past, just what the Victorians wanted. The poet can be experimental and very subjective but still culturally acceptable, allowing middle-class women to escape the 'passionless purity' that circumvented them, an appealing prospect for poet and reader.[71]

The concept of the fractured female voice propels Siddal into a wider philosophical debate. Nineteenth-century women poets were surrounded by knowledge of Christian philosophy that dictated that once Eve had spoken (and this is the key) to the serpent and acted on that, she had transgressed and henceforth all women would be punished with eternal silence. This dominant metaphorical framework informs Victorian culture and creates a language tradition that dictates only men have true power of speech, that women are unfit for poetry-writing, and have no right to even speak their own language.[72] If Siddal's poems are read in this light it would account for the references to deafness and elusiveness, as well as silence, found in all her ballads. Lines 7–10 of 'Speechless' encapsulate the theme, and here the apparent simplicity of the words and rhyme reinforces the bleakness of the speaker's situation. The use of alliteration emphasizes the awkwardness and hollowness of speech which cannot easily be enunciated or appreciated. Without an audience the speaker in these poems becomes necessarily introspective, hence the air of secrecy that pervades 'True Love', which sets up an implicit yet undefined relationship between the dead Richard and his still attentive and living lover. The latter has become an elusive figure by the end of the poem, one who promises to return to the graveside regardless of her travails in between; there she will be found 'watching or fainting, sleeping or dead' (19–20). Siddal also uses this blurring of edges in the last verse of 'Speechless' and throughout 'A Year and A Day', in which the contradictory images of the speaker as she redefines herself make it impossible to discern her state of mind or body. Behind the references to secrecy and elusiveness there lies the implication of unsanctioned love, already noted in 'Speechless', 'True Love', and 'He and She and Angels Three', but most evident in 'At Last'. In this poem the speaker is dying, having just delivered a child who will be brought up by his grandmother, not his father: 'And mother dear, take my young son, / (Since I was born of thee) / And care for all his little ways / And nurse him on thy knee' (5–8). The grandmother is urged to tell the boy (who may be the 'sweet Robert' of line twenty-three if this is not the absent parent) that his mother died of her 'great love' (27); it is open to conjecture whether this refers to her self-sacrifice once being 'great' with child, or to her simply being broken-hearted at a failed relationship. Either way, the punishment for her lone pregnancy is expected and accepted: 'And mother dear, when the sun has set / And the pale kirk grass waves, / Then carry me through the dim twilight / And hide me among the graves' (29–32). As a figure who hovers between life and death, she will be able to see if not be seen in her half-lit world.

The theme of illicit love is also explored by Swinburne, but this is to be expected as it features strongly in traditional ballads. 'The Sea Swallows' and 'Duriesdyke' both deal with its outcome, illegitimacy. In the former, two lovers meet on the banks of the Tyne where the girl foresees not only her own burial but those of her newly born son and her father. Their deaths are all connected with her actions; she dies in labour, and either kills the child or allows him to die. Her father is overcome by her shame: 'Oh Daughter if you have done this thing, / I wot the greater grief is mine; / This was a bitter child-bearing, / When ye were got by the sides of the Tyne' (49–52). 'Duriesdyke' begins with a sense of foreboding as again two lovers meet and she succumbs to his advances:

> The rain rains sair on Duriesdyke
>   Both the winter through and the spring;
> And she that will gang to get broom thereby
>   She shall get an ill thing. (1–4)

> The grass was low by Duriesdyke,
>   The high heather was red;

> And between the grass and the high heather
> He's tane her maidenhead. (37–40)

As she watches for her lover's return from the sea, having suffered 'mickle scaith' (much harm) and blame (62), she goes into premature labour during a violent storm that claims his life. The judgement is made clear in the final verse, where repetition of the first line of the poem reinforces the cyclical nature of sexual transgression: 'The rain rains sair on Duriesdyke / To the land side and the sea; / There was never bairn born of a woman / That was born mair bitterly' (105–8). 'The King's Daughter' deals with incest. Ten maidens, the last of which is the girl of the title, are occupied near a mill whose stream forms a literal current through the piece: 'We were ten maidens in the green corn, / Small red leaves in the mill-water: / Fairer maidens never were born, / Apples of gold for the king's daughter' (1–4). The king's son woos and then abandons the one that turns out to be his sister, who then prophesies their violent deaths in the final verse. The bitterness of the words here are at odds with the gently pastoral imagery of the opening stanzas; '"Ye'll make a grave for my fair body," / Running rain in the mill-water; / "And ye'll streek (lay-out) my brother at the side of me," / Pains of hell for the king's daughter' (53–6). 'May Janet' is a definite exception to the pattern. It concerns a couple who are forbidden to marry but despite somewhat drastic measures taken by her father, the pair remain defiant and their union succeeds. 'May Janet' is among Swinburne's more experimental ballads and its triumphalism contrasts sharply with Siddal's generally far more desolate tone.

There are only limited references to the physical body in Siddal's ballads, and far greater significance is given to the senses and their associated organs. This serves to reinforce the contention that the speakers are not fully alive and as such are unable to have a meaningful relationship with their (usually male) counterparts. 'A Year and A Day' is the most body-aware, but the parts mentioned tend to be associated with negativity: 'Wasted face' (9), 'tired brain' (12), 'a shadow lingering at the feet' (19–20) or across a face (29–30), or silence falling upon the heart (37). Even 'At Last', the ballad that celebrates fruitful communication between two women, still has 'pale pale hands', feet that are bound, and a body that may not rest (9–12). Swinburne's ballads on the other hand, exude the physicality Siddal's lack. This is particularly obvious in 'The Worm of Spindlestonheugh' where the text contains numerous references to Lady Helen's body in both her human and supernatural incarnations. However, the physical body also has to endure the pain of childbirth and in 'May Janet' Swinburne examines the different and sometimes violent attitudes of father and lover towards the female form, using the technique of modulated repetition:

> Her father's drawn her by both hands,
>   He's rent her gown from her,
> He's ta'en the smock round her body,
>   Cast in the sea-water.
>
> The captain's drawn her by both sides
>   Out of the fair green sea;
> 'Stand up, stand up, thou May Janet,
>   And come to the war with me'. (17–24)

In successive verses of 'The King's Daughter' Swinburne artfully juxtaposes the fate of the nine maidens with that of their one unfortunate counterpart by contrasting their situations, occupations, and physical treatment at the hands of the Prince:

> He's made her bed to the goodliest,
>   Wind and hail in the mill-water,
> A grass girdle for all the rest,
>   A girdle of arms for the king's daughter. (41–4)
>
> Nine little kisses for all the rest,
>   An hundredfold for the King's daughter. (47–8)

Kisses feature regularly in both Siddal's and Swinburne's ballads, but they use them differently. Swinburne associates the kiss with moments of high drama, episodes that seal the fate of the female character, as seen above. In 'The Sea-Swallows' six kisses are all that the father will provide for the upkeep of his daughter's illegitimate son, and in 'Duriesdyke', where the kiss acquires currency as a bargaining tool, the young man taunts his lover with their lack of sexual contact: 'It's I have served you, Burd Maisry, / These three months through and mair; / And the little ae kiss I gat of you, / It pains me aye and sair' (17–20). Under pressure she yields to him and becomes pregnant at a time when she is having to care for her mother and therefore cannot leave with her lover. Only in 'The Worm of Spindlestonheugh' does a kiss bring about a suitably happy ending, yet even here the vital act of love is enacted under duress. Helen entreats her brother to kiss her 'laidley' (loathsome) mouth to reverse the curse placed upon her by her evil stepmother that turned her from a beautiful woman into a foul beast that scorched the earth with its rank breath. Only with reluctance does he agree to do so. Siddal also uses the kiss as a sign of love, but under very different circumstances. Her mouths may not speak, but their lips can suggest private and intense passion. In 'True Love' the speaker kisses the dust from Richard's grave (3–4), a truly evocative image of devotion. In 'A Year and a Day' the speaker longs to kiss her lover 'in the old way' (4), and elsewhere ghostly beings pause to touch her on the cheek (17) in a manner reminiscent of the same action. The underlying emotions are regret, longing and sadness, but these kisses hark back to a time of happiness and pleasure with a resonance that Swinburne's ballads do not recognize.

In Siddal's poems sensory communication replaces the verbal. In 'He and She and Angels Three' once the woman has been borne up to heaven she waits, listening, for the angels to bring the soul of her lover to her, and once there all five pray and sing before God in an exclusive relationship. Watching and waiting are also the central tenets of 'True Love'. There is no dialogue with a second party in any of Siddal's ballads; instead her speakers find comfort in the self, as in 'Speechless', a poem that relies on the sensory perception of the speaker to relay her mood of impotent frustration. She feels the chill of the wind in a tactile sense and she can smell the vapours of decay in the place where she lies. She can imagine the comforting presence of her lover and also the all-embracing power of the spell that appears to be robbing her of conventional life. Despite her state of heightened sensory awareness, she still lacks the powers of speech and hearing that will enable her to communicate her emotions to another, and can only converse with herself – not that there appears to be much succour in this particular exchange. Swinburne uses dialogue to achieve a highly dramatic effect in 'After Death', where the four coffin boards, although posing individual rhetorical questions, act as collective foil to the bitter outbursts of the dead man. The delivery is cryptic from the outset and anticipates an intriguing, doom-laden *dénouement*. Each verse is vital to the development of the poem; irrelevancies are stripped away and the reader told only what Swinburne deems necessary, yet both parties make their viewpoints abundantly clear as their interchanges push the narrative forward. Dialogue between parent and child is regularly used in traditional ballads when the situation is macabre and 'The Worm of Spindlestonheugh' provides another, but varied, example of this. The interchange between daughter and newly acquired stepmother coupled with the supernatural overtone of the poem produces a comedic effect far removed from the anguished mood of 'The Sea-Swallows' for example, but the direct verbal communication between two parties is still a powerful motive force within the structure of the poem. The 'The Sea-Swallows' is another conversation piece but here it is hard to discern whether father or daughter is talking; the reader has to concentrate to unravel the twists of the plot, and this obscurity creates a contemplative element that echoes the mood of Siddal's poems where introspection replaces dialogue as the driving force. As per tradition Siddal's ballads do tell a story, but their narratives dwell on the pretext that their central female characters are essentially isolated and therefore reliant upon their own judgements and opinions.

The sense of separation or distance from extraneous contact found in Siddal's work is realized through variation and irregularity of rhythm. Swinburne uses this mechanism regularly; his poems appear to maintain a constant ballad metre and diction but he makes subtle changes in both rhythm and rhyme to highlight episodes of dramatic tension.[73] In 'The King's Daughter', for example, the rhythm changes as the incestuous relationship between the siblings evolves. Similarly, in 'Duriesdyke' the verse length is altered to draw attention to turning points in the narrative such as the arrival of a pivotal character.[74] Swinburne manipulates his audience by these means, directing their attention and establishing a line of communication with them. Siddal's texts are the antithesis of this; they argue that communication with others is at best fragmentary. Thus, rhythmic variations employed in their structure emphasize the differences between episodes of fruitful and barren intercourse. There are fewer examples of irregularity in Siddal's poems but where they do occur their effect is correspondingly more noticeable. In 'He and She and Angels Three' line 7 is given a smooth emphasis not found elsewhere in the poem: 'She shall stand to listen, / She shall stand and sing, / Till three winged angels / Her lover's soul shall bring' (5–8). The angels are the medium through which the speaker and her lover will talk to God, and their specific stylistic presentation here reinforces this special relationship. A similar smoothing effect is created in the fifth line of the second verse of 'A Year and a Day':

> I lie among the tall green grass
>   That bends above my head
> And covers up my wasted face
>   And folds me in its bed
> Tenderly and lovingly
>   Like grass above the dead. (7–12)

The speaker is lulled by the forces of nature that hide her from the harsh realities of life, and the unexpected change to two beats in this line draws attention to the escape being made. Later she becomes more agitated as she faces the uncertainty of a new relationship (or the rekindling of an old one) and the disturbed rhythm matches her mood:

> A shadow falls across the grass
>   And lingers at my feet;
> A new face lies between my hands-
>   Dear Christ, if I could weep
> Tears to shut out the summer leaves
>   When this new face I greet. (19–24)

Within the poem this is the point at which the speaker is most closely in touch with reality; hereafter she descends again into a daydream and the poem returns to the steady 4-3-4-3-4-3 iambic metre that represents it. There is just one more hiatus, as she remembers a time of happiness: 'Still it is but the memory / Of something I have seen / In the dreamy summer weather / When the green leaves came between' (25–8). The number of beats in the last two lines is inverted, and the reader recognizes a brief moment of optimism. Siddal places these changes strategically; when the speaker is self-absorbed the poem has an almost monotonous rhythmic regularity, but when she attempts to reach outside herself, the pattern varies and a moment of uncertainty hangs over the poem. The speaker could have maintained the effort to communicate with something outside herself, if only with the past; instead, she is defeated by her memories, and once more seeks only internalized comfort.

All Siddal's ballads contain references to barriers to communication and shared experience. Physical separation therefore acts as a metaphor for the failure of personal relationships, and the failure of women to express themselves emotionally. Only in 'At Last' is the barrier, death in this case, crossed, and this is the one poem that speaks of a successful relationship, that between two women. Siddal's ballads are economical in style and content and as such they have a distinctive form which contrasts with the poetics of expression and overflow.[75] This arguably means these poems are of a new type; the ballad has been redefined by the absence of narrative and the inclusion of a personal viewpoint so that it has become a ballad adaptation, but one substantially removed from the original. It may therefore be more correct to give Siddal's ballads a different generic name, considered at the end of this chapter. In these pieces reserve replaces excess and emotion is largely restrained and controlled.[76] There is a sense of liberation in the silence that surrounds the speakers, but that silence comes from the barriers of time, absence, death, sex and gender that Siddal erects. Her limited linguistic and colour palette offers a further message about abbreviated communication and would appear to have little in common with Swinburne's far more florid delivery. His use of dialect, on the other hand, can be seen as a limit or boundary that has echoes in her work. Time becomes a barrier through the emphasis placed on stasis rather than movement or progression, and the absence of incremental repetition, traditionally used to move the action of the ballad along. 'True Love', 'Speechless' and 'A Year and a Day' all revolve around speakers who lament the passage of time which has separated them from their lovers, and recall an earlier period when they had not been betrayed or deserted. In 'True Love' the speaker will leave the graveside in summer but promises to have returned, and then remain, by autumn, so that any physical movement here is certainly limited. In 'Speechless' the woman has been carrying a metaphorical cross 'for many a year' (6) and has no hope of relinquishing it. For her, time has literally stood still. Furthermore, the opening lines of 'A Year and a Day' specifically link stasis with isolation: 'Slow days have passed that make a year, / Slow hours that make a day, / Since I could take my first dear love / And kiss him in the old way' (1–4). Simple repetition puts an effective emphasis on the salient point: clock-watching has replaced the joy of human contact.

Repetition is used in 'At Last' to stress the idea that the burial instructions being given by the dying woman are singularly and collectively important. 'And mother' prefaces each quatrain, another simple but effective device. This is as close to incremental repetition as Siddal gets, as the commands arrive in a definite sequence.[77] They create a sense of movement, unique to this ballad, which celebrates successful communication. Swinburne uses incremental repetition in three of these ballads, one of which, 'After Death', also provides the best example of modulated repetition, a Swinburne characteristic. 'The King's Daughter' devotes each verse to a numbered maiden and similarly in 'May Janet' the last four verses refer to those towns visited by the captain and his lover as they celebrate their union and the moral defeat of her father. In all cases there is a definite sense of movement which is echoed elsewhere. It is literal in 'The Sea-Swallows': the number of paces required to mark out successive graves increases in multiples of three, and the migration of the birds of the title underlies the narrative. In the same way, the seasons of the year measure the passage of time in 'Duriesdyke', and draw attention again to the absence of such transience in much of Siddal's work. In Siddal's poems lack of physical movement is paralleled structurally by an abbreviated poetic style that can be seen to communicate a message about communication itself. Her delivery is pared down and terse, and in 'True Love' in particular it results in a cryptic form that leaves much open to interpretation. Limited word usage leads to ambiguity and a lack of resolution, and this is more readily appreciated if the poem is compared with 'At Last' in which clear instructions are given. Generally, Siddal prefers understatement and deceptively quiet disclosure; 'True Love' and 'Speechless' end with anti-climactic uncertainty and 'A Year and a Day' with the introduction of a seemingly random reference, the beaten grain of corn, that manages to summarize instantly the negativity of the entire poem. Swinburne achieves a similar effect in 'After Death'; the fusion of stylistic brevity and dialogue which centres on communication between the living and the dead echoes the contention identified in Siddal's work.

Siddal restricts references to colour to match this characteristically naive and economical linguistic structure. This serves to stress the introspection and isolation of the speaker, and contrasts vividly with Swinburne's worldly and sumptuous use of colour and material. Siddal's generally monochrome vision applies also to her paintings which rely on very specific injections of colour to lift salient points of the narrative out of their darkened context. In 'Speechless', 'red-brown' (14) is the only colour given, and it is linked with decay; the figurative landscape is otherwise 'chill and cold' (13), an image also found in 'True Love' where the white stone of the memorial above the body is the only specific colour reference. Elsewhere in these ballads hands and faces are merely 'pale'. Green and red, the typical Pre-Raphaelite shades, are rarely seen; the 'three berries red' (17) requested in 'At Last' are a unique citation, a startling intrusion upon the dim twilight death scene with its linen wrappings and 'empty bed' (15). Swinburne uses the colours of nature and precious metals extensively, and often without individual meaning. In 'The Sea–Swallows' the refrain 'Red rose leaves will never make wine' has no bearing on the story of the ballad, and the same applies to the warning given to May Janet by her father: 'He that strews red shall gather white, / He that sows white shall reap red, / Before your face and my daughter's / Meet in a marriage-bed' (5–8). Colour is generally used to create a rich visual tapestry which illuminates the narrative as a whole; only occasionally, when employed selectively, does he exploit its dramatic effect, as in 'Duriesdyke' where the young man courts his lover in extravagant fashion: 'He's happit her head about wi' silk, / Her feet with a gowden claith; / The red sandal (silk) that was of price / He's laid between them baith' (33–6). As the poem moves into the tragedy of the shipwreck and unwanted birth it is only the white of the rocks and foaming sea that dominates the visual image, and this reinforces the loneliness of the grieving woman.

Grief, parting and absence are further barriers to communication and shared experience in Siddal's poems. The concept of 'living death' that forms the nucleus of three ballads becomes the embodiment of such a barrier, a place from which the speaker can watch and comment but remain distant and untouchable. 'Living death', a sense of separation and removal that creates the possibility of fluidity between the self and the spectral nature of the self, is not restricted to Siddal's ballads but is thematically widespread throughout her work; here, a mixture of myth, illusion and reality can be discerned in 'A Year and a Day', 'Speechless' and 'True Love'. The latter is slightly different in that it injects an element of hope for the future into the last two verses. Neither does death have to be an insurmountable barrier; Siddal's poems allow for mediated communication beyond the grave that permits women and men to 'speak' effectively, if only through tokens. Without these, 'living death' keeps the protagonists apart. It can also reflect personal choice, as not all speakers in these poems find the ability to be an observer rather than a participant a disadvantage. Swinburne makes use of the concept in 'After Death', but to comedic effect. The man can physically speak to the boards of his coffin but they also act as the medium through which he can indirectly communicate with his surviving household. As such this poem coincidently encapsulates the suggested reading of Siddal's texts whilst not necessarily making any definitive philosophical statement itself. It also offers a solution to the problem of flawed communication central to their reading.

Victorian women poets needed to be both subject and object in order to locate themselves fully in the poetic world. Males could project themselves into female figures and become both poet and projection because of their much wider social experience, self-assertiveness and ability to overcome fears of self-display, whereas in a woman's poem the two figures blurred into one.[78] This was accomplished by substituting a flower (often a rose), child or animal to represent the object of male desire, because to voice the role directly would imply an unseemly knowledge of it. It is interesting that in Christina Rossetti's poems those animals are generally male, attractive but grotesque like the fat crocodile in 'My Dream' or the goblins in *Goblin Market*.[79] Alternatively, the two roles can be deliberately merged and this can be done when the speaker's voice comes from beyond or within the grave. Rossetti's speakers, like most of Siddal's, are on the border between waking and sleeping, life and death, where the female object of desire can become subject and speaker for a long transitional moment. 'Dreamland' (1849), in which a woman has travelled to a deathlike world, is about 'soul sleep', the state of the soul between death and Judgement Day when it dreams of Paradise, a time of waiting and reckoning. 'Song: When I am Dead, My Dearest' (1848), takes up the same theme, speculating about what would happen if the speaker dies and becomes the object of the song; she won't hear it but won't care, and furthermore won't worry about those left behind, even forgetting them entirely. The focus has shifted away from the mourners and towards the dead beloved and this is generally reminiscent of Siddal's poems which share the same 'shadowy' vocabulary and imagery. Rossetti returns to the concept of 'forgetting' several times such as in 'Remember' (1849) where the speaker won't mind if her lover forgets her if this banishes sadness, and in 'The Poor Ghost' (1863) where the latter comes back to find her lover over his grief and preferring she stay in her grave.[80] Siddal specifically refers to memory in 'A Year and a Day' and 'Lord, May I Come' and her speakers move seamlessly between past, present and future like souls in limbo to create a time continuum, a sense echoed in these Rossetti poems. Rossetti put her speakers between two worlds so they could comment on cultural limitations; a dead woman's body is reclaimed and made to speak instead of remaining a silent, passive object with the result that social marginalization in mainstream literary culture takes on a feminism mantle.[81]

Sex and gender become barriers erected by outside agencies, possibly parental, in 'He and She and Angels Three' and 'True Love' where, respectively, 'ruthless hands' (1) and 'that other' (11) have separated the lovers. Pregnancy has resulted in the death of the speaker in 'At Last', separating three generations. These women have been restrained in their choices, as have those in 'Speechless' and 'A Year and a Day'. In the former an uncontrollable supernatural element is implied in the 'spell' (15) that steals the power of speech, and in 'A Year and a Day' it is the suffocating weight of the failure of past relationships and a lack of desire to participate in the present that forces an acceptance of a half-life. This poem in particular illustrates the way in which in Siddal's ballads communication with the self replaces speaking to other people. Whether isolated by personal choice or by the behaviour or attitude of a second party, most of her speakers rely on rhetorical conversation and questioning to set up another level of communication, one which succeeds when conventional verbal contact has failed. By extrapolation, these texts therefore argue that women find communication with their own sex more profitable, that men are unable to appreciate their emotional needs. 'A Year and a Day' is made up of verses that could be reassembled in a different order yet still achieve the same effect; they are the seemingly random musings of one trying to deal with an indeterminate situation. There is little sense of a continuing narrative, and this is also the case in 'Speechless', though here the questions are directly posed rather than implied. In both cases the narrative is replaced by a representation of a mood, which allows Siddal greater freedom to express inner thoughts without censure, and also widens the scope of critical analysis. These two poems speak to the psyche; they express and query feelings that have led to a psychological state, and permit a multiplicity of interpretation through the use of deliberately distorted or unclear images such as those associated with a dream-state.[82] 'A Year and a Day' specifically refers to this several times and the dream or trance motif allows Siddal to explore and show understanding of women's subjectivity and sense of self without imposing definitive meaning on the poem. Language can therefore be obscure, and structure fragmentary, employing a form which readily poses questions for which Siddal has no answers. Her ballads generally lack a resolution, the fate of her speakers left open or seen as a projection of an undisclosed future. In 'He and She and Angels Three' various events 'shall' occur, but the repetition of this word reinforces the signs of waiting, and in 'True Love' there is only the promise of an unscheduled return to the graveside. Only in 'At Last' is there a foregone conclusion, while even here there is no certainty that death will bring an end to sensory experience. This points to a departure from the traditional ballad form in which there is a designated ending to the story. Swinburne's poems, representing an overridingly male tradition, provide the reader with an outcome, whereas Siddal's poems lack that sense of closure or certainty. The individual predicaments of her speakers can therefore be read as a collective metaphor for the political predicaments of women who have no effective voice in mid-Victorian society.

Only one of Swinburne's ballads has a speaker rather than a narrator, whereas Siddal, breaking with tradition, reverses the position. Her speakers reinforce the idea of the importance or necessity of communication with the self, and this gives a dramatic immediacy to their concerns which, along with their anonymous universality, draws the reader into the poem. Swinburne achieves a similar level of interactive intensity in 'The King's Daughter'. It is unclear whether the speaker is the eponymous and tragic maiden or simply an observer of her fate, but the personal viewpoint is important throughout and powerfully contributes to the unexpected vehemence of the final verse. This engenders a wider debate regarding the situation of the protagonists in all these works, and the extent to which they are, or believe themselves to be, victims. The king's daughter is a victim of family connivance, and recognizes that fact. The heroine of 'Duriesdyke' twice becomes a victim, at the hands of her lover who manipulates her into a sexual relationship, and, as a result, of misplaced loyalty to her mother. She chooses not to sail away with her lover because to do so would leave the latter unattended:

> 'Gin I should sail wi' you, Lord John,
>   Out under the rocks red,
> It's wha wad be my mither's bower-maiden
>   To hap (cover) saft her feet in bed?
>
> 'Gin I should sail wi' you, Lord John,
>   Out under the rocks white,
> There's nane wad do her very little ease
>   To hap her left and right. (53–60)

Lady Helen finds herself at the mercy of her stepmother in 'The Worm of Spindlestonheugh', a ballad which repeats the passive paternal complicity of 'The King's Daughter' but this time casts the brother in the role of rescuer and enactor of vengeance. Having travelled to find his sister and kissed her to return her to human form he confronts the older woman with her misdeeds, deflecting the curse back onto her:

> He's tane him to the witch-mother
> That sat by her bairn's bed;

> The gold was gone in her grey hair,
> Her face was heavy and red.
>
> 'Oh wae be wi' you, ye ill woman,
> And the young bairn at your knee;
> There's never a bairn shall die abed
> That comes out of your body'. (227–34)

Lady Helen puts up some resistance to her jealous persecutor, however, a stance copied by May Janet who takes matters into her own hands by publicly defying her father. Ostensibly a victim, she chooses not to see herself as one, and this attitude is shared by the women in 'True Love' and 'He and She and Angels Three'. Even in their silence or enforced isolation they exhibit a semblance of defiance, unlike those in 'Speechless' and 'A Year and a Day' who appear to have accepted their victim status and acknowledge a lack of will to alter it. There is, however, a parallel reading of the second poem that suggests the speaker might still be directing her own destiny; this woman has chosen to indulge her memories rather than face the loneliness of the present and she revels in the peace brought by simply lying in the silence. She has deliberately withdrawn herself from society and under those circumstances saved herself from being a victim; self-silence has become her liberation. It is not a question of her being unable to communicate with others, she is simply unwilling to do so, as is her prerogative. There is a double bind here: the speaker has chosen her way forward but recognizes her options were strictly limited; wider society holds nothing for her. At the same time this ironically emphasizes all that she has lost in making such a move, which in turn reminds the reader of the central tenet of these poems, that generally women have only a fractured voice, even when that voice is theirs.

Communication with the self is not the solution to the dilemma. Questioning the self merely results in evasive and indeterminate replies. Only where a second female party is involved, in 'At Last', is there true self-determination. The clarity and simplicity of the instructions given allows no room for interpretation; the speaker controls her destiny to the extent she believes she can overcome the separation brought by death itself. Her mother is her understanding audience, and the reader is confident that she will be responsive to the calm authority of the commands she is being given. 'At Last' is the only ballad to recognize the role of the audience and this further stresses the restricted nature of self-communication. Poems rely on interpretation to give them meaning, making their relationship with an audience fundamentally important. Siddal concentrates on expression of, and to, an inner self, but in 'At Last' there is awareness that an engagement with context cannot be avoided, even if its language and ethos might be at odds with those expressions. If that context is actually the self and not the material world, there is likely to be no resolution to the contradictions and conflicts that are uppermost in the psyche.[83] In Siddal's poems this means that her subjects largely speak to themselves, cannot answer their own questions, and remain hovering between life and death, unable to participate fully in either. The varied structure of Swinburne's poems similarly implies an understanding that ballad and audience were inextricable, that without an audience the ballad had no purpose. The subversive humour in 'After Death', the protracted and fanciful narrative of 'The Worm of Spindlestonheugh', the initially uncertain direction of 'The Sea-Swallows' and the deceptive tranquillity of 'The King's Daughter' all readily engage the reader. An audience signifies communication, which makes Siddal's failure to publish the greatest irony. In 'At Last' she gives a woman the power of true speech and arguably challenges the language tradition that dictated that this belonged only to male poets, but in keeping her feminist opinions silent she acquiesces to the existing stereotype that denied women a social and political voice. Bearing this in mind, it is also ironic that she was nicknamed 'Ida' by Ruskin who saw in her echoes of the heroine of Tennyson's 'The Princess', the advocate of women's higher education and the promulgation of knowledge.

Solving the dilemma of faltering communication

Siddal's poems do in fact offer a number of positive solutions to the problem of faltering communication. Women, as natural empathisers, can speak to each other as seen in 'At Last' where the language is unequivocal and purposeful, and explanations are given for what might otherwise seem to be random requests:

> And mother dear, Take a sapling twig
>   And green grass newly mown,
> And lay them on my empty bed
>   That my sorrow be not known.
>
> And mother, find three berries red
>   And pluck them from the stalk,
> And burn them at the first cockcrow
>   That my spirit may not walk.
>
> And mother dear, break a willow wand,
>   And if the sap be even,
> Then save it for sweet Robert's sake
>   And he'll know my soul's in heaven. (13–24)

The younger woman is calm because she is confident she has entrusted all these rituals, and her son, to the one in whom she has the most faith. Her mother is the centre of concern, not father or lover, and this child–mother bond is indicative of feminist thought. The all-female dialogue in 'The Worm of Spindlestonheugh' does not have such a positive outcome. The middle section (65–160) consists of bitter exchanges as Swinburne contrasts the status and physical situation of two feuding women; even the lowest of Lady Helen's expectations is thwarted as her new position in her father's household is made plain:

> 'O see ye not thae towers, Helen,
> Where ye gat meat and wine?
> It's I maun ligg (live) in the braw bride-chamber,
> And ye maun ligg wi' swine.
>
> O see ye not thae halls, Helen,
> Where ye gat silk to wear?
> It's I shall hae the gold gowns on,
> When your body is bare.'
>
> 'O ye'll sit in the braw guest-chamber,
> And ye'll drink white and red;
> But ye'll gar (make) them gie me the washing water,
> The meats and the broken bread?'

'Ye'll get nae chine (crust) o' the broken loaves,
The white bread wi' the brown;
Ye'll drink of the rain and the puddle water
My maids shall cast ye down.' (93–108)

Lady Helen survives this persecution, as does May Janet and the wife in 'After Death' but outside male agencies enable her to do so. The female protagonists in 'True Love', 'At Last' and 'He and She and Angels Three' demonstrate powers of endurance that emanate from inner moral strength which is, when necessary, supported by heavenly intervention.

Four of Siddal's poems contend that death and burial does not have to be an insurmountable barrier. This is most explicit in 'He and She and Angels Three' where two forms of verbal communication are given in the last verse: 'He and she and the angels three / Before God's face shall stand; / There they shall pray among themselves / And sing at His right hand' (9–12). This is a unique occurrence in these poems; both sexes are using a voice to speak to one another, implying that after death, in a utopian society, gender will not be a barrier to understanding. In 'True Love', there is less confidence that this will be the case as here only 'watching or fainting' (19) signify closeness. Similarly, 'At Last' is a monologue, so mother and son can only speak through a medium: 'Tell him I died of my great love / And my dying heart was gay' (27–8). 'Speechless' is the only poem entirely written in the past tense, which gives the speaker opportunity to criticize her lover for his tardy arrival. Ironically, in a piece which most clearly bemoans failed communication, death has given her a voice. She can speak from beyond the grave whereas she was unable to do so beforehand, even if she is restricted to speaking to herself. 'A Year and a Day' alone upholds the barrier; the speaker chooses the silence and emptiness of sleep to obliterate the pain that comes from the loss of physical and emotional contact. Communication beyond death is mediated via tokens that play an important part in Siddal's ballads. They are equivalent to the glass wand passed to Clerk Saunders in her painting of that name. In 'At Last' a 'sapling twig' (13), a stalk bearing three berries (17), and a 'willow wand' (21) are all instrumental in the laying-out ritual that enables the young woman to transcend death; they also indicate her faith in her mother. In 'True Love' the same role is given to the effigy close to which the woman is kneeling: 'Pray for me, Richard, / Lying alone / With hands pleading earnestly / All in white stone' (5–8).

The religious theme is hinted at in 'Speechless' but the underlying philosophy is inverted here; the 'cross' carried 'for many a year' (6) by the speaker cannot be handed over to one who 'came so ready to take and bear' it (7) because he cannot understand the words of her request; the token is redundant if there is no mutual understanding to accompany it. When Swinburne uses tokens, he usually does so in the traditional sense, as an indicator of a relationship between the living, a gift that reinforces communication that already exists. Their use is not always positive, however; in 'May Janet' the sumptuous clothes are part of a celebration whereas in 'The King's Daughter' the richness of the gifts is in inverse proportion to their effect on the recipient, and in 'The Sea-Swallows' only prosaic and useless items are pledged for the care of the illegitimate child: 'fen-water and adder's meat' (19) to eat, 'a weed and a web of nettle's hair' (23) to wear, 'two black stones at the kirkwall's head' (27) for bedding, and 'three girl's paces of red sand' (31) for land. The father's moralistic stance is thus made abundantly clear. The exception is in 'After Death' where the coffin is the medium that facilitates communion between the living and the dead. References to religion, superstition and the supernatural are generally negative in Swinburne's ballads and for obvious reasons this emerges most clearly in 'The Worm of Spindlestonheugh'. 'Speechless', in which an unspecified spell has rendered the speaker mute, is the only Siddal poem that shares this view. Elsewhere religious belief forms a channel that keeps communication between the sexes open, and there are specific appeals to Christianity to do this in 'He and She and Angels Three' and in 'A Year and a Day' where the speaker asks for Christ's help as she attempts to hold on to the fading memories of her lover (22–4).

The use of non-speech text and the non-human voice in Siddal's poems suggest ways in which the absence of speech need not necessarily be a barrier to successful communication. Alongside kissing, the grandmother in 'At Last' is encouraged to wash the hands of her daughter (9), an action that will bring physical comfort to one who can no longer see clearly. There are also several mentions of a touch that is welcome in 'A Year and a Day'. When humans cannot speak for themselves, inanimate objects may do it for them, a device employed by both Siddal and Swinburne. This occurs in 'The Worm of Spindlestonheugh' and Swinburne uses a similar device in 'The King's Daughter', where natural images are associated with incest. The subject's moods are projected on to nature in a 'pathetic fallacy', giving nature a persona which expresses the same views as the poet and implies the breaking of a boundary and an extension of consciousness.[84] By this reading, subject, poet and reader can be brought together in tripartite communication that relies on a non-human voice, a philosophy very similar to that suggested by Siddal's work. It is there in 'True Love', where hands plead earnestly (7), and 'Speechless', where 'the trees moaning overhead' (4) are the only 'words' the speaker can hear or remember. The most evocative usage is in 'A Year and a Day' where bird calls take the place of the human voices the woman cannot hear, or chooses to ignore:

> The river running down
>   Between its grassy bed,
> The voices of a thousand birds
>   That clang above my head,
> Shall bring me to a sadder dream
>   When this sad dream is dead. (31–6)

The onomatopoeic verb is cleverly chosen; the birds are sounding a death-knell that signals the end of contact with reality but the strident tone, so at odds with the rest of the poem, also briefly brings recognition of what is being lost. Its hollow and discordant note reminds the reader that this is the sound of the human voice when it cannot be properly heard or when its intrusion is unwelcome.

Siddal and Swinburne came together by social circumstance and forged a close friendship. Never associates in poetry, they independently engaged with the ballad tradition and brought to it diverse experiences and expectations. This is reflected in the way they individually and significantly contributed to the development of the tradition, modifying and experimenting with the existing format to produce work that is ostensibly very different even though it comes from the same root. Whether one made a greater contribution than the other is unimportant, of more interest is the role they simultaneously played in relation to it. Siddal took the ballad in a new direction by using it as a vehicle for a single philosophy that is evident in each of her texts. Swinburne dedicated himself to its ongoing preservation as a social and political tool. His immersion in ballad culture was scientific and purposeful, a deliberate attempt to source and rework or mimic ancient songs to prevent their being forgotten. This necessitated both innovation and conservation. He kept to established ballad technique because he felt its structure was vital for universal appeal but his ballads are a reflection of their contemporary context, a careful modulation of certain modern tones within the resurrected form.[85] The changes he made are more important than the parallels with his precursors and they include the use of highly individual decorative description, self-conscious manipulation of colour, and unexpectedly suggestive natural symbolism. He adapted traditional devices such as the refrain and the use of repetition to increase both dramatic intensity and audience participation and gave some of his heroines the opportunity to wax philosophical about their predicaments.[86]

Siddal was not writing for posterity and her texts are a looser and more varied interpretation of the age-old format. There are elements of tradition: verse structure, rhythmic and rhyming patterns, repetition, linguistic simplicity and themes of domestic tragedy are all historically identifiable, but in significant ways these texts show a departure from the stereotype. There is an absence of overt medievalism in their language especially, although it supplies a physical context for two poems and arguably informs the attitudes and behaviour of female characters throughout.[87] There is limited narrative propulsion, but greater psychological involvement with the speakers. These texts feminize the ballad by developing the complexities of their female characters and encouraging empathy with their situation rather than merely reporting on their misfortune. This focus on female subjectivity contradicts the prevailing thesis that the poet had to be male by testing men and showing that they are often wanting, not necessarily the chivalrous characters of the old ballads.[88] Siddal believed the male ballad tradition was insufficient as it pertained to women, omitting key details and perspectives. She responded by using a woman as a first-person narrator, but also saw the palimpsestic possibilities in the ballad so that her protest against what was expected of women could be hidden among other versions of the same tale.[89] Siddal's texts are full of ambiguity, and this encourages double readings. The reader is always unsure to what extent the speakers have actually been betrayed or deserted, or believe themselves to have been, likewise to what extent their inability to speak is self-imposed or the result of that betrayal. The presence of an underlying philosophical statement unifies these ballads, gives them a conjoined solidity, and opens them up to multiple interpretation. It also calls into question their collective name. They can be seen as part of the broadside ballad genre, poems that cut across the barriers of sex, class and politics.[90] Alternatively, they could be seen as veering towards the dramatic monologue because of the importance of the speaker, with or without an audience. Their personal tone could make them 'laments in ballad style', a term applied to Swinburne's later ballads that moved away from emphasis on a narrator towards a personal political standpoint.[91] It may be profitable to understand them not as ballads but rather as a hybrid form, a continuation of a sentimental female tradition that favoured abandoned or betrayed women.[92] A compromise is more satisfactory. They certainly have a substantial lyrical component not found in many literary ballads, and in view of their stylistic and philosophical dependence on the monologue, Siddal's adaptations could conceivably be labelled 'dramatic lyrics', as further indication of the extent to which her texts made a unique contribution to the ballad tradition.

Notes

1 Much that has been written about Siddal relies on supposition, the primary record being patchy and sparse. The shared interest in ballads is evident in her artwork, however, and their closeness is documented, hence the speculation above.
2 Francis James Child, ed., *The English and Scottish Popular Ballads*. 5 vols, 3rd edn 1882 (New York: Cooper Square Publishers, Inc., 1962 reprint), Vol. 1, p. 161.

3 Algernon Charles Swinburne, *Ballads of the English Border*, ed. William A. MacInnes (London: William Heinemann Ltd, 1925), p. 138.
4 W. M. Rossetti, *Burlington*, p. 273 refers to Siddal as 'alien from approach'.
5 Algernon Swinburne, *Letters*, 6 vols, ed. Cecil Y. Lang (Newhaven: Yale University Press, 1959–62), Vol. 1 1854–69, pp. 49–50.
6 Edmund Gosse, *The Life of Algernon Charles Swinburne* (London: Macmillan and Co. Ltd, 1917), p. 84.
7 Both as individuals and as a partnership, the ways in which Siddal and Swinburne have been represented as biographical constructs are remarkably similar. Focus has been placed on a supposed duality of personality, their inhabiting two parallel worlds, joint love of anonymity, and desire to escape into an inner self. She wrote in secret; he under a number of aliases. Such portrayals tend to be limiting and flawed.
8 Lucinda Hawksley, *Lizzie Siddal. The Tragedy of a Pre-Raphaelite Supermodel* (London: André Deutsche, 2004), pp. 175–6.
9 Marsh, *Legend*, p. 61.
10 Catherine Maxwell, *Swinburne* (Tavistock: Northcote House Publishers Ltd, 2006), p. 48.
11 Yopie Prins, *Victorian Sappho* (Princeton, NJ: Princeton University Press, 1999), pp. 174–245 explores the connection between Sapphic verse and nineteenth-century women poets at length. The chapter on Swinburne, pp. 112–73, suggests he like Sappho (and Siddal) had a disappearing and reappearing posthumous existence.
12 Joyce Zonana, 'Swinburne's Sappho: The Muse as Sister Goddess', *Victorian Poetry*, Vol. 28, No. 1 (Spring 1990), 39–50, p. 47.
13 Margaret Reynolds, *The Sappho History* (Basingstoke: Palgrave Macmillan, 2003), p. 112.
14 *Ibid.*, p. 123.
15 J.-A. George, 'Poetry in Translation', in Cronin, Chapman and Harrison, *Companion to Victorian Poetry*, pp. 262–78, pp. 274–7 discusses how translation gave many more women the opportunity to participate in the culture of poetry whilst sidestepping the vexed question of female poetic creativity.
16 Prins, *Victorian Sappho*, p. 192.
17 Maxwell, *Swinburne*, p. 48.
18 In 1882, when Swinburne was living with Theodore Watts-Dunton the latter purchased one of Siddal's finest watercolours, *The Ladies Lament* (1856), presumably at Swinburne's suggestion. Derived from another

Scott ballad, 'Sir Patrick Spens', this work, one of her most complete compositions, was still in the shared home when Swinburne died there in 1909. It shows a group of women and children looking anxiously out to sea as they await news of possible survivors of a shipwreck, just one insignificant episode in the ballad poem. Siddal's women are strong, patient and dignified and, interestingly, the brilliant blue, white, green and red/brown colours she uses are reminiscent of those Swinburne employs in his Sapphic poems.

19 Swinburne, *Letters*, pp. 131–2.
20 *Ibid.*, pp. 93–4.
21 *Ibid.*, pp. 131–2.
22 *Ibid.*, pp. 201–2.
23 W. M. Rossetti, *Burlington*, p. 291.
24 For discussion of Swinburne's Medievalist poems see, Antony H. Harrison, 'Arthurian Poetry and Medievalism', in Cronin, Chapman and Harrison, eds, *Companion to Victorian Poetry*, pp. 258–60.
25 Algernon Charles Swinburne, *Poems and Ballads 1866 and Atalanta in Calydon 1865*, ed. Kenneth Haynes (Harmondsworth: Penguin Books Ltd, 2000).
26 Sir Walter Scott, *Minstrelsy of the Scottish Border*, 4 vols 1802–03, ed. T. F. Henderson (London and Edinburgh: Oliver & Boyd, 1932).
27 Both volumes are held at the Fitzwilliam Museum, Cambridge.
28 Clyde K. Hyder, ed., *Swinburne. The Critical Heritage* (London: Routledge & Kegan Paul, 1970), p. 26.
29 *Ibid.*, pp. 31–3.
30 Rikky Rooksby, *A. C. Swinburne: A Poet's Life* (Aldershot, Hampshire: Scolar Press, 1997), p. 61.
31 Hyder, *Critical Heritage*, pp. 37–8.
32 *Ibid.*, p. 62.
33 *Ibid.*, p. 69.
34 Anne Henry Ehrenpreis, ed., *The Literary Ballad* (London: Edward Arnold Ltd, 1966), p. 9.
35 *Ibid.*, p. 86.
36 Jerome K. McGann, *Swinburne: An Experiment in Criticism* (Chicago and London: University of Chicago Press, 1972), p. 87.
37 Ehrenpreis, *Literary Ballad*, p. 9.
38 Anne Henry Ehrenpreis, 'Swinburne's Edition of Popular Ballads', *PMLA Publications of the Modern Language Association of America*, Vol. 78 (December 1963), 559–71, p. 564.
39 Armstrong, *Victorian Poetry*, p. 352.
40 Mermin, *Barrett Browning*, p. 91.

41 Rebecca Stott, 'Where Angels Fear to Tread: Aurora Leigh', in Simon Avery and Rebecca Stott, *Elizabeth Barrett Browning* (Edinburgh: Pearson Education Ltd, 2003), pp. 105–6.
42 Mermin, *Barrett Browning*, pp. 90–1.
43 Marjorie Stone, *Elizabeth Barrett Browning* (Basingstoke, Hampshire: Macmillan, 1995), pp. 108–9.
44 *Ibid.*, p. 92.
45 Harold Nicolson, *Swinburne* (London: Macmillan and Co., 1926), p. 108, separates the works of *Poems and Ballads* into nine categories, 'Pre-Raphaelite' and 'Incidental and Decorative but mainly Predominant Pre-Raphaelite Influence' being two of them. No attempt is made to explain what these terms signify and there is little analysis of any one poem, but all twenty-two that fall into the above categories are (ironically) criticized for being merely brilliant imitations of the work of others and as such rated below all others in the collection.
46 Clara Watts-Dunton, *The Home Life of Swinburne* (London: A. M. Philpot, 1922), p. 206.
47 Clyde K. Hyder, 'Swinburne and the Popular Ballad', *PMLA*, Vol. 49 (March 1934), 295–309, p. 9.
48 McGann, *Swinburne: Experiment in Criticism*, pp. 83–5.
49 Hyder, *Swinburne and the Popular Ballad*, p. 296.
50 Ehrenpreis, 'Swinburne's Edition of Popular Ballads', p. 559.
51 Hyder, *Swinburne and the Popular Ballad*, p. 295.
52 Ehrenpreis, *The Literary Ballad*, p. 12.
53 Texts are taken from the Lewis and Lasner edition. For the sake of argument and interest their dates can be applied; if they are accurate they do not indicate a progressive development of ballad style for Siddal's most experimental pieces come in the middle of the period and she returns to a more traditional pattern at the end.
54 Algernon Swinburne, *Posthumous Poems*, eds Edmund Gosse and Thomas Wise (London: William Heinemann, 1917), p. vi.
55 Hyder, 'Swinburne and the Popular Ballad', p. 305.
56 *Ibid.*, p. 304.
57 *Ibid.*, pp. 302–3.
58 *Ibid.*, p. 296.
59 Ehrenpreis, *The Literary Ballad*, p. 173.
60 Hassett, 'Elizabeth Siddal's Poetry', pp. 451–2.
61 *Ibid.*, p. 457.
62 Parkins, *Jane Morris*, pp. 57–65 looks at reasons for women being silent using Morris as a case study.
63 John M. Anderson, 'The Triumph of Voice in Felicia Hemans's

'The Forest Sanctuary', in Sweet, and Melnyk, eds, *Felicia Hemans. Reimagining Poetry*, pp. 55–72, p. 55.
64 *Ibid.*, pp. 61–8.
65 Constance W. Hassett, *Christina Rossetti. The Patience of Style* (Charlottesville and London: University of Virginia Press, 2005), p. 75.
66 *Ibid.*, p. 53.
67 Burlinson, *Christina Rossetti*, pp. 4–5.
68 Dinah Roe, *Christina Rossetti's Faithful Imagination: The Devotional Poetry and Prose* (Basingstoke. Palgrave Macmillan, 2006), pp. 12–14.
69 Ehnenn, 'Strong Traivelling', p. 252.
70 *Ibid.*, p. 256.
71 *Ibid.*, pp. 254–7.
72 Margaret Homans, *Women Writers and Poetic Identity. Dorothy Wordsworth, Emily Brontë and Emily Dickenson* (New Jersey: Princeton University Press, 1980), pp. 29–33.
73 Ehrenpreis, *The Literary Ballad*, p. 16 provides a useful outline of the most common ballad metres and their variations.
74 Maxwell, *Swinburne*, pp. 20–4 has extended discussion of how he uses metre, rhythm and language to charm or seduce the unsuspecting reader and dramatize symbolic meaning. Poetic form is shown to be an integral part of meaning in his work, vitalizing and liberating language while still giving it discipline.
75 Armstrong, *Victorian Poetry*, pp. 339–67 looks at the expressive aesthetic and the use of silence in women's poetry. It argues that expressive theory is the aesthetic of the secret and of overflow, a movement out of the self. It suggests that the overflow of hidden feelings sets up barriers which limit it, but that these barriers paradoxically enable the flow of feeling. The barrier is shown to be a fundamental structural principle of women's poetry, and the response made to it by women poets is shown through the various barriers they erect.
76 Mary Arseneau, *Recovering Christina Rossetti. Female Community and Incarnational Poetics* (Basingstoke and New York: Palgrave and Macmillan, 2004), has a third chapter that discusses the poetics of reserve in connection with Rossetti's novella *Maude: A Story for Girls* (1897). Siddal is not mentioned, but stylistic and thematic parallels can be drawn between the work of the two women.
77 Ehrenpreis, 'Swinburne's Edition of Popular Ballads', p. 56, explains the distinction between incremental and modulated repetition and shows how Swinburne successfully uses the latter in other ballad poems, and McGann discusses his belief that modulated repetition is one of

the specific changes Swinburne makes to ballad form in *Swinburne: Experiments in Criticism*, p. 85.
78 Dorothy Mermin, 'The Damsel, The Knight, and the Victorian Woman Poet', *Critical Enquiries*, Vol. 13, No. 1 (Autumn 1986), 64–80, p. 65.
79 *Ibid.*, p. 70.
80 *Ibid.*, p. 73.
81 Burlinson, *Christina Rossetti*, p. 27.
82 Cora Kaplan, *Questions for Feminism. Sea Changes, Culture, and Feminism* (London: Verso, 1986), pp. 95–114, looks at the dream-state poem in connection with Christina Rossetti, but cautions against its use as a biographical tool or substantiation of psychoanalytical theories of femininity.
83 *Ibid.*, p. 14, argues that the relationship between poet and readership it is so fundamental it actually renders the psyche of the poet and critical analysis of their work unimportant.
84 Maxwell, *Swinburne*, p. 23.
85 McGann, *Swinburne: Experiment in Criticism*, p. 84.
86 *Ibid.*, pp. 84–7 and Hyder, 'Swinburne and the Popular Ballad', p. 39, have more extended discussion of his ballad legacy.
87 Stone, *Elizabeth Barrett Browning*, p. 130 queries whether medieval times were attractive to nineteenth-century female poets because women then had some control over their property and destiny and could venture into male-dominated areas of politics.
88 *Ibid.*, p. 132.
89 Ehnenn, 'Strong Traivelling', p. 272.
90 Stone, *Barrett Browning*, p. 106.
91 Constance Rummons, 'The Ballad Imitations of Swinburne', *Poet Lore*, Vol. 33, No. 1 (Spring 1922), 58–84, p. 67. The term applied to those ballads that dealt with the Jacobite exile, a wrongdoing whose salvation lay in the 'music of lamentation'.
92 Stone, *Barrett Browning*, p. 105.

3

Siddal, Tennyson, Ruskin and the feminist question

Lady Clare

In early 1855 Edward Moxon commissioned a series of illustrations to accompany a volume of Tennyson poems. Siddal submitted sketches for six works but was unsuccessful in having them accepted in her own right even though her design for 'The Palace of Art', depicting St Cecilia, was adapted by Dante Gabriel Rossetti and used in the subsequent 1857 Moxon edition. Had Siddal's work been included it could have proved lucrative, providing a measure of financial and aesthetic independence that was central to her artistic endeavour. Book illustration afforded a valuable showcase to Victorian women artists whose access to exhibition space and multiple artistic genres was severely limited compared with their male counterparts. Under these circumstances there is a certain ironic inequality in Rossetti's use of Siddal's work, despite their personal and professional involvement and the recognition that the Pre-Raphaelites as a school not uncommonly shared ideas and their execution. Only one of the six pencil, brown ink and pen sketches was reworked as a watercolour, *Lady Clare*, which illustrates the eponymous Tennyson ballad published in *Poems* in 1842. Subtle changes between the two Siddal expositions strengthen the argument that this subject interested her more than the five that were left at the preparatory stage. *Lady Clare* offers a commentary on nineteenth-century feminist issues, and the 'Woman Question' also informs certain of Siddal's poems. Analysis of the latter draws Siddal into a closer literary relationship with not just Tennyson but also with Elizabeth Barrett Browning and John Ruskin, because although very different in form from their three texts, *The Princess*, *Aurora Leigh* and 'Of Queens' Gardens', her lyrics are part of the same early Victorian gender discourse. Siddal's personal involvement with three members of the Langham Place Group of early female campaigners, Barbara Leigh Smith Bodichon, Bessie Rayner Parkes Belloc and Anna Mary Howitt Watts, has hitherto been largely unreported but their personal, and for a time intense, concern for her welfare influenced her poetic thinking especially. The connections between all these individuals is intriguing and not perhaps surprising given the degree of social and professional mobility among the Pre-Raphaelites and their associates. More importantly, they position Siddal at the heart of a financial and philosophical debate that broadens interest in her poetry and further distances it from criticism that has rendered it slight, repetitive and self-consciously maudlin.

Tennyson's 'Lady Clare' tells the story of a young woman's discovery that Alice whom she believed to be her nurse was her mother, and that although apparently of elevated birth she is only of servant class, facts which will doubtless impact on her impending marriage to her cousin, Lord Ronald. Alice chooses the eve of the wedding to reveal her secret, and in seeing a solution to the problem of Clare's future position, seems relieved to do so: 'Oh God be thank'd!' said Alice the nurse, / 'That all comes round so just and fair: / Lord Ronald is heir of all your lands, / And you are not the Lady Clare' (17–20). Apparently she exchanged Clare with the old earl's own daughter who died while she was suckling her. Clare immediately decries what Alice has done and pledges to confess her change of status and unwitting deception to her betrothed, despite Alice's entreaties to keep her counsel:

'Nay now, my child,' Said Alice the nurse,
   'But keep the secret for your life,
And all you have will be Lord Ronald's,
   When you are man and wife.'

'If I'm a beggar born,' she said,
   'I will speak out, for I dare not lie.
Pull off, pull off, the brooch of gold,
   And fling the diamond necklace by.' (33–40)

However, before donning simple clothing ready to confront Ronald, Clare readily forgives her mother and elicits her blessing on her mission to regain the moral high ground: 'Yet here's a kiss for my mother dear, / My mother dear, if this be so, / And lay your hand upon my head, / And bless me, mother, ere I go' (53–6). Clare's course of action is justified when Lord Ronald, despite knowing the whole truth, immediately agrees to continue with the marriage on the grounds that it is after all better that they are not blood relatives, and that she will get to keep her title in any case as a reward for her honesty. The tone of the poem here is light-hearted, in recognition that disaster has been averted:

> He laughed a laugh of merry scorn:
>   He turn'd and kiss'd her where she stood:
> 'If you are not the heiress born,
>   And I,' said he, 'the next in blood—
>
> 'If you are not the heiress born,
>   And I,' said he, 'the lawful heir,
> We two will wed to-morrow morn,
>   And you shall still be Lady Clare.' (81–8)

The poem is satisfactorily complete, and the tale completed satisfactorily for all concerned. Moreover, Tennyson gives the reader a prophetic glimpse of the happy ending right at the beginning, as Clare muses upon her intended: 'He does not love me for my birth, / Nor for my lands so broad and fair; / He loves me for my own true worth, / And that is well,' said Lady Clare' (9–12). For Clare there could be no dispute about her decision; as a female she needed to maintain the unimpeachable character Tennyson's audience would expect at a time when middle-class women were defined in literature by their guardianship of all that was considered noble, righteous and ethereal.

The poetic form allows an entire history to be explored, unlike a drawing. The artist must select one moment of high drama to capture the essence of a situation or the written word, and as in the case of *Clerk Saunders* Siddal focuses on an aspect of the narrative which does not feature in the poetic source. Her Clare is captured in a moment of uncertainty, to lie and behave unethically or to speak the truth and disobey her mother. In the poem there is no pause for such thought, the matter is clear-cut. Both the sketch and the watercolour (figure 13) are identical in this regard. Both show the figures of the two women entwined in a medieval setting that entirely suits Tennyson's ballad; their clothing and relative positions make them almost indistinguishable, even in the colour version. Mother and daughter are interdependent and therefore depicted as one, but the implication is that once the deceit is exposed their togetherness will be destroyed, and how they appear to each other and to others will be radically changed.[1] The nurse's arms are reaching up around her daughter's neck as she pleads with her; they simultaneously appear to be physically and metaphorically dragging her down. Lady Clare is covering Alice's face with her one hand, pushing it away in a physical rejection of her speech and actions. Her other hand rests on the handle of a door that is half open; she has yet to decide whether to go to Lord Randal or maintain the façade. Her face is averted from her mother, her expression unreadable. Her head is bowed in thought, her eyes staring as she fights for understanding and control of a complex situation.[2] There is a strong physical resemblance to Siddal's self-portrait, provoking an autobiographical interpretation; Siddal was of lowly background herself yet was most probably by this time engaged to a man who was her social superior, with no wedding date in prospect. The changes that appear in the 1857 working of the subject, however, create a convincing case for a revisionist reading.

The original sketch is likely to have been begun in 1853.[3] It is heavily worked in much corrected pen and pencil but the enclosed space is lightened by the view of other buildings and a garden through the half open door to the left of the figures and the sunlight permeating through the open lattice of the casement to the right. There is a markedly enhanced sense of claustrophobia in the watercolour. The view through the door is now restricted and indeterminate, and the lattice has been replaced by a stained glass window that depicts the Judgement of Solomon which creates a parallel with the central subject. Here a mother's true identity is revealed by her willingness to forgo her claim to a child to save it from death. The jewel-like Pre-Raphaelite colours throw the tiny figures into sharp relief making this an essential part of the narrative: to show that a woman is not just called upon to sacrifice her

13 Elizabeth Siddal, *Lady Clare*, c.1854–57, watercolour

social position when faced with a moral dilemma. The watercolour portrayal of Clare also places greater emphasis on her endurance and strength of character. Her expression is less wistful and the whiteness of her neck against her dark gown suggests its power and tension. Her pose is even more awkward, as if captured the second before the action of the sketch, and more deliberately frozen in a moment of agonizing indecision. She has a choice to make but will make it without external pressure, hence the violent rejection of her mother and her lack of overt sexuality. She is clearly female, her long hair undisguised, but her body shape is enfolded in slabs of solid dull colour, the eye instead drawn to her face which appears very pale in contrast to the darker contextual shades. In this subtle but incisive critique of Victorian gender ideology the impact of the emotional female drama is not dissipated by anatomical detail that would in all probability have been supplied by a male artist.[4] In Tennyson's poem Clare is redeemed by love and Ronald's ability to see beyond Alice's lie, but Siddal's pictures cannot show this. There is no resolution and furthermore the viewer is disconcertingly aware of her precarious ethical and social predicament. However, Siddal has empowered her and in this metaphorical exploration of the Victorian 'Woman Question' allows her independence to be celebrated, regardless of her decision. The consequences of her stepping away from convention could be severe, but still acceptable to a woman determined to pursue her chosen course in whatever field.

The Langham Place Group

A melancholy subject is typical of Siddal's artwork and a moment of anger and frustration features in several pictures where a single female figure is the focal point. Lady Clare is seen rejecting authority and this reflects Siddal's attitude to Ruskin who became her patron in 1855 and who is central to the literary web of connections alluded to earlier. His controlling influence led to his urging Siddal to abandon drawing certain subjects in favour of those he deemed more suitable. Perhaps as a result, Siddal appears to have allowed their financial arrangement to lapse by 1857, but not before he had bestowed upon her the nickname 'Ida', seemingly in reference to the heroine of Tennyson's *The Princess*. Ruskin was accustomed to using pet names with his correspondents and indeed Siddal and Dante Rossetti used them between themselves, but this case is interesting because the literary Ida was a spirited advocate of the feminist cause, some shadow of which Ruskin arguably saw in paintings and sketches like *Lady Clare*. At some stage Ruskin presented Siddal with a specially bound edition of Barrett Browning's *Casa Guidi Windows* (1851), inscribed 'To Elizabeth Eleanor Siddal with John Ruskin's sincere regards' and he seems to have seen her as some kind of soul-sister to the poet's artistic heroine Aurora Leigh as well as feminist Princess Ida.[5] Ruskin knew Tennyson less well than the Brownings; the latter enjoyed his praise and remained friendly with him despite his occasional storms of criticism of their work. Tennyson had been an admirer of Ruskin since 1843 when his *Modern Painters* was first published. Tennyson did visit him at home in 1855 to view his considerable collection of Turners but otherwise theirs was a relationship conducted via polite notes in which Ruskin made occasional comments about Tennyson's poetry.[6] Coincidently, 1855 also saw the publication of the third volume of *Modern Painters* which extensively linked the worlds of poetry and art. Ruskin's acknowledgement of Siddal's feminist sympathies, however grudging, was of course based only on her work as an artist at this point but inadvertently he has opened the way for examination of her poems 'Dead Love', 'Love and Hate' and 'The Passing of Love' alongside *The Princess* and *Aurora Leigh* (1856). His own views on the 'Woman Question' were made known in book form in 1865 with the publication of 'Of Queens' Gardens', part of *Sesame and Lilies*; the texts of all three can be used to identify a feminist poetics within Siddal's work, especially when they are contextualized by an issue that by mid-century was becoming a political as well as a social cause.

The greatest oppression was clearly against working-class women and was undeniably materially brutal. However, literate middle-class women, especially writers, social critics and reformers, suffered a particular abuse because patriarchal dominance involved the suppression of women's speech outside the home, as well as censorship of not only what they could read and write but also their behaviour.[7] The traditional subjection of wife to husband was still emphasized at this time by her having to pass to him all property she might have had before marriage, by the impossibility of divorce except through a prohibitively expensive Act of Parliament, and by a legally enforced double standard of morality which made adultery a worse offence in a woman than in a man. The Married Women's Property Acts (1870, 1882 and 1890) would eventually allow women to sue for divorce, own property, have rights over their children, and charge their husbands with rape or abuse. Until then they were subject to the concept of 'civil death' in marriage, despite their becoming increasingly audible in their demands for legal, political, educational and professional status from the 1840s onwards. Initially simply a gathering of like-minded friends, what became known as the Langham Place Group would be instrumental in this process and for a brief period Siddal came within the sphere of influence of three of its founder members.

Barbara Leigh Smith was of independent means, courtesy of her father, a radical MP who had given her a personal allowance to enable her to devote herself to art and social reform. By 1854 when she was introduced to Siddal she was already a journalist and poet, had travelled unchaperoned in Europe, undertaken art training in Munich, and made her exhibition debut. In that same year she would open a pioneering school for girls and begin working on a petition to Parliament as part of her campaign for the reform of married women's property laws. Her London home after her 1857 marriage would become the headquarters of the Langham Place circle, whose extended membership would be central to various key reform movements by the end of the century. Her closest friend, Bessie Parkes, was similarly progressive and came from a Whig and Liberal background influenced by Benthamite thought. She had early ambitions to be a poet, and accompanied Smith throughout Europe. In 1854 she published a pamphlet on the education of girls and would go on to focus her attention on the issues of professional employment and property. Anna Mary Howitt was the daughter of radical Quakers, and had also undertaken art training in London and Germany. In 1853 she published *An Art Student in Munich* containing plans for a 'sisterhood-in-art' based on her experiences there. Both her parents were prolific writers and espoused many emancipatory and humanitarian causes; her father supported an extension of the 1834 Reform Act and the abolition of slavery and, along with her mother Mary, founded *The Howitt Journal* in 1847 which offered contributions on women's issues. Both signed Smith's 1856 petition, as did Smith's father. Mary Howitt was a member of the Health of Towns Association, and in that capacity worked alongside Octavia Hill, Harriet Martineau and Elizabeth Gaskell, all of whom contributed to *The Howitt Journal*. The two elder Howitts were also well-known poets with close ties to Rossetti and the PRB, so it was through Rossetti that Siddal met Anna Mary and her fellow campaigners.

By 1862 when Siddal died, the Langham Place Group, just one strand of an emerging feminist movement, had been successful in publicizing the plight of middle-class women and had initiated reformist and pioneering schemes in the fields of property, work, education and the arts. Siddal was never an active member but a feminist reading of her poems encapsulates much of what the Group was attempting to change, or at least bring to public attention. In 1854 Smith published a pamphlet entitled *A Brief Summary in Plain Language of the Most Important Laws of England Concerning Women*. It succinctly showed the extent to which married women were subject to their husband's authority: a wife was his property whether she was abandoned or not; marriage was inequitable even if happy; in rich marriages there was some evidence of financial settlements to protect women from spendthrift husbands, but this did not apply to the poor. Smith set up a committee of protest, of which Parkes and Mrs Howitt were members, and this led to the 1856 petition to Parliament to reform married women's property law in view of the hardship suffered by women of station and professionals involved in the arts. There were 24,000 signatories, including Elizabeth Barrett Browning. Parliamentary reaction was more positive than anticipated, but in fact the only change to directly result from it was in the law of marriage and divorce. The campaign, however, revealed Smith as arguably the most radical member of the Group; whereas others struggled to improve the status of women within the framework of traditional values, she challenged the values themselves.[8] Parkes assumed it was Rossetti who was reluctant to marry Siddal because of his fear of commitment.[9] There remains the possibility that given this intellectual climate Siddal was not prepared to surrender such freedom as she had; her poems can certainly be read as an indictment of the prevailing system and attitude.

Langham Place was otherwise known as the headquarters of the Society for Promoting the Employment of Women, a vexed question to which the attention of the Group formally turned in 1857. Smith published her 'Women and Work' pamphlet in which she insisted on the female right to paid work, saying women were not degraded by financial independence, but by dependence on the benevolence of their nearest male relative. Women were not purely the 'helpmate' in all areas of masculine life, and should not be seen as, or consider themselves to be, charity cases. Women needed an occupation beyond marriage and were not necessarily content to be financial dependants. Women wanted to work for the sake of their minds and bodies, because they must eat, and because others were dependent upon them.[10] Siddal initially supported herself as a shop worker and later as an artist's model; the former was generally considered a reputable job, the latter was not, and this prejudice illustrates the dichotomy facing the women's movement, largely comprised of representatives of middle-class 'respectability'. Both sexes generally considered the professional art world unsuitable for women; Siddal may have left dressmaking/millinery to gain access to its opportunities and materials but modelling was intermittent, poorly paid and stigmatized, so that her decision to go down that path was certainly unconventional.

During Siddal's lifetime the group opened up several new work opportunities for women under their own auspices, to be staffed entirely by them: a Law Engrossing Office, a Telegraph School run by Isa Craig, the Victoria Press and *The English Women's Journal*, which was edited from 1858 by Parkes and Adelaide Procter. The *Journal* was designed to highlight female misery, chiefly centred on the lack of female employment. It was a means of informing its readership of relevant legal and political issues but its primary purpose was to open up the workplace to women, which in turn led to a call for changes in female education and training. Christina Rossetti published two poems in the *Journal* in 1861 and 1863 and this gives some indication of her opinion of the mid-Victorian women's movement, assuming she was sympathetic to the *Journal*'s overall purpose and tone. Rossetti knew Smith and Parkes personally and was happy to have her name associated with a publication that had an obvious political message: to employ, educate and organize middle-class women and to extend a woman's sphere of action outwards from the home.[11] However, both radical and conservative attitudes pertained. She attacked the under-privilege of women, worked with prostitutes and stressed feminine strengths such as support and forbearance, but credited men with 'keener, tougher and more work-worthy gifts' and claimed curiosity would be the downfall of an independent woman.[12] She was cautious about social equality, arguing that a wife was the foremost possession of her husband, but also equated a mutually beneficial unity in marriage with the relationship between Christ and the Church. The latter was essentially patriarchal and didn't encourage women to discuss theology or hermeneutics, yet in 'The Face of the Deep' (1892) she stated gender should not restrict religious vocation or the duty of women to teach the scriptures, a clever blend of Christian principles and a demand for more forward thinking that also lay behind her advocacy of Anglican Sisterhoods in which women lived in chosen celibacy without having to renounce debate or writing poetry.[13] Despite this she did not support access for women to higher education or suffrage, as she explained in a contradictory letter to Augusta Webster. She argued that the doctrines of Christian orthodoxy would not allow such an extension, and that because men formed the army they deserved to govern, but that if women's rights were overborne for lack of female voting influence then female MPs were only right and reasonable, and married women should be included in suffrage because of their caring, protective role. Rossetti seems to have been claiming feminism was both too ambitious and not ambitious enough, that nothing short of universal female suffrage was her goal, but a second letter to Webster appeared to settle the matter. As supporters of women's rights were doing so for social not Christian reasons, morally she could not join the movement, the implied criticism one explanation perhaps for why the Langham Place Group never called her one of their own.[14] Christina's personal situation differed greatly from that of Siddal who did not have a secure income or parental support. As an artist and modelling only for Dante Rossetti she had little choice but to secure herself a patron, making Smith's call for monetary independence very pertinent. The issue of money lay at the heart of her complex relationship with Ruskin who offered her a financial arrangement in 1855. Siddal needed his backing but she resented his artistic and personal interference, and would choose independence over his controlling male influence.

Procter, Craig and Parkes were all members of the Langham Place Group, and in 1854 Parkes, Howitt, Smith and her two sisters formed the Portfolio Society, to exhibit sketches and listen to poetry on prescribed themes. Procter was central to the debate on women's suffrage and also principal poet for the *Journal*, using her position to empathize with women facing childlessness, a loveless marriage, or an illegitimate child that could never be acknowledged, as in 'A Comforter' (1860). In 'A Woman's Last Word' (1861) she advocates leaving an unhappy marriage and 'A Woman's Question' (1858) looks towards honesty and equality in a relationship. She was also secretary to the Society for Promoting the Employment of Women which was linked to the Victoria Press run by Emily Faithfull, so her involvement in the feminist movement was both pragmatic and philosophical. Jean Ingelow wrote fairy tales that revised the dominant representations of femininity and challenged the limitations imposed on women and their movements.[15] Her heroines are independent and resourceful and display superior intellectual and physical skill, as in 'Gladys and Her Island' (1874) in which a young pupil-teacher uses her initiative to find her idea of heaven when forbidden to go on a seaside picnic with the rest of the girls. Gladys makes the most of adverse circumstance to ultimately achieve far more than she could have imagined. Like all good fairy tales, it has a moral, a rallying cry: the future may be uncertain but what has already been gained can never be taken away and will live on in the hearts of those women who seek change.

Published poets figured prominently within the circle, yet to be a woman writer at all brought difficulties. The comparative reticence of women poets can be linked to the feminist question by showing how a high proportion of women's poems are about the right to speak and a desire to have parity of 'high' or poetic language with men. This desire is thwarted by prejudice against women's use of such language and a patriarchal definition of what constitutes ideal femininity: the ideal woman is silent. Once she speaks she will only talk nonsense, so she is better off being mute so she can be truly loved. As human beings women have access to language but as females they cannot use the very form, the poetic, which would enable them to be emotionally expressive.[16] This generic argument fits the mid-Victorian period well. *The English Women's Journal* published women's poetry and the Portfolio Society offered encouragement and a platform to a few women poets. Siddal recognized the potency of poetic language in female hands, but in failing to publish she also fell victim to the prevailing patriarchal ethos that deemed women unfit for involvement with that artistic genre.

Smith and Howitt were friends at the centre of a group of Pre-Raphaelite artists before they took up the ideas of early feminism, and art would remain an important means of communication for that cause. The debate on gender issues actually stimulated the production of many compelling images of women by male artists because the question of women's status was being opened up to more radical interrogation than ever before. Pre-Raphaelite male artists were also less likely to have intentionally promoted patriarchal ideologies than the vast majority of their nineteenth-century counterparts.[17] Dante Rossetti seems to have believed Siddal had creative powers equal to that of a man, even if his treatment of her in other ways was dismissive and even cruel. Both he and Ruskin encouraged Smith in her artistic endeavours, but Howitt did not fare so well in Ruskin's hands. She completed *Boadicea Brooding over her Wrongs* in 1856 but it was rejected by the Royal Academy and then had a mixed critical reception chiefly because of its over-embellished forest setting, but also because of its openly feminist stance. Ruskin sent his verdict in a letter, not in published form: 'What do *you* know about Boadicea? Leave such subjects alone and paint me a pheasant's wing.'[18] Stung by the force of Ruskin's misogyny, Howitt reputedly never worked again.[19] Bearing in mind that Siddal's sketches and paintings frequently depict protagonistic women in historical settings, the relationship between artist and patron was bound to be tense. The *Boadicea* episode illustrates wider issues to do with the identities and activities of women artists at this time. History painting was especially contentious as women began to challenge the traditional belief that this most prestigious category of painting should automatically be undertaken by men. It was important for women artists to take on female historical subjects as this also challenged the Whig view that all history was that of great men. Ruskin believed that women should occupy a secondary, dependent role in culture and society and that there had as yet been no great women painters, so *Boadicea*, which elided contemporary feminist activity with a defiant warrior queen, was a direct affront to his thinking.[20]

As 'sisters-in-art' Smith, Parkes and Howitt extended mutual support to Siddal, but they also undertook a more maternal role in the spring of 1854 when Siddal was temporarily living in Hastings, a town already familiar to all parties.[21] Siddal's first visit to the Howitt household had seemingly coincided with the first evidence of an unexplained illness that would be regularly incapacitating thereafter. Mrs Howitt insisted Siddal be sent to her homeopathic doctor and this appears to have led to her daughter and Smith taking over the management of Siddal's complaint. Smith, who had already failed to persuade Siddal to enter the Harley Street sanatorium run by her cousin Florence Nightingale, wrote to Parkes in Hastings in early April, asking for her help in securing temporary accommodation for Siddal there:

> I have got a strong interest in a young girl formerly model to Millais and Dante Rossetti now Rossetti's love and pupil. She is a genius and will (if she lives) be a great artist ... I do not doubt if circumstances were favourable [Rossetti] would marry her. She is of course under a ban having been a model ... ergo do not mention it to anyone ... Will you ask ... where there is a room with <u>sun</u> and a good woman ... for a few shillings a week ... It must be big enough to do for eating and drawing and sleeping.[22]

Smith's use of the word 'genius', according to its mid-century definition, carries an implication of artistic potential even Siddal is unaware of. Smith recognized Siddal's inability to expose this artistry in herself as something natural; rather, Siddal needed someone such as Smith herself to bring it out. Siddal had the native intellectual power to be an artist, but as yet she was 'unformed' and without an agency to enable her to perform. Smith, Parkes, Rossetti and Ruskin all speak of Siddal as a genius in which case presumably they all believed themselves to be that controlling agency, and Siddal to be primarily a victim, unable to enact her own destiny without their intervention. Smith would appear to have thrown herself wholeheartedly into this project as part of her mission 'to champion society's strays of every class and religion throughout her life'.[23] Siddal needed space to recover and be shielded from gossip and also to work, but there is still a distancing here, from one whose background is considered slightly below par. Her 'championship' of Siddal is a form of patronage or short-term philanthropic concern, not an equal interchange. A subsequent letter to Parkes, written as Siddal set out for Hastings with Rossetti, carries similar sentiments, as well as a hint of prophecy:

> I think Miss S. is a genius and very beautiful and although she is not a lady her mind is poetic ... He [Rossetti] wishes her to see Ladies [sic] and it seems to me the only way to keep her self-esteem from sinking. I do not think she will recover and perhaps this prevents one from thinking much about the future for them. The present is all we have, do not let us or them cast it away.[24]

By 'poetic' Smith means Siddal is 'full of poetry', but yet again her agency is removed, leaving her poetics to be demonstrated by others.

Bessie Parkes recorded her first impressions of Siddal in her journal shortly after the latter's arrival. Her relationship with Siddal would last until Siddal died and is notable for its perceptive compassion:

> April 24th
> Dante Rossetti brought Miss Siddal down on Saturday. Together they form the most touching group I ever saw in my life ... Every line of her face is spiritual grace but I fear there is no hope for her ... I never saw a creature who seemed to be so full of poetry ... I don't know when anything has so deeply affected me, as to see her and that poor young lover ... This girl 'Elizabeth' is intellectual whatever her education may have been; and now there is a strange satire about her; a half-joking way of speaking of her own state, most peculiar. It does not deem want of depth to me; rather a way of saying 'Oh of course I shall suffer', a sort of mocking at fate, even under the conviction of ill.[25]

Parkes never refers specifically to Siddal as an artist nor does there appear to have been any collective effort made to acquire her work; this stance is repeated in her memoirs, published in 1897. It is as a model for Rossetti that Siddal makes her greatest impression, which reinforces the stigma Smith cannot fully ignore and yet which also contradicts a central tenet of the Langham Place Group, namely that women have a right to paid work. Only Rossetti was able to animate Siddal, and this in itself is problematic for modern feminists. Parkes would recall:

> an unworldly sympathy and purity of aspect which Rossetti recorded in his pencil drawings of her face ... a remarkably retiring English girl ... [whose features Rossetti transfused] with an expression in which I could recognise nothing of the moral nature of Miss Siddal. She had the look of one who read her Bible and said her prayers every night, which she probably did.[26]

The contradictory accounts here are illuminating; Parkes saw the Siddal she wanted to see but was unsettled by the dubious accuracy of Rossetti's interpretation of latent sexuality. Siddal's identity is mutable and can be fashioned by others as they want; she becomes different when different people look at her, just as she herself became different when she donned a costume as an artist's model. Both Parkes and Smith seem reconciled to Siddal's premature death despite there being no firm diagnosis of her illness. Theirs was evidently to be a supportive role, without further proactive intervention. Smith's comment about Siddal having a poetic mind without being a lady implies the two were normally assumed synonymous, and the class difference between Siddal and the other women does seem to have been an issue. Perhaps Parkes, Smith and Howitt merely saw Siddal as an invalid requiring their charity, her reduced social status mitigating against her being regarded as a fellow professional. Friendship networks were still at this time based on familial alliances, and their egalitarian feminism was still class-specific, which explains why they did not promote her work or secure commissions for her. Even the drawings done by two of the group during the stay at Hastings emphasize her lowly status: her face with its averted gaze presents a blank and passive mask of beauty that fails to fully connect lower-middle-class model with upper-middle-class artists.[27]

On 4 May Siddal wrote to Smith asking if she and Rossetti could visit her and Howitt at Smith's family home outside Hastings. The suggestion was not welcomed; in a letter to Parkes, Smith indicated she and Howitt, with weightier matters occupying their attention, were already finding irksome the company of those who would not heed her advice:

> Anna Mary Howitt and I are just now returning from seeing Miss Siddal and Mr Rossetti ... As for the hospital plan they do not like it and will not think of it for the present. On Saturday they propose to come and see us at Scalands ... This day A. M. H. and I consider as a terrible cut up of our valuable time and their coming over will be another cut up as we must look after Miss S.[28]

That Saturday was the occasion of the drawings of Siddal mentioned above from which it can be inferred that the artists believed painting and 'looking after' were part of the same healing process. Siddal arguably had a need to be watched, which creates another paradox: her unpublished poems are kept internal because they are her property, yet she allowed multiple interpretations of her public face. Smith, Howitt and Rossetti simultaneously sketched Siddal in profile and their work gives a unique opportunity to see Siddal through their different eyes. All three pencil portraits are identical in technique but Smith brings out Siddal's dignity and pride, Howitt her resilience and pathos, and Rossetti her surprisingly wide-eyed seriousness and determination.[29] Drawing as a group was a common activity within the PRB, where a sense of community in art was essential to its ethos, yet Siddal's detachment is palpable and cannot merely be put down to her recovery from recent illness. The individuality that typifies her own art prevented her becoming an integral part of this new female circle, even if elements of their political philosophy can be found in her poems. Rossetti refers to the day at Scalands in one of several letters he exchanged with Parkes around this time. Whereas Siddal's health is the ostensible reason for the correspondence (Parkes is considerably more worried about it than he), on two occasions Rossetti goes on to speak of literary matters on which he sought her opinion.[30] Parkes's interest in Siddal was undoubtedly genuine, but her refusal to believe his behaviour had anything to do with her illness or

14 Anna Mary Howitt (later Watts), *Elizabeth Siddall*, 1854, pencil

15 Barbara Leigh Smith, *Elizabeth Siddall*, 1854, pencil

eventual death smacks of hero-worship, and makes her motive slightly less altruistic.[31]

Ruskin and Tennyson were leading exponents of the 'separate and supportive' creed that emerged as the male counter-attack to

16 Dante Gabriel Rossetti, *Profile Portrait of Elizabeth Siddal with Irises in her Hair*, 1854, pencil

the demands for the reform of women's social and economic position. As part of this philosophy, Ruskin put forward an education plan for girls in 'Of Queens' Gardens' that contrasts sharply with the ethos behind the Portman Hill School opened by Smith in 1854, the same year Parkes produced her *Remarks on the Education of Girls*. It had no uniform, punishments or creed, and encouraged a mix of social classes. It was co-educational up to the age of 11 but the sexes followed a different curriculum; thereafter boys were not permitted, to avoid distraction as the girls embarked on a rigorous teaching programme to equip them for a more progressive role in society. Lessons in English, French, drawing, music, physiology, health and hygiene, elementary physics, reading and arithmetic provided a wide educational focus; the lack of specific religious teaching did, however, cause some controversy despite the strong moral tone of the school.[32] Although it only survived for ten years and had no widespread effect on the education of women, Portland School epitomized the stance and aspirations of those peripheral members of the Pre-Raphaelite group that espoused the cause of the early women's movement.

Ruskin, patronage and female educational reform

Ruskin was a patron of a number of artists, both male and female, and his involvement with them throws further light on his attitude to women and makes apparent the connection between art and its power to do social good. His over-paternalism, evidenced in his dealings with Siddal and Rossetti, contributed to the breakdown of relationships with individual male artists and the PRB as a whole, but his involvement with women artists and collectors would prove more substantial. Octavia Hill, a former drawing pupil, became a more significant channel through whom Ruskin could direct his social policy. From 1853 Ruskin gave financial aid to her Working Ladies Guild which trained and found jobs for single women, and in the early 1860s he invested more than £10,000 in her schemes for working-class housing management.

If Hill represented the public face of Ruskin's patronage of women, then Ellen Heaton, Lady Pauline Trevelyan and Louisa,

Marchioness of Waterford constituted the private.[33] From 1855 he acted as mentor and mediator for Heaton and Lady Trevelyan in their purchase of Pre-Raphaelite works and this gave his love of control full rein; he overrode their instructions to artists and took for himself works they had commissioned.[34] Significantly, Heaton and Ruskin corresponded about her possible purchase of works by Siddal, and the letters from Ruskin give some indication of his relationship with the artist, and his role as her patron. In February 1855 Ruskin wrote to Heaton suggesting in passing that she could be of support to his new interest: 'by the bye there is one of Rossetti's pupils – a poor girl – dying I am afraid – of ineffable genius – to whom some day or other a commission by encouragement and sympathy be charity – but there is no hurry as she don't work *well* enough yet, and Rossetti and I will take care of her till she does, if she lives.'[35] The lack of urgency and the appeal to Heaton's kindness rather than to her artistic acumen would tend to support the contention that Ruskin was more interested in Rossetti at this point, but his offer of financial support for Siddal did follow in May; he would give her £150 per year for first refusal on all her watercolours and drawings, and he would also take all her work to sell at a profit to herself, or to keep. In November he reminded Heaton of Siddal again in passing, without actually naming her, as he reported on a Rossetti painting *Rachael and Leah* that Heaton was to view: 'I think the face of Rachael beautiful in expression ... It is the portrait of the young girl I told you of – who draws so well herself.'[36] Heaton had obviously responded positively to this prompting because on 30 December he wrote again, but his tone is pessimistic and hardly supportive of one in whom he has made an investment. He actually goes on to point Heaton in another direction, though whether this was to retain tight control over what Siddal was producing, or to protect his buying client is difficult to say:

> Best thanks about Miss Siddal ... I am afraid you can't help her – yet – for the simple reason that she is still too ill to draw ... I have given her the means of going to Nice for the winter ... she being sanguine of being able to paint there and send me home beautiful drawings of blue sea and orange groves – I encouraged the idea – or she would not have let me help her – but I have no drawings yet and I much doubt when they come they will be as such as I could fairly put

into your hands ... She believes me, as she may, when I tell her *I* like them, but ... I don't hold them, yet, fit to sell again: I think therefore for the present, you must still leave her to me: and I think you can help me better with one of my [male] pupils.[37]

Ruskin had recognized that Siddal was not always compliant; she could also directly disobey him. On 12 April 1856 he wrote to Heaton agreeing with her about her notion of sending Siddal to Switzerland for the summer from Nice,[38] an instruction he had already passed to Siddal.[39] In May Siddal, whom Ruskin refers to as 'Ida', was actually back in England, but Heaton's involvement is interesting and has become more personal, having been put in charge of delivering the August instalment of Ruskin's allowance to Siddal whilst he was abroad.[40] By October Ruskin was evidently seeing Heaton as a definite purchaser of Siddal's work, which could explain such direct intervention. Having invited Heaton for a viewing Ruskin cancelled it and proposed posting Siddal's drawings to her instead. It transpired that this was because he had yet to receive them himself, and the correspondence ends with a further cancellation and vague proposals for a rearranged meeting.[41] Ruskin appears not to have been a proactive patron of Siddal, but Heaton also allowed him to dictate her taste. She owned numerous sketches and vignettes by Turner, and this, rather than promoting Siddal's interests, could have been why Ruskin was interested in writing to her. His relationship with Siddal was different, which may account for its brevity. He was her conspicuous patron, yet between 1855 and 1857 she was not producing the meticulous and accurate works he demanded from his other women protégées. Her small watercolours and often over-worked pencil sketches were idiosyncratic, with strange spatial configuration. His influence on her was evidently and frustratingly limited as his letters show. By rejecting his money Siddal escaped the master–servant relationship that applied to his other women artists, and her poetry, secret, unpaid and unpublished, also remained free of restriction.

Ruskin appeared not to see the inherent contradiction between wanting to control artists like Siddal at a time when the whole idea of patronage ran contrary to emerging feminism. He advised, instructed, commissioned, bought and sold their work for others but did little to publicize their efforts or bring them to a wider audience, and rarely bought pieces for himself.[42] The extent of his engagement is visible when the cases of two pairs of siblings are considered: he gave active encouragement to George Price Boyce yet virtually ignored Joanna who was more talented, and the same applied to John and Rosa Brett. Both devoted themselves to the depiction of nature as Ruskin demanded, yet only the brother got Ruskin's endorsement. Ruskin insisted that the copying of old masters should be an essential aspect of his patronage of women, but other critics argued that it held back individual and collective artistic development and doomed women to an amateur status not expected of men.[43] Siddal did have his financial protection, but she still remained hidden because she did not sell on the open market. As a result, she was not fully introduced to the art world, and lacked its validation. Ruskin did not see women artists as a separate entity; they were there merely to support the work of men. In any case their gender and overt sentimentality barred them from certain aspects of formal instruction; men and women therefore needed a different artistic curriculum, a theory Ruskin extrapolated into a much wider social context in 'Of Queens' Gardens'.

For Ruskin the role of patron was synonymous with that of moral and artistic educator. He never considered those he mentored his equals, instead he saw artists and protégés as children in need of guidance, and this, applied to women in general, is the prevailing stance of this essay, the classic statement of the doctrine of the 'Woman's Role':

> The perfect loveliness of a woman's countenance can only consist in that majestic peace, which is founded in the memory of happy and useful years ... and from the joining of this with that yet more majestic childishness, which is still full of change and promise ... Woman and child, and past and present, are linked through physical beauty; woman is at the epicentre of art, but as its image, not its producer.[44]

Men and women were intended to fulfil entirely different but complementary functions in life, a familiar thesis that Ruskin made more unusual by managing to suggest her function was more attractive and noble than his. In listing the functions of each sex he implies that neither partner is superior, a wife can direct her husband whilst still being his subject. In reality his text firmly places women in a submissive role, one philosophically opposed to that suggested by Siddal's poems.[45] The woman's sphere was to be the home and its governance. Only philanthropy, the dispensing of charity within the locality, should allow her to step beyond it. Ruskin makes it clear, however, that she needed to be properly prepared for both these spheres of influence, meaning that education was of paramount importance. As the latter had to be designed to reflect the essential qualities of womanhood, sentiment, compassion, supportiveness and etherialism, it would of necessity encompass a different set of principles and body of knowledge from those required by men, making female education automatically restrictive. Education therefore defined the secondary role Ruskin envisioned for women and ensured the continuation of their childlike status and dependence; it was the key to his social philosophy.[46] As an artist Siddal broke away from such dependence by resisting Ruskin's attempts to amend her style and by refusing his money. As a poet she further emphasized his failure as a patron by withholding her work, the texts of which are testament to women who are both socially and poetically independent.

Ruskin's theories of female education are predicated upon the central tenet that women only need to be taught such as will enable them to understand and support the work of men, and to learn to empathize with the suffering of those around them. A woman therefore has no need for a specific linguistic, scientific, geographic or historic curriculum; instead, through a general appreciation of these subjects she must be taught to understand the insignificance of her life compared with the vastness of God's entire creation, in other words to be grateful for her lot.[47] Theology itself however, is considered off limits; women are not intellectually or morally capable of grasping its concepts, despite their automatic assumption to the contrary. Ruskin is especially vituperative on this point, suggesting that the petulant woman/child has brought patriarchal religion to the point of calamity: 'They dare to turn the household Gods of Christianity into ugly idols of their own; – spiritual dolls, for them to dress according to their caprice; and from which their husbands must turn away in grieved contempt, lest they be shrieked at for breaking them.'[48] As men and women are intellectually unequal, even if both sexes should follow a similar curriculum its direction should be quite different. 'His command of it should be foundational and progressive; hers, general and accomplished for daily and helpful use.'[49] As such a woman is denied any love of learning per se, especially as a girl should be led earlier than a boy towards the: 'deep and serious subjects ... and her range of literature should be, not more, but less frivolous ... to keep her in a lofty and pure element of thought ... [lest] by its excitement, it renders the ordinary course of life uninteresting, and increases the morbid thirst for useless acquaintance with scenes in which we shall never be called upon to act.'[50]

As a patron and mentor of female artists Ruskin could be seen to be advocating literary censorship, denying access to sources of imaginative inspiration and disallowing freedom of artistic expression, but all the while sugaring the didactic pill. He states that only 'good' novels, those with 'serious use' as studies of human nature, should be considered worthy of reading: 'Whether novels, or poetry, or history be read, they should be chosen, not for their freedom from evil, but for their possession of good ... and if she can have access to a good library of old and classical books there need be no choosing at all. Keep the modern magazine and novel out of your girl's way ... she will find what is good for her; you cannot.'[51] Formal education for girls is considered a waste of time, and whereas freedom of choice is enticing, in reality such a curriculum was deliberately designed to be superficial and decorative. As such it entirely suited the wider female social role Ruskin envisaged. The artistic curriculum was similarly curtailed: 'Let her practice in all accomplishments be accurate and thorough, so as to enable her to understand more than she accomplishes.'[52] By such means achievement would be held back, and Ruskin's protégées experienced this first-hand. In art and music truth, simplicity and usefulness were deemed the guiding principles in the creation of pieces that were accurately observed, using the fewest strokes or notes, and guaranteed to beautify experience or memory. There was no room here for personal or critical expression. This was an educational ideal that acted to censor experience and blunt aspiration. It created 'the most ingenious system of mental enslavement known to history' in an attempt to ennoble a system of 'subordination through hopeful rhetoric'.[53]

The first reference to Siddal in Ruskin's correspondence occurs in a letter to Rossetti written when the two men were barely acquainted. In May 1854 Ruskin promised to come and see some of her drawings; she was not even named.[54] A year later the relationship between all three had become more substantial. Rossetti and Siddal had visited Ruskin and his parents who were impressed with her demeanour. Shortly after, Ruskin approached Rossetti with two suggestions for financial support for Siddal, and Rossetti, overriding her preference for being paid for individual works, decided upon the more conventional £150 per annum sponsorship. Siddal was to be 'sternly coerced if necessary' into compliance.[55] In an attempt to finalize this arrangement Ruskin wrote to Rossetti several times in April 1855, addressing him in a less formal way and involving himself in the management of Siddal's health by suggesting she visit Wales, Jersey, and later, the Continent.[56] Ruskin's sympathy is as much with Rossetti, the concerned lover, as with his new artistic interest, a point clarified in the altogether more dramatic idea Ruskin put before him shortly after: 'My feeling at first reading is that it would be best for you to marry, for the sake of giving Miss Siddal complete protection and care, and putting an end to the peculiar sadness, and want of you hardly know what, that there is in both of you.'[57] This attempt to interfere in the private lives of Siddal and Rossetti came to nothing, but Ruskin persisted, offering her, again indirectly, the run of his house and garden and, for the first time, his artistic judgement: 'and I want to talk to you about her, because you seem to me to let her wear herself out with fancies, and she really ought to be made to draw in a dull way sometimes from dull things'.[58]

Two letters from Ruskin to Siddal written in the spring of 1855 continue the combined themes of concern over her health, instruction, and an attempt to persuade her of the benefits of accepting his financial help.[59] The second of these is the more forthright; Ruskin exerts a greater degree of emotional pressure on Siddal than previously: 'and if you will put yourself in my place, and ask yourself what you would like any other person to do who was in yours, I believe you will answer rightly, and save both me and yourself much discomfort'.[60] Having thus swept aside any remaining objection to his financial plan, Ruskin continues with numerous professional stipulations: Siddal must not even consider working or recuperating in Italy or France, only in Wales where the air was bracing, not relaxing; she must only draw at an easel placed so that she need not stoop; she must only work in colour: 'The slightest blot of blue and green is pleasanter to me than a month's work with chalk or ink.'[61] The recipient is addressed as 'Miss Siddal' in the more complete of the two, but this formality ceased a month later, when she became 'Ida'. There is no specific reason for the change, but it occurs at the same time as correspondence begins between Ruskin and Dr Henry Ackland, whom Ruskin had persuaded to look into Siddal's case, apparently without her or Rossetti's permission.[62] In fact one of the earliest mentions of 'Ida' is made not to Siddal herself but is used in reference to her in a letter to Ackland's wife; Siddal stayed with the family whilst being medically assessed and appears to have created a negative impression. Ruskin's comments about Siddal are arguably his most illuminating, and a connection with the Tennyson heroine achieves some substance:

> I don't know how that wilful Ida has behaved to you. As far as I can make out, she is not ungrateful but sick, and sickly headstrong ... But I find trying to be of use to people is the most wearying thing possible ... These geniuses are all alike, little and big, I have known five of them – Turner, Watts, Millais, Rossetti, and this girl – and I don't know which was, or which is, the most wrongheadedest.[63]

Ruskin continued to find both Siddal and Rossetti exasperating. Siddal was making an elongated stay in Paris when Rossetti asked Ruskin for funds to visit her there; the latter refused to supply them: 'You are such absurd creatures both of you. I don't say you do wrong, because you don't seem to know what *is* wrong, but just do whatever you like as far as possible – as puppies and tomtits do. However, as it is so, I must think for you.'[64]

According to W. M. Rossetti, Siddal's absence from England prevented her from working, and this occasioned the opportunity to free herself from the monetary agreement with Ruskin in October 1855.[65] Ruskin's presumptive treatment of her and Rossetti may also have influenced their decision. In January 1856 he wrote to 'Ida' in Nice, insisting she move on to the Alps because of the vibrancy of the colours she would encounter there, and because she had already defied him by going to Paris in the first place. He ends in the following patronizing tone: 'Now do be a good girl and try Switzerland, and believe me always affectionately yours, J. Ruskin.'[66] The payments to Siddal did in fact continue until at least August, hand delivered in this case by Ellen Heaton, but by June 1857 the arrangement had ceased, apparently at Siddal's instigation.[67] Ruskin would continue to directly involve himself in her work despite having lost the moral control he had had. Writing again to Rossetti, he reproaches himself for the loss of that more personal involvement:

> I shall rejoice in Ida's success with her picture, as I shall in every opportunity of being useful either to you or to her. The only feeling I have about the matter is of some shame at having allowed the arrangement between us to end as it did, and the chief pleasure I could have about it now would be her simply accepting it as she would have accepted a glass of water when she was thirsty, and never thinking of it any more.[68]

By implication, Siddal and Ruskin parted on acrimonious terms, and given the demands Ruskin had placed on her it is difficult to imagine their relationship continuing along the lines Ruskin was envisaging. Later that year he was still calling her by her nickname, but also still attempting to be of influence: 'I must see Ida; I want to tell her one or two things about her way of study. I can't bear to see her missing her mark only by a few inches, which she might as easily win as not.'[69]

After Siddal and Rossetti were finally married Ruskin offered his congratulations, saying he wished he could have done so personally. He begged them to visit him as soon as possible, assuring them both of his continuing affection. In the postscript he comments on how much more beautiful are Rossetti's drawings of 'Ida' than of anybody else: 'She cures you of all your worst faults when you only look at her.'[70] There is a sense of estrangement here, and Siddal is seen as possessing an elusive power that Ruskin himself was unable to harness. In the last surviving letter to mention Siddal, she is no longer 'Ida' and the aforementioned affection has vanished: 'I wish you and Lizzie liked me enough to – say – put on a dressing gown and run in for a minute rather than not see me; or paint a picture in an unsightly state, rather than not amuse me when I was ill. But you can't *make* yourselves like me, and you would only like me less if you tried.'[71] Neither was there to be correspondence with Rossetti after her death in February 1862, only an oblique reference to the latter's 'great sorrow' in a letter sent the following July.[72] In Ruskin's eyes Siddal and Rossetti are once again the children he tried, and ultimately failed, to manipulate. Ruskin's relationship with Siddal was fluctuating and complex. She was not alone in being given a pet-name: his letters to his cherished student Rose La Touche are addressed to 'Rosie-Posie', her sister Emily was 'Wisie', and their mother 'The Lizard'. He took pleasure in the company of girls and young women, but in the majority of all his dealings with others he is either child or mentor, never an equal, and this is reflected in the playful names he employs.[73] Siddal appears to have quickly tired of this, but not before Ruskin had likened her to a fictional character who was ostensibly mounting a challenge to expected social norms. For her part Siddal withheld from him poems that adopted a similar stance, the implication being that it was the protégée and not the mentor who in this case had the upper hand.

Feminist issues in Siddal's poems, *The Princess* and *Aurora Leigh*

The Princess is an extended way of discussing Siddal's relationship with Ruskin, as the question of funding or patronage is one of several issues that seek to contain Ida's poetic voice. Ida represents the contemporary debate on the 'Woman Question' and parallels can be drawn with Siddal's attempts to claim artistic independence. Both *The Princess* and *Aurora Leigh* also provide a platform from which to examine the contention that the feminist perspective of Siddal's poems can be extrapolated to explore the inherent potency of female poetry and the role it plays in political change or reform. Ruskin associated Siddal with Ida, the spirited character who represented challenge and independence, for similar reasons. This in itself does not elicit parallels between Ida the fictional heroine and the texts of Siddal's poetry, as *The Princess* is structured in layers of ventriloqual and gendered voices. Rather, the connection between

Siddal and Tennyson's poem operates on a different level, merely suggested by Ruskin's perception of his protégée. Ida herself does not define feminist thought because she is voiced by male narrators. Arguably, the female voice can best be found in the interpolated lyrics, although controversy surrounds the degree of feminist sympathy they actually exhibit, especially when they are read alongside the poems delivered by Ida in the mainframe poem.[74] However, regardless of the political sentiments they carry it is these eleven songs that draw Siddal the poet into feminist dialogue with *The Princess*. 'As through the land at eve we went', 'Sweet and low', 'The splendour falls on castle walls', 'Thy voice is heard through rolling drums', 'Home they brought the warrior dead', and 'Ask me no more' act as divisions between successive parts of the poem, whereas 'Tears, idle tears', 'O, Swallow, Swallow', 'Our enemies have fallen', 'Now sleeps the crimson petal' and 'Come down, O maid' form part of its narrative. The female poet/singers in Tennyson's poem become commentators on a range of issues affecting women and as such they fulfil the same function as Siddal's texts and throw the strength of feeling in the latter into perspective.

Tennyson's tale is comic and medieval but it shares its focus on women's role in the world, including that of the female poet, with Barrett Browning's nineteenth-century context. Both works are therefore topical, but with a crucial difference: *Aurora Leigh* is written from a woman's perspective as Barrett Browning shows her rejection of Tennyson's male version of female experience. Her approach to the 'Woman Question' was conditioned by Mary Wollstonecraft's *A Vindication of the Rights of Woman* (1792) in that it advocated a more enhanced female role that considered all aspects of their condition, cultural, political and socio-economic. *Aurora Leigh* discusses the relationship between middle-class women's experience, politics and creativity and Barrett Browning admired the strong call for change in educational provision, for middle-class women especially, that Wollstonecraft spearheaded. Barrett Browning and Leigh benefited from access to an extensive home library and used it to become proficient in ancient and modern languages. Both asserted their right to be poets of politics, tackling controversial subjects like nationalism, liberalism and the use and misuse of power. Women had an absolute right to work and follow a career and therefore bring about change, and marriage and motherhood should be no disqualification. As Siddal's three poems are also written in the first person their texts can be read in the light of Aurora's experience as both poet and champion of women's independence. Ruskin, who had recommended *Casa Guidi Windows* to Siddal, declared *Aurora Leigh* to be 'a genuine work of feeling' and 'as far as I know, the greatest poem which the country has produced in any language', when advising his students what to read in his 1857 essay 'The Elements of Drawing'.[75] In a letter to Robert Browning in late 1856 when the poem first appeared Ruskin declared it unsurpassed by anything but Shakespeare, and emphatically not his sonnets. He liked it all: 'familiar parts and unfamiliar, passionate and satirical, evil telling and good telling, philosophical and dramatic'. He was better for reading it but 'crushed' by it; like breathing the purest air, it made him 'healthier'.[76] He wrote again in late December specifying which elements he liked best: chiefly and significantly these were references to natural history, geology and Italy, and moments of comedy, intense emotion and pathos. He does not mention Aurora's feminist stance; on the contrary, it was her confession of love to Romney that moved him especially.[77]

The three lyric poems that illustrate Siddal's feminist perspective are structurally very similar, but vary according to their deployment of anger, irony and self-blame. 'Love and Hate' (1857) consists of five quatrains, each with a regular abcb rhyming pattern and 4–3–4–3 iambic metre. It is a passionate outburst from a deserted lover that uses powerful imagery to express a fury whose specific cause is not given. 'The Passing of Love' (1857) is close in form, but it has slight variations in rhythm that are matched by a wider emotional span. The speaker berates herself for her stupidity, yet harks back to a time of happiness with her ex-lover. 'Dead Love' (1859) is more ambitious in structure and tone. It has three sestets with an abcbdb rhyme and repeated iambic 4–3 beat, but the flow of the language tends to negate such stricture. The poem, which again reacts to the ending of a love affair, is deeply sarcastic and exhibits a greater degree of self-confidence than 'Love and Hate' or 'The Passing of Love'. In all three poems feminist sentiment is equated with the move from victim-status to self-determination via the acquisition of self-control, and deconstructed they allow the argument for self-determination to be explored more fully. They may be scrutinized for images of subjugation: tears, loss, innocence, remorse, foolishness, limitation and enslavement, or pain. As is the case with all of Siddal's poems such things are dealt with generically; there are no assaults on identifiable political targets, which lends these examples an air of timelessness. Correspondingly, there are also images of female potency: courage in speaking, unconventionality, pride, self-determination, and the rejection of love as a political act. The poems may be read as an attack on the 'ideal' partnership. Siddal tends to forge negative images of men as liars, betrayers, belittlers, creators of disillusion and upholders of convention. She counters this with signs of female retaliation, of struggle, and a possibly changing role for women which could encompass heterodox relationships. They can also be analysed for what they say about women's poetry and its potency. There are direct references to speech and singing, and the use of the first person stresses a 'right to write', but there is also a more complex subtext to these outwardly simplistic verses: they are not necessarily berating men; they also set their sights on those female poets who do a disservice to women in accepting a secondary role. As a result, Siddal's relationship as a poet with the womanly types most often found in Victorian poetry, the daughter, the dutiful wife, the stereotypically subjected one, can be considered.

These approaches allow Siddal's work to be profitably read alongside *The Princess* and *Aurora Leigh* because they establish a dialogue between texts that are on face value incompatible. 'Love and Hate', 'Dead Love' and 'The Passing of Love' are substantially different in scope, language and structure, and are the product of a very different class and educational background. Siddal's father owned two ironmongery shops in working-class Southwark in London and the family of ten lived above one of them. As such, he was in an insecure position in an economically fluid and class-conscious age. He had already moved from Sheffield presumably to consolidate his business, but could not be described as prosperous; he employed no live-in servants and all his surviving children went into trades for a living. There is no record of how or where any were educated, but possibly apocryphal stories tell of novels and poetry being read aloud at home.[78] Siddal's love of art and poetry may have had its origins here; it certainly reflected a middle-class aspiration shared with her father who had some pretension to past grandeur as a landowner.[79] There remains the possibility that Siddal believed herself to have been objectified because she was perceived as being from a different class background once she became involved with the PRB; *Lady Clare* is not unique among her paintings and drawings in challenging established social norms. Only very little can be gleaned about what books Siddal read at any point in her life from the evidence of her art she was an avid reader of Romantic poetry, Keats and Wordsworth especially, as well as Tennyson, Browning and Dante Rossetti. She owned two volumes of the 1802 edition of *Minstrelsy of the Scottish Border* and was fascinated by the Border ballads in general.[80] She was still in contact with Ruskin in 1857, the year in which he wrote of his admiration for *Aurora Leigh*, because he helped her mount her pictures for the exhibition at Russell Place that June, so it is feasible to think he recommended 'the perfect poetical expression of the age' to his then protégée.[81]

Once associated with Rossetti Siddal would have been exposed to any number of authors; *The Improvisatrice*, *The Golden Violet* and *The Venetian Bracelet*, all by L. E. L., are known to have been in the Rossetti library in 1848 and Christina both admired and respected her.[82] Christina was a close role model for Siddal since they shared the Pre-Raphaelite interest in colour, shape, form and simple Medievalism. They also both offer a woman's perspective on loss, the fickleness of masculine love for a muse or model and the hopelessness of a restricted female existence, such commonality suggesting a relationship strongly inflected with poetry.[83] Women poets regularly read each other and it is possible to map their connections by way of allusions and cross-references. Rossetti knew Dora Greenwell, Procter, Ingelow and Webster; Greenwell and Michael Field wrote sonnets and Amy Levy wrote an essay on her.[84] Membership of the Portfolio Society that circulated texts between women readers facilitated discourse about female experience and it would be interesting to know if Siddal read Hemans and Landon as it's understood others did. As her poems are entirely non-specific and refer only to generic circumstances they cannot be related to external events or stand as commentary on, for example, specific feminist issues. By comparison, the reading habits of Elizabeth Barrett Browning are widely known. She read from hundreds of women writers as well as British, European and American male novelists and poets, and from childhood was familiar with the classics, transgressing the cultural law that deemed only boys capable of such understanding.[85] Her letters make this clear and constitute the kind of invaluable primary record Siddal does not possess.

The fluidity of Siddal's family circumstances finds, perhaps, a correlate in the open-endedness of poems in which back-stories and outcomes are uncertain and meanings are obscure. This is not in itself problematic as the absence of context coupled with the fragmentary condition of her manuscripts permits multiple readings of verses that are open to multiple levels of meaning. The apparent simplicity of these poems may mark the lack of knowledge of classical modes of composition, but it also lends itself to their enigmatic and troubling nature. Their brevity and deliberate ambiguity precludes their being revelatory. Instead, these texts have to be approached for what they do not say; they hold their meaning close, tantalizing the reader into believing that the outward image also reveals what is inside. The poems often take an unexpected turn: an abrupt change of mood, an awkwardness of language that draws attention to a pivotal point, the juxtaposition of pathos and self-parody. They are passionately self-centred even when directed elsewhere, and their mocking tone becomes another layer of protection, paradoxical feminist armour against betrayal by her own gender. Siddal was defined by her reticence yet her poems speak on a subject that was topically significant and in doing so they provide her with a different, more politically charged, face. When the mask of anonymity is translated into non-publication of her work, conscious withholding of meaning then becomes the ultimate feminine wile. The significance of these three short poems lies in their rhetorical nature, and their essence would be dissipated if their meaning were obvious or immediately understood. As it is, they can make a contribution to a debate traditionally dominated by markedly different texts like *The Princess* which have already been the subject of intense feminist scrutiny.

However bold the language, these three poems all deal with loss, whether it is of a lover, or love itself, or of self-respect. 'Great love' has been replaced by 'great hate' (15) in 'Love and Hate' and 'tears of anguish' (3) accompany the realization of rejection in 'The Passing of Love'. In 'Dead Love' the addressee is urged not to weep for something that will never occur (13), and here as elsewhere what has happened in the past is linked to premature death (5). The anger that ripples through 'The Passing of Love' and 'Love and Hate' is undercut with remorse; 'The Passing of Love' opens with a cry of pain that quickly grasps the reader's attention as the speaker expresses regret for her stupidity: 'O God, forgive me that I ranged / My life into a dream of love! / Will tears of anguish never wash / The passion from my blood?' (1–4). Following this outburst the poem abruptly changes tack, and for three verses it soliloquizes love and its transformative power to hold a woman captive, only to resume its sharpness and pace in the final stanza: 'O Heaven help my foolish heart / Which heeded not the passing time / That dragged my idol from its place / And shattered all its shrine! (17–20). The speaker cannot help recalling how love held her in thrall, even if she now deplores her slavishness, and this marked contrast of mood also comes out in the use of cold or frozen imagery for lost or unrequited love, compared with images of fire or burning for anger and passion. This appears to have been an erotic or at least sensual relationship so that loss of innocence is also implied: 'Love kept my heart in a song of joy, / My pulses quivered to the tune; (5–6) / Love held me joyful through the day / And dreaming ever through the night' (13–14). The same is true of the last line of 'Love and Hate' where the speaker accuses her lover of stealing her life away (20). 'Dead Love' is outwardly less vitriolic but it still offers a critique of cultural conditions that limit the actions of a woman, as emphasized in the opening verse:

> Oh never weep for love that's dead
>   Since love is seldom true
> But changes his fashion from blue to red,
>   From brightest red to blue,
> And love was born to an early death
>   And is so seldom true. (1–6)

Elsewhere in the poem the 'merest dream' of love can transport a woman heavenward (15–16), and even true words 'pass on and surely die' (10). Love is thus portrayed as male, fickle and transient, and woman has been taken in by it.

In *Aurora Leigh* Barrett Browning translates the same sentiment more literally, and connects prostitution with the issue of funding for the single woman. Marian is duped by Lady Waldemar into going to France where she is drugged and multiple-raped in a brothel (VI:1207–18). Taken in as a servant in Paris she is sacked once her pregnancy becomes apparent (VII:43–8), then as a lone parent she can only find pitifully paid employment as a seamstress (VII:108–13). The connection between money and independence is also made in *The Princess*; the university is funded by Gama, so Ida is reliant on his tolerance and good will, but in developing her relationship with the Prince Tennyson extends the gender stereotype. In 'Now sleeps the crimson petal' (VII:161–74) and 'Come down O maid' (VII:177–207) Ida is forced to acknowledge her destiny as a marriage partner. Even the words are no longer hers; she has to resort to quoting someone else's. Their eroticism becomes a vehicle for her seduction, but they largely negate the feminist cause. 'Now sleeps …' evokes a world of suspended dreams in which sleep is non-threatening despite the heavy overtones of penetration. The many references to light reinforce this; gold, the firefly, the milk-white peacock, the stars, the meteor, the shining furrow and the lily. Woman is incomplete without man and longs for the promised sexual relationship: 'Now folds the lily all her sweetness up, / And slips into the bosom of the lake: / So fold thyself, my dearest, thou, and slip / Into my bosom and be lost in me' (VII:171–4). 'Come down' reaches the same conclusion but takes a different approach: happiness lies not in the lofty heights of academia but in the verdant valleys of domesticity. Ida must therefore 'cease to move so near the Heavens' (180) and embrace the land of 'Plenty in the maize', and 'red with spirited purple in the vats' (186–7). The white and icy mountains are seen in the distance and are full of danger, but the valley, 'the hearth' (201), is full of sweet sound that is infinitely more alluring. By the end of the poem the torrent that arose in the hills and 'danced' the woman down to find love below (194–5) has become 'myriads of rivulets hurrying through the lawn' (205), and this echoes the disintegration of Ida's feminist Utopia.

Not surprisingly, references to female potency are more abundant. In 'The Passing of Love' it is the passion in her blood that rules the woman's tears (4), and there is violence in the wording of the last verse. 'Dead Love' uses sarcasm to achieve a similar effect, addressing the ex-lover patronizingly as 'my dear' (11,17) and 'Sweet' (13,16), while assuring them of their punishment for an unspecified crime: 'And you will stand alone, my dear, / When wintry winds draw nigh' (11–12). Alliteration and repetition are used as metaphorical weapons. The subtle repositioning of key words in the last verse allows the speaker to deliver a final deadly blow which establishes her unanswerable moral supremacy. More importantly, by extrapolation it also celebrates the power of the lyric in female hands:

> Sweet, never weep for what cannot be,
>   For this God has not given.
> If the merest dream of love were true
>   The, sweet, we should be in heaven,
> And this is only earth, my dear,
>   Where true love is not given. (13–18)

In 'Love and Hate' the references are less cryptic. When the speaker tells the addressee to 'take thy shadow from my path' (5), she instantly puts herself in a dominant position and the sunshine is 'gay' (12) since she has become oblivious to the pain she has been caused. The language deployed is quite masculine and bombastic in tone: 'blasts of heaven' (3) and 'wild wild winds' (7) are invoked, and the hatred she now feels sits 'grimly' in the place of love (16). The last verse, again, delivers the *coup de grâce*; the speaker is so dismissive of her ex-lover she is feigning sleep, or at least looking away, and using silence as a means of defiance. At four points in the poem (2, 5, 13, 14) she actually forbids her lover to look at her, which neatly reverses the motif and shifts the balance of power, hinting at the onset of political and social change for women. In saying she cannot or will not speak she is of course contradicting herself, but by this device she can stress her right to choose: 'All changes pass me like a dream, / I neither sing nor pray: / And thou art like the poisonous tree / That stole my life away' (17–20). Unlike Siddal, Tennyson places women in a specific domestic context and it is through this that their changing role can be measured. 'As through the land at eve we went' (I<II: −14) describes a husband and wife who 'fell out' (3) but 'kissed again with tears' (5) above the grave of the 'child ... lost in other years' (10–11). The poem reinforces the traditional dependence of the sexes upon one another, and the need for children to cement a union, but their combined and ongoing grief breaks down the male stereotype and hints at further sharing in the future. Siddal's three poems do not reflect on children, they focus on broken adult relationships, but like this lyric they expose the heightened complexity of a situation many women were likely to face. In 'Sweet and low' (II:1–16) a mother attempts to reassure her young charge that her father will 'come to his babe in the nest' (13) safe from the perils of the sea. There is an emphasis on the family being incomplete without the male figure; in the first verse the woman asks the wind to 'blow him again to me' (7) whereas the child and its wellbeing are not mentioned. There is latent feminist sentiment in the sub-text, however; the husband has yet to return and is in fact not needed at home because the woman, having no choice, is coping alone.

'Love and Hate' contains a number of emotive yet negative images of men that are testament to their wrongdoing. If the speaker is indeed addressing a male then he is 'foolish' (1) and 'false' (9, 13). In the third verse he is depicted struggling, face down, among dying leaves: 'Lift thy false brow from out the dust / Nor wild thine hands entwine / Among the golden summer leaves / To mock this gay sunshine' (9–12). The evocative image of the grasping, twisted hands reverses the gender stereotype, and this is reinforced in this poem, as it is in 'Dead Love', by the use of other physical features more often associated with women: lips (1), face (2, 4) and eyes (13).[86] The final couplet is far from enigmatic in its language, but its sense is deeply emotive. The words used stress the insidious nature of loss compared with the sudden explosive fury of the first four verses. The branches and roots of the tree have stealthily moved to squeeze life out of the speaker, leaving her utterly changed. In the middle section of 'The Passing of Love' love and a male lover become synonymous. The poem lauds one who can calm the elements and avert evil, but this same individual has lulled the speaker into a false sense of security. In her enslavement to love she has failed to see that over time his passion has dimmed, leaving her to worship at an empty 'shrine' (20). The same concept appears in the opening lines of 'Dead Love' where the fickle male lover seems to oscillate between the two objects of his amorous attention at whim (3–4). *The Princess* adopts a more open-ended and subtle stance. 'Ask me no more' (VI<VII:1–15) comes at the point at which Ida is almost ready to surrender her feminist philosophy in favour of capitulation to the Prince, and the repetition of the four words at the beginning and end of each verse presumes that the pressure to do so has been intense. There could still be an element of withholding in the plea; Ida will indeed submit but it has yet to happen, meaning the surrender is not yet complete. The last verse does, however, stress the inevitability: 'Ask me no more: thy fate and mine are sealed: / I strove against the stream and all in vain: / Let the great river take me to the main: / No more, dear love, for at a touch I yield. / Ask me no more' (11–15). The words are tinged with regret, implying that the forthcoming union is not something to be welcomed because Ida has not chosen it, and moreover, despite its being a moral duty to offer support to a wounded man, there is an element of blackmail in his 'hollow cheek' and 'faded eye' (7). This lyric is closest in temperament to Siddal's poems, which use anger and sarcasm to rail against the indignities women can suffer within a relationship. This piece in particular tells a literal story, a narrative of solemn domestic reality which contrasts sharply with the mock-heroics of the story proper and the embedded male songs.[87]

Autonomy and independence

Siddal's poems speak of changes in the attitude and circumstances of individuals, but these specific narratives can then be read as metaphors for more far-reaching changes in the condition and role of women as a whole. Experience has acted upon the woman in 'Love and Hate' to make her wiser about relationships; she will not allow herself to be deceived again because henceforth, in her dream state (17) she will distance herself from emotional entanglement. 'Dead Love' celebrates the moral superiority she has gained, and this confidence is expressed through the use of superlatives: 'brightest blue'

(4), 'deepest sigh' (8), 'truest lips' (9) and 'merest dream of love' (15).[88] In the last verse the message is even stronger; God cannot give 'true love' (18), neither by implication can he give women freedom; women must fight for these themselves. By the same token the higher powers invoked in 'The Passing of Love' have to be interpreted metaphorically, as an appeal to intuition or self-reliance, not literally. Exactly what constitutes 'true love' is uncertain, but given the erotic undercurrents of these poems a sexual relationship seems likely to be part of it. Women are therefore being encouraged to break with orthodoxy, and this can be widely defined because these poems are largely ungendered. Love is an important focus in each case, but it is more than a male/female romantic involvement. These poems can all be read as inter-feminine communication or simply as a furious interchange with the self. In 'The Passing of Love' the object of scorn in the first and last verses could even be a different individual from that recalled in the intervening three. In whatever form, love is depicted as a force that threatens to entrap so needs to be rejected, much as Siddal felt it necessary to break away from Ruskin's artistic and personal control. This is clearly indicated in the dream state at the end of 'Love and Hate', the violent self-criticism in 'The Passing of Love', and the denial of religion in 'Dead Love'.

A woman having to take up responsibility alone is also the focus of 'Thy voice is heard through rolling drums' (IV<V:1–8):

> Thy voice is heard through rolling drums,
>   That beat to battle where he stands:
> Thy face across his fancy comes,
>   And gives the battle to his hands:
> A moment, while the trumpets blow,
>   He sees his brood about thy knee:
> The next, like fire he meets his foe,
>   And strikes him dead for thine and thee. (1–8)

The man is protecting his family by going to fight, but it is the woman and her domestic role that inspires him morally and physically to do so, a situation already seen in the philanthropic ideal envisioned by Ruskin. Marital love is given a different and more poignant face in 'Home they brought her warrior dead'

(V<VI: 1–16), a ballad that considers the emergence of the more powerful woman. Although sharing a similar back-story to 'Thy voice' this poem is not centred on male glory or sacrifice but is instead written much more from a woman's perspective. Grief strikes the widow mute and emotionless: 'She must weep or she will die' (4), even when her husband is eulogized and his dead face shown to her. The turning point does not come until the final verse: 'Rose a nurse of ninety years, / Set his child upon her knee— / Like summer tempest came her tears— / "Sweet my child, I live for thee"' (13–16). It takes the female voice of experience to bring about the catharsis and show her charge that the future lies in the child, the fruit of the union. This poem succinctly captures several potentially conflicting images: the dependent wife, but one who will also have the strength to survive this domestic tragedy, and the capable woman whose timely intervention ensures the continuity of civilized life. 'Our enemies have fallen' (VI:17–42) can be read as Ida's clearest feminist message. It speaks of evolutionary political hope: 'The little seed they laughed at in the dark, / Has risen and cleft the soil, and grown a bulk / Of spanless girth' (18–20), and tells how men have disregarded women at their peril: 'they came ... they heard a noise of songs they would not understand ... marked it with the red cross to the fall ... and are fallen themselves' (23–6). Much promises to come from this metaphorical battle: 'A night of Summer from the heat, a breath / Of Autumn, dropping fruits of power' (38–9), and men and women will build a future together, turning adversity to advantage (28–31). That said, sympathy for Ida's views is diluted by the context. She is made to carry a stolen child as she speaks of war, and immediately after her rendition she and her followers take up traditionally assigned roles as nurses and carers as the university is finally overrun by men.

Aurora Leigh makes the issues of funding and financial independence central to signs of an emerging new order for women. Marian retains her purity and nobility despite her sexual past, and simultaneously a step is taken to stir up dissent with a view to changing attitudes towards women who unavoidably break established codes of behaviour. Aurora takes on paltry writing so, somewhat like Siddal, she will not need a patron. Her pen then becomes 'a spade' (III:294), equating her work with good honest toil. As a writer she needed an education, yet ironically she has to sell her father's books, those that provided that very thing and inspired her taste for poetry, in order to finance her move to Italy, the source of poetic inspiration. Concern with the reform of the condition of women draws Barrett Browning back to the work of the Langham Place Group, Smith and Parkes especially, with whom she was acquainted, and references to education and employment for women permeate *Aurora Leigh*. Aurora describes her experiences of learning in Book I (385–481) and relates how she had to work on periodical articles to support herself in London whilst trying to write her epic poem (III:306–28). She wants women to work so they can equal the dignity of men even if what they do might be considered demeaning (VIII:712–15), a view shared by Siddal who probably became an artists' model, an occupation also tinged with immorality, in an effort to be financially independent, and who chose artistic integrity rather than Ruskin's patronage.

The potency of women's poetry and its ability to effect change is mooted differently in each of Siddal's poems. In 'Love and Hate' the poet is speaking, yet she can choose to withhold her speech as Siddal did. She forbids speech, and even prayer, from the second party and so becomes doubly powerful. When that party is allowed to speak they can only voice a 'dirge', a lament for the dead. 'The Passing of Love' exemplifies a contrast between the form and sense of a poem. Its very simplicity lends itself to the succinct conveyance of complex ideas and encourages the artful placement of individual words. The third line of each verse contains a reference to something negative even when the overall sense of the verse is positive, and this juxtaposition is most apparent in the inner three stanzas:

> Love kept my heart in a song of joy,
>   My pulses quivered to the tune;
> The coldest blasts of winter blew
>   Upon me like sweet airs in June.
>
> Love floated on the mists of morn
>   And rested on the sunset' rays;
> He calmed the thunder of the storm
>   And lighted all my ways.

> Love held me joyful through the day
>   And dreaming ever through the night;
> No evil thing could come to me,
>   My spirit was so light. (5–16)

By this means the poem injects a note of concern into what is ostensibly a perfect male–female relationship. The framing verses destroy that impression, making them a powerful poetic tool. It can be argued that 'The splendour falls on castle walls' (III<IV:1–18) takes a similar position regarding the singular and important role of women's poetry. The passage of time with perhaps little associated change appears to be its central tenet; events are seen to be recurring and echoing across the centuries, never really dying, and this is poetically emphasized in the almost identical repetition of the last two lines of each verse: 'Blow, bugle, blow, set the wild echoes flying, / Blow, bugle; answer, echoes dying, dying, dying' (5–6). The old order is both physically and metaphorically retained via the many references to the constancy of the landscape over which the sounds roll, snowy summits, the wild cataract, cliff and scar and purple glens, but there are hints that this may not always be the case as verse three does celebrate the eternal might of the female singers' voices: 'Our echoes roll from soul to soul, / And grow for ever and ever' (15–16). A specific female presence can be found that 'venerates music as an alternatively powerful means of non-verbal speech' and reinstates value to this aesthetic form traditionally associated with women.[89] Epic poetry is an essential part of the curriculum at the university (II:253–7), and linked particularly with women; Homer may rank as the greatest male epic poet, but Sappho and others have vied for a place beside him as representatives of the 'arts of grace' upon which civilization depends (II:144–8 and 161–4). Aurora, similarly, muses over what she should or could write, although unlike Ida she wants to be judged as a poet per se rather than a woman poet specifically. In consequence she dismisses lyric mode as static (V:84–138), choosing instead the male stronghold of the epic poem as her goal. In turning away from the female preserve of the lyric Aurora then becomes a nineteenth-century Homer, a writer of a dramatic narrative poem that has a complete story and points to a new future with identifiable heroes.

Siddal's poems are resolutely lyric. Their shortness and subjectivity make them ideal vehicles for the personal thoughts and feelings Siddal needs to express and this is particularly apparent in 'Dead Love' where the brevity of the poem contrasts with the weight and importance of its subject, the gap between the reality of the cultural situation for women and the presumption of what love is supposed to mean. Only the 'merest dream of love' (15) is called for, yet even this is beyond reach. The infinite desolation of this discovery is cleverly reinforced by the use of controlled anger and the deployment of surprisingly seductive language. Terms of endearment give a sarcastic touch and intensify the sentiment. The message is unequivocal and its attack is formulated to allow little time for retaliation between verbal blows that fall swiftly. The poem is littered with superlatives and their ironic use draws attention back to the essentially compact and restricted format of the piece. Elsewhere, the language is sparse and cryptic, and occasional repetition makes this seem more so. As with most of Siddal's work, words of one or two syllables predominate. There are no vivid or rolling descriptions, and this focuses attention on personal sentiment. Individual images are rare, and merely suggested: 'wintry winds' (12) hint at the bleakness that underlies the deceptive levity of the delivery. Beneath the latter is a gritty determination which is most obvious in Siddal's use of absolutes: empty words will 'surely die' (10), and true love is 'not given' on earth (13 and 18). In the narrative of this poem an adverse situation is controlled without an outpouring of emotion, just as the piece itself is controlled by the simplicity of its structure. 'Love and Hate' reaches an emotive and very personal climax at the end of the fourth verse: 'Great love I bore thee: now great hate / Sits grimly in its place' (15–16), but the speaker then disassociates herself from whatever or whoever has caused such intensity of feeling. The barrier thus erected ensures her spiritual survival at this pivotal moment. The language of this poem is largely uncompromising and again predominantly monosyllabic which gives pace to an already confrontational delivery. 'Poisonous' (19) is the exception and its elongated sound creates contrast and gives immediate emphasis to its contextual meaning: betrayal has been slow and silent. Recognition of this has brought empowerment, but also a suggestion of vulnerability. Something of the character of the speaker is glimpsed here and an empathetic relationship is begun with the reader, but the poem resists any development of this by allowing the speaker to step away from the cause of her anger, lest such intensity of emotion be seen as a sign of weakness. The use of an archaic form of the personal pronoun introduces a quasi-religious element which stresses her moral superiority and gives the poem a medieval ambience, but in this context it signifies the end of chivalry and courtly love, so admired by the PRB yet here considered irrelevant to the social situation of Victorian women.

'The Passing of Love' addresses the consequences of a temporary loss of self-control. Its central section explores experiences of love with reference to more traditional love lyrics: 'sweet airs' blow upon the speaker (8) whose love 'floated on the mists of morn' (9), but the framing verses make it obvious that this buoyant and positive picture was only temporary, and their rapid changes of mood emphasize what has been lost. They also provide a commentary on the intervening narrative in which the mask of self-control has again slipped to reveal feminine vulnerability. The man is not to blame, rather the speaker takes responsibility for becoming love's victim and this ultimately makes her the more powerful individual. This short lyric quickly achieves a range of emotion which prevents its being purely melancholic; it also demonstrates the complexity of female response to an already emotive situation. The anger evident in all the poems is directed at those parties who have betrayed or deserted the speaker. Given that the latter is female, her targets are those women who have allowed themselves to be victimized by love and the relationships that define it. If the speaker identifies herself as a woman poet, the focus of her attention then can shift to those other women writers whose poems have proliferated the stereotypical image of femininity engendered by a male-dominated society. This is again apparent in 'Love and Hate' where the poetess is scorned for the 'dirge' (and now this word assumes its greatest significance) that leaves her lips. 'Dead Love' too rails against the conventionalist woman poet, promising her that the influence and legacy of her work will be short-lived once attitudes to women begin to change:

> Then harbour no smile on your bonny face
>   To win the deepest sigh.
> The fairest words on truest lips
>   Pass on and surely die,
> And you will stand alone, my dear,
>   When wintry winds draw nigh. (7–12)

Ida also berates a female poet for over-sentimentality and lack of progressive thinking, but Tennyson is quick to limit the impact of her criticism. 'Tears, idle tears' (IV:21–40) laments the passing of time and the ambiguity of memory: 'Tears from the depth of some divine despair / Rise in the heart ... thinking of the days that are no more' (22–5), days that are 'sad and strange' (31), as indeterminate as those immediately before death, and 'wild with all regret' (39). This is a very strong emotional response to loss, especially as the speaker appears to be regretting what she never had. Neither is there a sign that the future will hold out hope of change, as Ida's achievements at the university are not acknowledged by her followers. Ida, in turn, is very quick to condemn the poem as anti-aesthetic and overly concerned with a reactionary past that needs to be discarded in favour of an egalitarian future: '... for all things serve their time / Toward that great year of equal mights and rights' (IV:55–6), which should have brought her closer to Siddal's argument. However, her abrupt dismissal of the poetry of another woman reinforces the perspective of the male storyteller; a woman's voice has failed to carry Ida's philosophy, implying that Ida has limited support even amongst those closest to her. 'Tears, idle tears' is intrinsically retrospective, and contextual reaction makes it metaphorically more so.

Felicia Hemans's characteristically sentimental and melancholic poems also demonstrate these opposing forces. They celebrate domesticity, female duty and heroism, but within an acceptance of the limitations of a gendered sphere of influence. She takes a personally pertinent theme of absent or lost love and extrapolates it to voice experience of loss and the enacting of vengeance at turning points in history, especially when individuals, communities or whole nations died in repeated cycles of male domination. *Tales and Historic Scenes* (1819) has been criticized for romanticizing the many deaths during the Napoleonic Wars but it can also be judged as an early attempt to reconstruct history from a female viewpoint, allowing domestic ideals to begin to alter attitudes to war.[90] Two later collections, *Records of Woman* (1828) and *Songs of the Affections* (1830) extended the premise, proposing a feminist negotiation of the tension between brave deeds and domestic ties with an emphasis on the importance of peace for women, the conventional guardians of the home. Women were posited as important historical figures, upholding cultural values but always victims of men's rivalries and political contentions. Their fate could encompass suffering, abandonment, suicide, even infanticide, especially odious when juxtaposed with domestic bliss. The conflicts thus generated, family versus fame, affection versus ambition, home versus career, were played down by contemporary readers who were uncomfortable with any challenge to the ideology of feminine virtue, but Hemans's poems tap into and voice the feeling of uncertainty and revolutionary challenge post-1815.[91] Hemans was no radical, but as an example of more subversive feminism, in 'The Restoration of the Works of Art To Italy' (1816) she took a complex political situation and made it a legitimate arena for female debate by focusing attention on art, a feminine sphere of influence, which allowed her arguments to be framed in an acceptable way.[92] She regularly depicted women as the bringers of order out of chaos and Tennyson arguably found her judgement persuasive. 'The Chamois Hunter's Love', published in *Records of Woman*, shows how the young protagonist dutifully balances her desire to live in a valley with her husband's love of the mountains by going to live in a lonely hut somewhere between the two locations, and there are distinct parallels with 'Come down, o maid' and 'Sweet and low.'[93] Hemans provides a platform whereby Tennyson's and Siddal's lyrics can be brought together again, one that throws Siddal's 'feminism' into sharp relief.

Siddal's three poems certainly deal with loss, but they also deal with transformation, or a realization that change is at least possible; indeed, change is built into the structure, sense and tone of each one. Just as her women are transformed by love as in 'The Passing of Love', so they can become empowered through recognition of their victim status, as in 'Love and Hate' and 'Dead Love'. Siddal does not argue for the acquisition of named political or economic rights as demanded by the Langham Place Group. Instead, her poems begin to make women aware of their own moral independence. Tennyson's interpolated lyrics comment upon aspects of female existence in which men play a large part. *Aurora Leigh* focuses on the trials of a woman poet who encounters male prejudice. Siddal's poems adopt a different 'feminist' stance; rather than placing emphasis on the treatment women receive at the hands of a male-dominated society, they celebrate female self-determination by urging women to look at themselves for reasons for their subjugation.

Notes

1 Starzyk, 'Siddal and the Soulless Self-Reflections of Man's Skill', p. 15.
2 The significance of 'women looking' is discussed in Deborah Cherry, *Painting Women. Victorian Women Artists* (London and New York: Routledge, 1993), pp. 109–91.
3 Elizabeth Prettejohn, *The Art of the Pre-Raphaelites* (London: Tate Publishing, 2000), p. 76.
4 *Ibid.*, pp. 74–7 has extended discussion of dual interpretations of this work.
5 Marsh, *Sheffield*, p. 6.
6 Timothy Hilton, *John Ruskin. The Early Years 1819–1859* (New Haven and London: Yale University Press, 1985), pp. 213–14.
7 Elizabeth Barrett Browning, *Aurora Leigh and Other Poems*, ed. Cora Kaplan (London: The Women's Press Ltd, 1978), p. 9.
8 Candida Ann Lacey, ed., *Barbara Leigh Smith Bodichon and the Langham Place Group* (New York and London: Routledge & Kegan Paul, 1987), p. 3.
9 Girton College Library and Archive, Cambridge University, GCPP Parkes 15/70, letter quoted in Margaret Crompton, 'Prelude to Arcadia', unpublished biography of the early life of Bessie Parkes (*c.*1970), p. 87.
10 Lacey, *Bodichon and the Langham Place Group*, pp. 13–14.
11 Diane D'Amico, 'Christina Rossetti and the English Women's Journal', *Journal of Pre-Raphaelite Studies*, No. 3 (Spring 1994), 20–4, pp. 20–2.
12 Hassett, *Christina Rossetti*, p. 227.
13 Burlinson, *Christina Rossetti*, p. 68.
14 Anthony H. Harrison, *Christina Rossetti in Context* (Brighton: Harvester Press, 1988), p. 207 (n. 4).
15 Burlinson, *Christina Rossetti*, p. 37.

16 Cora Kaplan, 'Language and Gender', in Dennis Walder, ed., *Literature in the Modern World. Critical Essays and Documents* (Oxford: Open University Press, 1990), pp. 310–16, p. 315.
17 Prettejohn, *Art of the Pre-Raphaelites*, p. 210.
18 Quoted in Cherry, *Painting Women*, p. 187.
19 Mary Howitt, *An Autobiography edited by her daughter Margaret Howitt* (London: Isbister and Company Ltd, 1889), p. 231.
20 Cherry, *Painting Women*, pp. 187–8.
21 Jenny Ridd, *A Destiny Defined. Dante Gabriel Rossetti and Elizabeth Siddal in Hastings* (Pett, East Sussex: Edgerton Publishing Services, 2008) has a narrative of Siddal's two month visit in 1854.
22 Girton College Library and Archive, Cambridge University, GCPP Parkes 5, Correspondence between Bessie Rayner Parkes and Barbara Leigh Smith Bodichon, GCPP/Parkes 5/172.
23 Sheila R. Herstein, *'A Mid-Victorian Feminist', Barbara Leigh Smith Bodichon* (New Haven and London: Yale University Press, 1985), p. 100.
24 Girton College Archive, GCPP Parkes 5/173.
25 Girton College Library and Archive, Cambridge University, GCPP Parkes 1/35, Parkes, Bessie Rayner, Bessie Parkes' Journal 1852–4.
26 Bessie Rayner Belloc (née Parkes), *A Passing World* (London: Ward and Downey Ltd, 1897), p. 24.
27 Cherry, *Painting Women*, p. 189.
28 Girton College Archive, GCPP Parkes 5/174.
29 Prettejohn, *Art of the Pre-Raphaelites*, pp. 77–8.
30 Girton College Library and Archive, Cambridge University, GCPP Parkes 9, Correspondence between Bessie Rayner Parkes and Dante Gabriel Rossetti and John Ruskin *et al.*, GCPP Parkes 9/55–57.
31 Belloc, *A Passing World*, p. 23.
32 Herstein, *Mid-Victorian Feminist*, p. 14.
33 See John Ruskin, *Sublime and Instructive. Letters to Louisa, Marchioness of Waterford, Anna Blunden and Ellen Heaton*, ed. Virginia Surtees (London: Michael Joseph Ltd, 1972).
34 In 1855 Heaton was to have bought a watercolour by Rossetti, possibly *Dante's Dream of the Death of Beatrice*, but Ruskin kept it and offered her a choice of two others instead. He argued that Heaton had probably forgotten what she had ordered anyway and that via his 'trick' she was now able to pay less for the replacement even though she would not like it so well. Letter from Ruskin to Rossetti in William Michael Rossetti, ed., *Ruskin: Rossetti: Pre-Raphaelitism. Papers 1854–1862* (London: George Allen, 1899), pp. 59–60.

35 Ruskin, *Sublime and Instructive*, pp. 157–8.
36 *Ibid.*, p. 174.
37 *Ibid.*, pp. 181–2.
38 *Ibid.*, p. 185.
39 W. M. Rossetti, *Ruskin: Rossetti: Pre-Raphaelitism*, pp. 119–21.
40 *Ibid.*, p. 141 has a letter from Ruskin to Rossetti telling him of the arrangement. There is no evidence of Siddal being personally informed.
41 Ruskin, *Sublime and Instructive*, pp. 189–91 has four letters from Ruskin dated 7–14 October 1856.
42 Pamela Gerrish Nunn, 'Ruskin's Patronage of Women Artists', *Women's Art Journal*, Vol. 2 (1981), 8–13, pp. 10–12 has a breakdown of how and where Ruskin reviewed women's art between 1855 and 1875.
43 *Ibid.*, p. 10.
44 John Ruskin, 'Of Queens' Gardens', in E. T. Cook, and Alexander Wedderburn, eds, *The Works of John Ruskin, Vol. XVIII Sesame and Lilies* (1865), *The Ethics of Dust* (1866), *The Crown of Wild Olives* (1866) (London: George Allen, 1905), pp. 109–44, p. 125.
45 Patrick Conner, *Savage Ruskin* (London and Basingstoke: the Macmillan Press Ltd, 1979), pp. 141–2 explores Ruskin's verbal manipulation of neutral ideas into weighted phraseology to disguise their conservatism.
46 From 1859 Ruskin was closely associated, as patron and visiting lecturer, with Winnington Hall School for Girls, described in Ruskin, *Works, Vol. XVIII*, pp. lxiii–lxxiii. His extensive conversations with the young women there would form the backdrop to the imaginary dialogues of *The Ethics of Dust* and re-emphasize his adopted position as moral tutor.
47 Ruskin, 'Of Queens' Gardens', pp. 126–7.
48 *Ibid.*, p. 128.
49 *Ibid.*
50 *Ibid.*, p. 129.
51 *Ibid.*, pp. 130–1.
52 *Ibid.*, p. 131.
53 Kate Millett, 'The Debate Over Women. Ruskin vs. Mill', in Martha Vicinus, ed., *Suffer and Be Still. Women in the Victorian Age* (London: Methuen and Co. Ltd, 1980), pp. 121–39, p. 130. Linda H. Peterson, 'The Feminist Origins of "Of Queens' Gardens"', in Dinah Birch and Francis O'Gorman, eds, *Ruskin and Gender* (London: Palgrave, 2002) considers an opposing interpretation.
54 Ruskin, *Works*, Vol. XXXVI *The Letters of John Ruskin 1827–1869* (London: George Allen, 1909), p. 167.

55 Letter from Rossetti to Ford Madox Brown in W. M. Rossetti, *Ruskin: Rossetti: Pre-Raphaelitism*, pp. 67–8.
56 *Ibid.*, p. 70.
57 Ruskin, *Works*, Vol. XXXVI *Letters*, pp. 200–1.
58 *Ibid.*, p. 201.
59 W. M. Rossetti, *Ruskin: Rossetti: Pre-Raphaelitism*, pp. 62–7.
60 *Ibid.*, p. 65.
61 *Ibid.*, pp. 66–7.
62 Ruskin, *Works*, Vol. XXXVI *Letters*, p. 205.
63 *Ibid.*, p. 217.
64 *Ibid.*, p. 226.
65 *Ibid.*, p. 227, footnote no. 6.
66 W. M. Rossetti, *Ruskin: Rossetti: Pre-Raphaelitism*, pp. 118–21.
67 *Ibid.*, pp. 166–7.
68 *Ibid.*, p. 167.
69 *Ibid.*, pp. 183–4.
70 *Ibid.*, pp. 245–6.
71 *Ibid.*, pp. 342–3.
72 Ruskin, *Works*, Vol. XXXVI *Letters*, p. 411.
73 Jeffrey L. Spear, *Dreams of an English Eden. Ruskin and his Tradition in English Social Criticism* (New York: Columbia University Press, 1984), p. 31.
74 Terry Eagleton, 'Tennyson: Politics and Sexuality in *The Princess* and *In Memoriam*', in Rebecca Stott, ed., *Tennyson* (London and New York: Longman Ltd, 1996), pp. 76–86, pp. 82–3 suggests they do little to weaken the dominant masculine stance of the poem because they have only a subordinate role as 'punctuators'. Their collective voice has no dialogue with the seven narrators which renders their contribution to the feminist debate limited and internalized. Any hint of feminist sympathy remains with the male narrative where it can be diluted or removed. Alisa Clapp-Intyre, 'Marginalized Musical Interludes: Tennyson's Critique of Conventionality in *The Princess*', *Victorian Poetry*, Vol. 38, No. 2 (Summer 2000), 27–48, pp. 229–30 contends that the lyrics were added to reassert Tennyson's mastery as a poet in the face of contemporary criticism, to redeem his misread poem by showing he was not belittling women and to counter the parody of women's political endeavours given in the men's narrative.
75 John Ruskin, 'The Elements of Drawing' (1857) in E. T. Cook and Alexander Wedderburn, eds, *The Works of John Ruskin*, Vol. XV *The Elements of Drawing* (London: George Allen, 1904), pp. 224 and 227.
76 Ruskin, *Works*, Vol. XXXVI *Letters*, pp. 247–8.

Siddal, Tennyson, Ruskin and the feminist question 195

77 *Ibid.*, pp. 252–3.
78 Marsh, *Pre-Raphaelite Sisterhood*, p. 22.
79 *Ibid.*, p. 18.
80 Deborah Cherry, 'Elizabeth Eleanor Siddall (1828–62)', in Prettejohn, *The Cambridge Guide to the Pre-Raphaelites*, pp. 183–95, p. 184.
81 Stone, *Barrett Browning*, p. 141 quotes this in a letter from Ruskin to Robert Browning.
82 Hassett, *Christina Rossetti*, p. 71.
83 Trowbridge, *My Ladys Soul*, p. 15.
84 Blain, *Victorian Women Poets*, p. 12.
85 Stone, *Barrett Browning*, p. 145.
86 This verse does not appear in the Lewis and Lasner edition of Siddal's poems. See Trowbridge, *My Ladys Soul*, p. 81 for history.
87 Clapp-Intyre, 'Marginalized Musical Interludes', pp. 238–9.
88 Hassett, 'Elizabeth Siddal's Poetry', p. 461.
89 Clapp-Intyre, 'Marginalized Musical Interludes', pp. 238–9.
90 Felicia Hemans, *Selected Poems, Prose and Letters*, ed. Gary Kelly (Canada: Broadview Literary Texts, 2002), p. 28.
91 *Hemans: Selected Poems*, ed. Wolfson, p. xvii.
92 *Felicia Hemans*, ed. Kelly, p. 22.
93 Richard Cronin, *Romantic Victorians. English Literature 1824–40* (Palgrave: Basingstoke and New York, 2002), pp. 68 and 81.

4

Siddal, Keats and Pre-Raphaelite relations of power

A Woman and a Spectre

Elizabeth Siddal's drawings frequently depict women in a state of agitation. One very rough and unfinished pen and brown ink sketch attributed to her and referred to as *A Woman and a Spectre* (figure 17) is a case in point and shows two female figures, one superimposed over and possibly arising from the other. The more substantial of the two is clothed in a plain gown and could be seated or lying partly on her side, as in the absence of any background there is no indication of how the drawing was expected to be viewed. The figure has her left arm raised and bent outwards whilst the right is resting in her lap. Her hair, in typical Siddalesque format, is plainly and severely dressed, either side of a centre parting, pulled away from her face so that attention is drawn to well-defined brows and eyes that even in this small, simplistic composition can be seen as being open. The face is reminiscent of Siddal's as painted in her 1857 *Self Portrait*, but here it is partially obscured by a combination of wash and the heavy-handed application of an eraser. The second female figure appears to emerge from the first at right angles to it so that if the clothed woman is lying down it is this erect, barely evident form that dominates the sketch. It has no body, just the suggestion of a shroud-like garment that flows down from the neck, and the head is disproportionately large, framed by bent arms that end in hands with clearly delineated fingers that tear at strands of long, dishevelled hair. The eyes are rounded, wide open and wildly staring, the mouth skewed into a lopsided grimace. There can be no doubt that this 'woman' is alert and in extreme emotional turmoil,

17 Elizabeth Siddal, *A Woman and A Spectre*, date unknown, pen, brown ink and some wash over pencil

and as such she makes an immediate contrast with her more restful and inert host-figure. She is by no means unique as a stereotype of passionate and even violent womanhood in Siddal's artistic oeuvre, but it is unusual to see two such opposing characters in the same composition.

The relationship between the two figures is intriguing and the interpretative possibilities it throws up lie at the centre of this chapter. The second female figure appears to represent a 'wraith', Siddal's frustrated Spirit leaving her body at the point of death.[1] The drawing could reflect the artist's preoccupation with issues of gender and power, and Siddal's belief that 'a demure Victorian woman in an unguarded state may release a terrified and terrifying spectre'.[2] Again it could be illustrating Siddal's relationship with her own hated and unhealthy body; the latter physically incarcerates the artist and prevents her achieving independence and self-fulfilment.[3] There seems little doubt that the two forms are widely differing images of the same person; their lines may be sparse and quickly executed and therefore only roughly committed to paper, but they are drawn with a conviction that invites direct comparison, notably in the treatment of hair, a trope that is examined later with reference to the poems of Siddal and Keats, arguably the most significant literary influence on the Pre-Raphaelites and their ethic. An ego and an alter-ego are involved in a struggle of sorts, yet the latter doesn't appear to be rooted in fear or revulsion. The woman is not raising her right arm, the one closer to the spectre, in an effort to push it away; similarly, the one that is raised, the left, is not shielding her face from attack. Indeed, there is a certain passivity in her body-language as a whole that suggests an acceptance of the dualism that the sketch portrays. Ruskin and members of the Langham Place group referred to Siddal as 'a genius', a largely untutored artist whose potential for greatness needed an outside agency to channel and mentor her budding ability. It is worth noting here that in the nineteenth century 'genius' was still also used to indicate the presence of two mutually opposed spirits, good and evil, which were released by frailty of the body and by whom every person was supposed to be attended. The Romantics envisaged the 'evil' aspect of this dichotomy more as a malevolent Puck-figure than a devil-character, which gave greater scope for literary application. If this is taken into account there can be a rather different interpretation of *A Woman and a Spectre*: the sketch depicts a recognition of there being two aspects to a woman's persona, and that a 'genius' is capable of powerfully influencing another for better or worse. This simple and outwardly naive drawing encapsulates a fluid internal conflict as well as an awareness of the essential nature of both spirits. In parallel, it also points to the more obvious yet deep-seated struggle between the physical and the spectral body, the contention upon which this chapter hinges.

Keats, Siddal and the PRB can be drawn together by showing that Keats was, to a certain degree, a Pre-Raphaelite construct and that his image was manipulated by the Brotherhood. This symbiotic relationship with the PRB (and the artwork of Rossetti, Hunt and Millais in particular) via four of his poems provides a context for Siddal and her relationship with that same group. In other words, the dualisms and juxtapositions that pervade *Isabella or the Pot of Basil*, 'La Belle Dame Sans Merci', *Lamia* and *The Eve of St Agnes* provide a platform for the reading of Siddal's three works: 'Shepherd Turned Sailor', 'Gone' and 'Worn Out'. In outline, these three poems point to a power struggle between the physical body and the spectral body, of the type seen in *A Woman and a Spectre*, and this forms the basis of a literary relationship with Keats. This struggle is paralleled by the recovery and interpretation of her work by W. M. Rossetti in that all such interpretations are spectral by definition. Siddal's poems are enigmatic and are reluctant to yield meaning, creating a poetics of withdrawal due in part to her use of paradox which bridges the gap between the physical and the spectral. A poetics of sensation such as the Pre-Raphaelites found in Keats's work fulfils the same function, blurring the edges between the two worlds and the ways in which they are experienced. Added to this, Siddal was deeply conscious of the image that she created in the physical world and of the way this was manipulated by her Pre-Raphaelite contemporaries. In consequence, she set up a counter-image that demands to be considered as spectral or wraith-like.

In this artistic and poetic context the physical body registers emotion, sensation and needs, but is wasted by disease and sexual attraction despite being erotically powerful. It lacks permanent identity but can change repeatedly, even its gender. It is also a source of meaning-production through its hair in particular. It is a means of communication that implicates the poet's voice, and the balance between silence and speech is central to reading Siddal's poems in general. The physical body can therefore also be used as a metaphor for their structure and chameleon-like variation in punctuation, tense, rhythm and form. By contrast the spectral body allows for an awareness of uncertainty, or a version of 'negative capability'. It creates an elusiveness or dreamy otherness that equates to being half-alive, which in turn allows for an extended range of emotions and the exploration of experience beyond the physical, such as posthumous existence and the possibility of genius. It allows grief and disillusionment to be analysed and rationalized through withdrawal, and an alter-ego to be constructed. Dreams and the concept of sleep can be explored and silence turned into a positive force. It can therefore be transformative, developing the power of imagination through the use of colour and texture in language. There is evidence of struggle between these two body forms in Siddal's three poems, manifest through the recognition that experience of sensation requires withdrawal from, and opposition to, the physical world and its needs, which makes the poet melancholic of necessity. It emerges too in the internal conflicts and polarities within her work that reflect tension between, for example, reality and illusion, or physical health and disease. On a more tangible level tension can also be found in the posthumous reworking of her poems and her refusal to share the latter through publication. By this means Siddal indicated a resistance to interpretation by others and a championing of poetic individualism and independence.

Siddal, Keats and the PRB

The 1857 Moxon edition of Tennyson's poems contains a small pen and ink illustration by John Everett Millais which accompanies 'St Agnes' Eve' (1836) in which a young nun waits with longing for spiritual union with God. The poem begins by immediately setting the physical and emotional context: 'Deep on the convent-roof the snows / Are sparkling to the moon: / My breath to heaven like vapour goes: / May my soul follow soon!' (1–4).[4] The speaker is counting the hours to her death and the absolution it will provide, as stressed throughout by references to things that are white: snow, frost, snowdrops, the moon, even her bosom. The juxtaposition of sin and salvation, shadow and brightness, underlies verse 2 where the lines form couplets of contrast:

> As these white robes are soiled and dark,
>   To yonder shining ground:
> As this pale taper's earthly spark,
>   To yonder argent round;
> So shows my soul before the Lamb,
>   My spirit before thee;
> So in mine earthly house I am,
>   To that I hope to be.
> Break up the heavens, O Lord! And far,
>   Thro' all yon starlight keen,
> Draw me, thy bride, a glittering star,
>   In raiment white and clean. (13–24)

Even the first and last lines are balanced to illustrate an opposite. The final verse ushers in the spiritual consummation of a hitherto earthly relationship with God, using startling images of light:

> He lifts me to the golden doors;
>   The flashes come and go;
> All heaven bursts her starry floors,
>   And strows her lights below,
> And deepens on and up! ... (25–9)

It culminates in an ethereal marriage as the nun anticipates passing through the gates of heaven to meet her Husband. The snow on the shadowy convent roofs has melted to create a 'shining sea' (35), illuminated not by the moon but by God, the light of the world. Millais's illustration depicts the young nun standing on a spiral staircase, holding a candle in her outstretched hand and gazing through an open window over the snow-covered roofs of her convent. He captures the asceticism of the poem through a number of contrasts: light and dark, animate and inanimate, breath and stillness, warmth and coldness, interior and exterior, hope and anxiety. These dualities provide the structural skeleton of Tennyson's lyric, and may also be found in most Pre-Raphaelite art and its poetry, Siddal's included.

There are several small crude pen and brown ink Siddal sketches of this poem in existence (figure 18) which probably all date

18 Elizabeth Siddal, *Study for St Agnes' Eve*, c.1855, pen and brown ink over pencil

from 1855 when she was encouraged to tackle Tennyson subjects with the forthcoming Moxon edition in mind. They are compositionally similar; the noviciate is either leaning on or kneeling by the side of an open window below which is a low, rounded or almost circular doorway giving access to her cell, which contains a few items of simple furniture. The anatomically grotesque figure is wearing vestments but curiously her arms, awkwardly outstretched along the deep sill, are bare. These pieces are childlike and very heavily worked, with many strident straight or solid lines and little finesse, but the facial expressions are startling; whether directed down or towards the barely realized landscape, the eyes are fixed and wide open, and the mouth is grimly and uncompromisingly set. This nun is a tortured being, not one longing for a rapturous heavenly marriage. Something is clasped in her hands and is the focus of her attention, but her body is not in an attitude of prayer in any drawing. Siddal appears to envisage the prospect of religious commitment differently from Millais; the scribbled and rubbed shading of the walls of the convent and the dark texture of the habit suggest earthly containment and fear rather than spiritual liberation. She has offered a personal reflection on Tennyson's poem, in itself an interpretation of the first verse of Keats's work, drawing all three together in collaboration typical of the PRB.

Tennyson's 'St Agnes' Eve' is clearly influenced by Keats's *The Eve of St Agnes* written in 1819. The first verses of both refer to 'breath taking flight for heaven' on a frozen winter's night, and Keats's Beadsman is also occupied with religious devotion, telling his rosary and holding an icon whilst saying his prayers (5–9). Structurally the poems are very different; Keats narrates an entire story with great colour, movement and sensuousness whereas Tennyson concentrates on one imaginary moment voiced by one individual, yet both are derived from the same legend, that of St Agnes who aged 13 was raped before execution after her refusal to marry. By a miracle she remained a virgin, and thereafter any maiden who fasted on the eve of her feast day, 20 January, might see a vision of her destined lover. The story of fourth-century St Agnes partly connects a complex web of nineteenth-century artistic and poetic associates. Keats's poem appealed to Tennyson, and both these poets captivated the Pre-Raphaelites who illustrated their works extensively, especially those with a mythical or spiritual or medieval context, and a female protagonist. Dante Rossetti and William Holman Hunt would both lay claim to the rediscovery of Keats nearly thirty years after his death, and Pre-Raphaelite artistic interpretations of some of Keats's poems would strongly influence Victorian critical opinion well beyond the lifespan of the Brotherhood. Both Dante Rossetti and William Morris acknowledged Keats as a source of inspiration; Christina Rossetti and her brother wrote eulogies to him in 1849 and 1880 respectively, and William Michael in his 1887 biography referred to the 'large and abiding debt [owed] to him and his well-loved memory. He has given us something of beauty to permanently treasure.'[5] Several of Christina's poems reference the varying states of consciousness found at the edges of the known. 'At Home' (1849) and 'After Death' (1858) speak from the afterlife and 'Dream Land' (1848) is about a quest to reach a 'purple land' and the shelter of sleep. The heroine has come far to enter a twilight zone where physical stimuli have little impression. The reader is allowed some sensation even if the subject herself cannot experience it; she is present but can't feel the rain on her hand or see the grain ripening.[6] 'Repining' (1847) has Keats's medievalism and altered states of consciousness as well as the piety and asceticism of Tennyson's Beadsman. Rossetti has a 'Madeline' but as in Tennyson's poem she is awakened spiritually not sexually, and the man doesn't stay in her chamber. Instead he guides her out into a world full of tragedy, and her subsequent experiences turn her previous longing for physical love into a pining for a better relationship with God.[7] Given this intellectual climate it is unsurprising that Siddal attempted sketches that were derived from both 'La Belle Dame' and *The Eve of St Agnes*. Jean Ingelow would return to a similar theme, multiple lives lived in dreams outside of normal existence, in 'Divided' (1863). Two lovers walking side by side become separated by a stream that becomes a mighty river and they lose opportunities to cross over as well as each other and their love, the female voice becoming a metaphor for both companionship and division.

In Pre-Raphaelite hands Keats became a specific construct, designed to support and substantiate the philosophy of the Brotherhood. This was a symbiotic relationship that was modified over the life of the Movement to reflect Pre-Raphaelite concerns and aspirations, but admiration for Keats was constant, and this is reflected in the deference paid to his poetry and in the sense of responsibility the PRB demonstrated towards his legacy. As well as *The Eve of St Agnes*, *Isabella or the Pot of Basil* (1818), *Lamia* (1819) and 'La Belle Dame Sans Merci' (1819) were regularly visited and these texts will be read alongside those of Siddal's poems to discuss their collective involvement with the imagination, the spectral nature of the self, the physical body and the nature of disillusionment. Siddal was herself a Pre-Raphaelite construct, and one that was also manipulated over time. She like Keats was supposedly 'discovered' separately by two people, the artist Walter Deverell and his father, and Hunt, Millais and Rossetti each saw themselves as being responsible for putting her in the public domain. When Hunt published an account of his position in the PRB in 1905 he was retrospectively bidding for its leadership, challenging Rossetti's pre-eminence and staking a claim for Siddal, the icon and muse for the Brotherhood.[8] She has virtually no primary record beyond her own artwork and poems, meaning any Pre-Raphaelite construction has tended to be merely rewritten or reinterpreted. W. M. Rossetti, as official historian of the PRB, recorded her presence and was the first to put her poems into print, but he added titles that gave them an emphasis Siddal herself may not have wanted or recognized. His family archive provides glimpses of humour, wit and self-deprecation not found elsewhere; less positively he also records her unapproachable demeanour and exaggerated reserve.[9] He saw Siddal only infrequently so this was a remembered relationship based on his personal observations, yet his early assessment continues to influence Siddal's biographers because of its rarity and authoritative voice. Keats was reconstructed posthumously, as indeed was Siddal, but in her case the process began while she was still alive, when Dante Rossetti laid exclusive claim to her as his model and muse shortly after she sat for Millais's *Ophelia* in 1852. As with Keats, Rossetti exerted influence over her career as an exhibited artist and he also held himself at least partly responsible for her psychological and physical welfare, marrying her in 1860 after a suicide attempt prompted by his alleged infidelity. Siddal and Keats share this unique affiliation with the PRB, a relationship that tipped the balance of power in favour of the Brotherhood, creators of their largely posthumous images. Voluntarily distancing herself from social interaction and positing herself as an observer rather than a participant potentially made Siddal susceptible, but such a stance is arguably also akin to the 'negative capability' envisaged by Keats whereby the individual psyche becomes a conduit for collective emotion. Being distanced could be empowering if the individual poet or artist then channelled their absorbed responses to outside stimuli into their own work.

Both Keats and Siddal were born into relatively humble middle-class backgrounds. Keats resented his lowly affiliations, especially when they were seized upon by his detractors who claimed his poetry was similarly plebeian, read and imitated by manual workers and, even worse, women. Class and gender were thus negatively linked, a situation compounded by Keats's complex and paradoxical relationship with women readers.[10] The latter would surely have sympathized with Keats who shared their lack of university education and social and political opportunity, and indeed Keats did posit poetry as a female, maternal creative force, but he also believed his power as a poet would be diluted by any relationship with women, and this is reflected in his obvious antagonism.[11] He blamed women readers for poor book sales, and as they had become the biggest consumers of literature this became a self-fulfilling prophecy. They were also likely to be from a higher class than he so class difference became a specific bone of contention. He was deeply scornful of 'blue-stockings', condemning them as pretentious Sapphos, and reserved especial distain for writers of historical romance.[12] He considered a revised, much more explicit, ending for *The Eve of St Agnes* that might have repelled the very women readers he needed, which rather confirms his ambivalence. At the end of his life Keats was feminized, and therefore of lower class, deserted by his poetic muse and by his physical body dying from tuberculosis, itself no respecter of gender or class. He was feminized by disease, which for Victorian women could also be a class issue. Middle-class women were meant to espouse the ideal of 'non-verbalized suffering' and never be seen to protest too much because illness was just a part of normal life, otherwise an affectation, probably with psychosomatic elements.[13] Alternatively, it was a transgression, a way of shirking a domestic role, gaining sympathy or manipulating men's emotions.[14]

Public reference to the body and its condition was generally taboo so it is very difficult to say what was actually wrong with Siddal. Spinal, neurological, digestive and gynaecological conditions were all implicated in her air of malaise, along with the ubiquitous 'hysteria'. Letters between Rossetti and Jane Morris reveal recurring general concerns about their health but both Barrett Browning and Christina Rossetti suffered from serious identifiable illness.[15] The former was treated for tuberculosis and spinal disease which left her with long-term physical and emotional disability, and Rossetti, ill for most of her life, had Graves' disease which brought facial disfigurement and accompanying shyness and reticence. She wore a veil in public and lived in a kind of twilight between what is seen and unseen, where attempts at concealment enact the nineteenth-century contradiction of illness as a sign of the feminine, and illness as a sign of spiritual disorder; she acknowledged both the anonymity of twilight and the spiritual beauty of suffering in her letters and her preoccupation with death is a reflection of Romantic writers like Keats.[16] If Keats can in some ways be considered feminine then it can also be said that Siddal's poems have their masculine elements. Her speakers are mostly ungendered, with only 'At Last' and 'True Love' containing references suggesting they should be spoken by a woman. The recipients are more varied, for example 'A Year and a Day' and 'Speechless' refer to a man but the speaker/lover could be of either gender. Only 'Gone' and 'The Lust of the Eyes' specifically address a woman. The reader assumes the poems are spoken by a woman because the author is known to be female, but ignore that and they could be describing a same-sex relationship or be words written for a male for, or about, a female. As for Siddal herself, her persistent illness and the way she may have exploited it in her relationship with Rossetti would suggest Victorian femininity, whereas the independence she showed in temporarily moving to Sheffield to study art and later in travelling in Europe (albeit at Ruskin's suggestion) might indicate a more masculine spirit.

The earliest manifestation of Pre-Raphaelite identification with Keats is in their artwork so when Siddal began her very individualistic illustrations for 'La Belle Dame' in 1855 she would already have seen finished works taken from *Isabella* and *The Eve of St Agnes*, but her several slight sketches have little in common with the rich, sumptuous, highly detailed and critically acclaimed paintings of Hunt and Millais. Instead they sensitively explore one single aspect of Keats's poem of mythical bewitchment which is itself different from the other three under consideration here. None of Siddal's drawings appear to relate directly to the text, but each focuses on the same point in the narrative: a man and a young girl stand or sit close together while he lifts her hair away from her face. In two of the sketches this takes place by water, but Siddal's interpretation of the water meadow of the fourth verse is far from literal in one case which clearly depicts a stone basin into which a fountain in the form of a human figure is disgorging. Regardless of their exact posture the figures are always positioned with the man on the left, and taller than the woman whose closed eyes are set in a demure and down-turned face. She is submissive and passive; her straightened arms are unwelcoming and tend to be somewhat awkwardly conjoined at the wrist, and her loose simple robe effectively disguises her female form. The heavy pencil lines imply a certain latent male aggression; in one piece in particular the two figures are compressed together, yet the faerie-child leans away from the man as if uneasy at his proximity or even repelled by his attentions. Spatial distance thus becomes a metaphor for the preservation of self-image and a resistance to its being externally manipulated. Siddal's women are not predatory or voluptuous, neither have they bewitched an innocent Knight with their elfin ways; he is to blame for his entrapment and banishment. The focus on female hair in these drawings picks up a common Pre-Raphaelite trope but Siddal does not use the former as a fatal snare. Rather, the long straight locks form a lifeless shroud that is being perhaps roughly handled by the man in order to uncover the woman's neck and shoulders for his own purpose and delectation. Keats's 'La Belle Dame Sans Merci' is richly enigmatic and open to a number of readings and Siddal's sketches capitalize on this to the extent that some doubt has been cast on their identification with the poem, especially as no watercolour or finished drawing is known to exist.[17] In withholding the meaning of these drawings it can be argued that the balance of power shifts in Siddal's favour and away from Ruskin and Dante Rossetti who sought to influence her artistic direction. Her silence echoes her reluctance to put her poems up for public scrutiny and points to an awareness of the positive importance of feminine reticence. The sketches do however speak of the manipulation of women and their image, an inversion of Keats's narrative whereby the Knight-at-Arms was in thrall to the sorceress.

Locks of hair had long since been exchanged as love tokens and used to signify female sexuality, but Pre-Raphaelite artists extrapolated this to allow hair to speak of desire and eroticism in a way actual language could not. In reality loose hair was rare beyond childhood because it implied a state of being undressed in public, but in art it could be put on glorious display as in Millais's *The Bridesmaid* (1851) in which a young girl is lost in dreams of her own husband, her untied and luxuriant hair flowing about her upper body and acting as a veil that gives an element of secrecy to the intimacy already present. Rossetti made a sketch of Siddal as Delia in 1851, her hair again long and loose but in a deeply suggestive addition she has a lock of it in her mouth. He painted many female figures with bejewelled or decorated hair and attention is further drawn to it because the women in these overtly sexualized portraits remain fully clothed, *Monna Vanna* (1866) being a prime example of his fetishizing of hair, making it an erogenous zone upon which he was apparently 'fixated'.[18] Golden hair became a Victorian obsession, linking it with money, sexual power, and different types of woman such as the immobile, who uses her hair to shelter lovers and whose locks take on their own magic persona.[19] The combing of hair is connected to spinning and weaving and because hair is also synonymous with the female pudenda combing takes on a potent sexuality, something to be feared. Webs are woven to snare a victim but weaving is also an art associated with story-telling and music, and one Greek word, *pecten*, can mean comb, pudenda or an instrument for striking a lyre, making a woman's hair her instrument, important if she cannot speak for herself.[20] Silence is then overtaken by self-expression, a proclamation of identity in which art speaks for women just as ballads spoke for a silent Siddal. Her illustration of 'The Lady of Shalott' depicts the heroine like a spider caught in her own web sat at a loom whose threads look like long pieces of hair as they fly off the frame. Nineteenth-century writers were fascinated by the idea of 'reading' women's hair and its physical attributes, using it to explain character, or seeing it as a part of her body that existed separately from her, like the 'hair tent' found in lyric poetry. Rossetti uses the image of a girl lying on top of a man letting her hair down around his head in 'The Stream's Secret' (ll. 73–84) but it makes a cocoon, a place of shelter and healing rather than a love nest, and this reflects the generally ambivalent attitude to golden hair itself. It could be a radiant halo or a deadly weapon, a beautiful attribute or a lure for the unwary, or a means of dubious exchange as Laura finds when she trades it for fruit in *Goblin Market*. Because of its parallel association with genitalia women's hair was thought to conceal an underlying filth and this is perhaps why Victorian poets used the image of buried golden hair flourishing in the graves of dead women.[21] In 'The Poor Ghost' by Christina Rossetti it has extended beyond her knees, terrifying the lover who thinks it will murder him, in Rossetti's 1855 sketch for 'La Belle Dame' her hair is strangling the knight, and Siddal's hair purportedly grew after death with some sort of supernatural force.

The Pre-Raphaelite role in Keats's critical heritage

When the Pre-Raphaelite artists were reading Keats in the 1840s literary criticism was still directly affected by his early death and the supposed part played in it by his contemporary reviewers. Such opinion was polarized; Keats was genius or charlatan, the subject of extravagant praise or merciless, derogatory condemnation as a member of the 'Cockney School', a term coined by *Blackwood's Magazine* in October 1817. His earliest works were presented as a kind of manifesto against the prevailing rules of literary taste; he was using a poetic method and vocabulary that was so unlike Pope in particular that it was merely uncouth and affected by comparison. There were political overtones to the controversy because his work overlapped a period of social and political unrest and its repression by Tory governments, and this further coloured critical opinion for almost a decade after his death in 1821. Nineteenth-century literary magazines such as the (Tory) *Quarterly Review*, the (Whig) *Edinburgh Review* and *Blackwood's Magazine* wielded great power, meaning that a writer whose political views were associated with one party could never get a fair literary criticism from a rival publication, and this affected how Keats was perceived until about 1830.[22] After this date reviews were less prejudiced but even then his early death led to a suspicion that his was an undeveloped talent, poetry to be wondered at without analysis. Until the 1860s his work was largely read by small groups who admired him as a poet of sensation rather than thought; it was his life and death that attracted more public comment. Therefore, because until mid-century critical material is sparse and scattered, the Pre-Raphaelites were able to latch on to his progressive reputation with impunity, and use him as a writer on whom they could impose their particular interpretation of his poems.

When Keats's first volume of poems was published in 1817 it was largely ignored critically; the full backlash came with *Endymion* the year after. This was parodied in the *Quarterly* and *Blackwood's* for its lack of true sensuous vitality and ludicrous and idiomatic phraseology and combed for its supposed 'Cockneyisms'. It was these attacks, together with the campaign of personal abuse mounted also by *Blackwood's*, that were reputedly responsible for his death. *Lamia, Isabella, The Eve of St Agnes and Other Poems* (1820) did not receive such antagonism, but neither did its 500 printed copies sell out. Only at this point did *The Edinburgh Review* publish a critique, adding to Keats's slow public recognition. In 1829 The Apostles (Tennyson, Richard Monkton Milnes and Arthur Hallam) emerged from an underground group that largely consisted of young practising poets to express their enthusiasm for the Romantic poets, Keats and Shelley in particular. This strengthened Keats's reputation because he became assimilated into a living poetic tradition even before he was widely read.[23] The connection between Tennyson, Keats and the Pre-Raphaelites has already been noted, but its theoretical basis was initiated in an article written by Hallam for *Englishman's Magazine* in 1831.[24] In it he substantiated his belief that Keats was the forerunner of Tennyson by giving a rationale for Keats's poetry and laying down his aesthetic principles. Milnes's *Life and Letters of John Keats* (1848, the first biography published after his death) and the stimulus provided by the Pre-Raphaelites via their paintings marked the critical dividing line between obscurity and fame for Keats, but the affinity Hallam saw between Keats and Tennyson, which was later extrapolated to include Dante Rossetti, provided a fused philosophy which was mutually beneficial.[25]

Hallam described Keats's poetry as that of sensation not reflection; it was emotionally charged with colour, sound and movement. He believed he had a 'fearful and wonderful constitution' that enabled him to produce poetry which was 'a sort of magic' that could reflect Nature in its entire bewildering array. This same constitution enabled him to feel the exquisite pain and pleasure denied most people, but it also meant he was derided as a visionary by those without the ability to understand his ethos and philosophy. Keats's poetics was challengingly new, a genuine advancement, but his audience needed to work at appreciating it; his public disregard came as a result of the majority not being prepared to do this as it was easier for them to criticize than try to understand. Keats had the additional ability, by the 'magnetic force of his conception', to elevate inferior intellects and bring together the separate energies of sensitive, reflective and passionate emotion in order to reinstate a wider appreciation of a poetics that was progressive and authoritative. Hallam believed Keats's way of looking at poetry could be used to prepare the way for Tennyson; Rossetti, Hunt and Millais believed it could also provide the PRB with a gravitas and a theoretical base, with the result that they used Keats for their individual ends whilst simultaneously ensuring the steady rise of his posthumous popular appeal, arguably begun by Hallam some fifteen years before the inception of the PRB.

In 1848, and before the publication of Milnes's biography, Keats was regarded as unfashionable, effeminate, coarse and presumptuous, but the founders of the PRB were irresistibly drawn to the rich immediacy of his poetry and its subversive elements. They and Keats set out to be confrontational, a stance enforced by their position as outcasts. Rossetti aside, they all came from relatively lowly backgrounds and this gave the potential for radical expression without loss of privileged artistic or social status.[26] In Keats the Pre-Raphaelites found the power of imagination, the worship of love and beauty, a youthful idealism that put paid to any half-heartedness of expression, and an insistence on intensity:

> The excellence of every art is in its intensity, capable of making all disagreeables evaporate from their being in close relationship with beauty and truth ... at once it struck me what quality went to form a man of achievement, especially in literature ... I mean negative capability that is when a man is capable of being in uncertainties, mysteries, doubts, without any irritable reaching after fact or reason.[27]

Two things are significant here, the envisioning of art that includes literature, and the notion that uncertainty does not have to mean negativity, and both of these resonate with Pre-Raphaelite philosophy. The Pre-Raphaelites similarly aimed to explore their subjects through sensation and watchfulness in the pursuit of truth, and by being always open to impression. Keats's vivid pictures and powerful images, and his readiness to be impulsive, provided a springboard for their fresh enquiry into cultural traditions. He showed the PRB how to construct a symbolic language to convey tensions between social demands and inner emotional states, using rich material settings and body language, respectively.[28] In return they popularized him for Victorian contemporaries. Victorians probably knew his poems when they saw their interpretation as Pre-Raphaelite paintings, and they probably thought of the paintings when they read the poems; words were thus applied to pictures both figuratively and literally. This forced a comparison between the two texts, yet showed their dependence on each other.[29] Pre-Raphaelite paintings did not illustrate the texts, even if they became popular images of them, but they did illuminate the texts whilst simultaneously carrying their own agendas.

The PRB initially never had Keats's letters so they only knew him through his poems, and how they read the latter conditioned their response. They were intrigued by the psychology behind them and they telescoped their narratives to heighten the dichotomies and paradoxes they contained.[30] This joint interest in Keats the poet and the concerns of his poems opened the way for art and poetry and the individuals involved in their production to become intimately associated. This is paradoxically illustrated by the change in attitude to Keats that emerged after the publication of his letters to Fanny Brawne in 1878. This destroyed both the image of Keats that Milnes had created, and the PRB construct, and replaced them with one that W. M. Rossetti found deplorable: 'unbalanced, wayward, and profuse; he exhibits great fervour of temperament, and abundant caressingness, without the inner depths of tenderness and regard. He lives in his mistress for himself ... he abandons all self-restraint.'[31] Codell speculates that once the old 'untarnished' Keats had gone the PRB felt its loss keenly, which would account for their comparatively small interest in him thereafter.[32] Keats is controversial because he was fought over by reviewers and by those such as Hallam, Hunt and Rossetti who laid claim to his posthumous recovery, and this is reflected in his publication history and especially his inclusion in serious nineteenth-century anthologies, which tended to be conservative in outlook. Keats's work was rumoured to be morally unsound and therefore unsuitable for collections aimed at the female reader, with the result that between 1819 and 1859, of the thirty-three published anthologies containing nineteenth-century poetry, twenty-six ignored Keats altogether and the two most generous exceptions were compiled by personal friends. Fairer representation did follow, but even in *The Golden Treasury* (1861) edited by F. T. Palgrave and Tennyson only eleven poems were included, far fewer than works by Shelley, Wordsworth and Tennyson himself.[33] Selections from Keats's poems alone were similarly rare, and this creates an impression of him as a fragmentary poet, a position similarly occupied by Siddal both as a poet and as an artistic interpreter of poems. The PRB adopted this same fragmentary approach in their illustrations of *Isabella* and *Eve*, taking one scene and developing it to the exclusion of others to satisfy economic and political as well as artistic demands.

According to his brother, Rossetti began reading Keats's poems around 1845 and thereafter he considered himself one of his earliest and most strenuous admirers, responsible for his later fame.[34] In a letter dated August 1848 he indicated he had now acquired the recently published *Life and Letters of John Keats* by Milnes, arguably as responsible as the Pre-Raphaelites for the resurgence of interest in its subject. Rossetti took an immediate liking to Keats who 'seems to have been a glorious fellow' because he too appeared to have admired artists before Raphael.[35] He went on to make quite an extensive study of his poetry and notes on individual works can be found in his letters, especially those to Henry Buxton Forman and William Allingham, and in marginal comments made in a personal anthology.[36] Of the poems under consideration here *Isabella* and *Lamia* receive little or no attention but analysis of their influence on Rossetti's poetry has thrown up certain exact parallels, despite Rossetti's determination to avoid the charge of having imitated him; indeed he censured his brother and sister for this very thing.[37] Rossetti appears to have agreed with Keats's picturesque medievalism and made his whole approach to poetic experience a natural development of some of the lines laid out by Keats.[38] From his reading of Keats Rossetti believed they shared a common philosophy whereby individuals, not revolutionary or philanthropic ideas, were more important to poetry. It was not necessary for Keats to be a philosopher, or an advocate of science, or a participant in the debate between science and faith, or a political visionary. Instead, Keats was valued as a provider of aesthetic intensity, of beauty that transcended mere words, of imaginative fire and excitement, of the weird, all of which linked poetry with art (for Rossetti the ultimate goal) through vivid story-telling. Rossetti described 'La Belle Dame Sans Merci' as: 'a masterpiece of condensed and hinted order so dear to imagined minds'.[39] He associated himself with Keats's sense of isolation and temporariness, requesting that like Keats his epitaph might be: 'Here lies one whose name was writ in water', and this is echoed in the last line of his 1880 sonnet 'John Keats':[40] 'Thou whom the daisies glory in growing o'er— / Their fragrance clings around thy name, not writ / But rumour'd in water, while thy fame of it / Along Time's flood goes echoing evermore' (11–14). 'Water' refers to Keats and his belief in transitoriness both in life and afterlife, but it also points to the posthumous reputation Rossetti created for Keats. The latter's epitaph, written in water, is being washed away to be replaced by an identity Rossetti has conceived. Keats is therefore not immortalized via his own words but through their reworking by someone else, Rossetti in this case. This will continue for 'evermore', an apt and resounding final word. By this token, poems only ever exist as the reading of one critic or generation.[41] If posthumous significance is a mixture of a silenced voice and one reinterpreted by another, then this applies precisely to Siddal, as an artist and particularly as a poet.

Rossetti singled out 'La Belle Dame' and *The Eve of St Agnes*, poems of intensity and highly finished pictorial power, for special consideration. Evidence for this emerges in his correspondence with Thomas Hall Caine, one of many young satellites with whom he shared passionate feelings for Keats and other male poets in later life.[42] Speaking of these two works in particular he wrote to Caine: 'All poetry affects me deeply, and often to tears. It doesn't need to be pathetic or tender to produce this result'.[43] Rossetti is actually speaking about himself through Keats to show his emotional susceptibility. He credits the ability of Keats's poems to stimulate his heightened responses, but he sees Keats as a channel through which his latent aestheticism can be realized, rather than its source. Thus, Keats became another young man to be saved and celebrated as the 'father' of the PRB, to be separated from any hint of the commonplace, and awarded a sentimental image reserved for poets who meet an early death. Keats's poetry was praised for its ability to beautify simply by its existence, and as such it was placed above that of Coleridge who was given similar treatment. Rossetti was obsessive about Keats, contriving a portrait of him in later life that represented an ideal by which Keats's life must be made to conform to the image Rossetti created.[44] The same has to be said of the relationship between Rossetti and Siddal.

Keats was considered one of the 'Immortals', placed within a declaration drawn up by Rossetti and Holman Hunt that almost qualifies as a Pre-Raphaelite manifesto. It lists principally those authors and artists 'who illustrate the character of our tastes and aims at this time', a prophetic and apt statement considering the way in which their interpretations of Keats would vary over the next fifty years.[45] It was intended to be deliberately shocking; no national or religious heroes other than Christ were included. Keats was awarded two stars along with Shelley, Christ has four, and Shakespeare three. Tennyson is given one, but Wordsworth and Byron are mentioned purely by name. All the Pre-Raphaelites shared with Keats a fondness for medieval and Celtic themes and the rendering of richly coloured pictorial detail, and this is particularly apparent in the work of Millais and Hunt whose paintings epitomized mid-century interpretations of Keats's poems. Hunt literally found Keats in 1846; at a time when no other copies of his works than those published in his lifetime had yet appeared, he acquired his from a book-bin labelled 'This lot for 4*d*'.[46] Shortly after, he made his first attempt to communicate his enthusiasm for Keats to Millais when he read *Isabella* to him, but he was forced to admit this was a 'ludicrous failure'. Millais objected to Hunt's delivery, finding the poems boring, but Hunt persisted, showing Millais his designs for *The Eve of St Agnes* which he had decided was 'a good subject which was likely to sell'.[47] Hunt may have been fascinated by a poem that had the potential to allow him to experiment with revolutionary techniques and to illustrate 'the sacredness of honest responsible love and the weakness of proud intemperance', but an economic motive was clearly important. He was looking to capitalize on his connection with Keats's legacy by appropriating market forces at a time when the PRB were seeking public recognition in the face of criticism from the Royal Academy. This supposition is supported by his stated aim to imbue his painting with a look that would 'make an audience take notice', providing elements of surprise on faces that would display 'a variety and an individuality of emotion'; the more widespread the emotional and aesthetic appeal, the greater the chance of a sale.[48] Hunt recognized that the poem was inspiring what he believed to be a radical line of thought, so that early on Keats was bound up in the discussions he had with Millais about the contrast between vigorous and moribund art. Art needed to be seen to address contemporary issues to make it relevant, combining classical or medieval revivalism with, 'strong modern physical and mental force of character'.[49] A potential anxiety emerges here: in memorializing Keats there exists a tension between 'old art' preserved for its own sake, and its modern interpretation designed to appeal to contemporary social circumstances and to reflect the aspirations and economic motives of a new generation of artists. This paradox runs through the work Hunt did from Keats's poems. He was less *avant-garde* than Keats so he retained certain conventions such as the use of engraving and the iconized female figure to keep in with the Academy and to tie his paintings to market expectations.

Pre-Raphaelite interpretations of Keats's poems

The combination of past and present can be made to work very effectively in the translation of one artistic medium into another. Hemans used ekphrasis in many of her poems but extended the traditional Romantic focus to include portraits, sketches, watercolours and funerary monuments as well as classical sculpture to invoke an immediate emotional response that bypasses concern with the technical qualities of the original artwork. 'Properzia Rossi' (1828), which draws together several artistic media and plays on silent female voices, was inspired by a painting that depicts the making of a bas-relief of Ariadne and Theseus. Ekphrasis particularly suited Keats's aesthetic and he used it to describe and animate classical objects as well as richly decorated interior scenes. The

Pre-Raphaelites borrowed from this artistic and poetic legacy but inverted the process, integrating poetry into their narrative paintings through metaphor and allegory and literally framing the results with quotations. Keats is central to this because the philosophical arguments between Hunt and Millais were a precursor to the decision to form the PRB, and both artists would go on to use tiny visual detail translated from Keats's sensuous language and explore his paradox between sexual desire and established social conventions. During 1847 Hunt continued to work on *The Eve of St Agnes* and meanwhile had converted Millais to be as ardent an admirer as he was. They were already involved in a combined illustrative project of 'magnificent' *Isabella* about the time Rossetti presented his portfolio to the Cyclographic Society.[50] It would appear that Hunt and Rossetti had developed a parallel independent interest in Keats because when *Eve* was displayed at the Royal Academy in 1848 Hunt recorded Rossetti's enthusiasm: 'for I think no-one had ever before painted any subject from this still little-known poet'.[51] Thus this work brought the original PRB triumvirate together in early appropriation of a newly rediscovered Keats; the latter became their emblem at the same time as Rossetti became Hunt's pupil in painting.

The Pre-Raphaelites took single elements of Keats's poetry and froze them in time so they could be examined for meaning, and this coincided with the growth of museums and galleries as part of Victorian municipal culture. Keats's 'Ode on a Grecian Urn' (1819) epitomized the Romantic conception of ekphrasis whereby fairly modest museum objects from antiquity were presented in such a way that those without means to experience the Grand Tour could still appreciate them on paper. The urn, partly Keats's own creation and partly a composite drawn from his reading about and viewing of classical art, is the outcome of the contemporary debate about the relationships between poetry and the visual arts, and those between the ideal, unchanging world of art and beauty and the death, decay and fleetingness of human life. Keats admires the 'unravish'd' nature of the images of perfection it depicts but suggests its silence and coldness is limiting and unhuman; he extrapolates a physical description of an object into a philosophical discussion about beauty and man's role in its creation. Such objects came to symbolize an aspect of the past, but without a precise context, and this again appealed to Pre-Raphaelite painters who put great store in a mythologized history, or one of their own making.[52] Romantics and Pre-Raphaelites both used nostalgia to reinvent an idyllic past via an alternative artistic stimulus. The context did not have to be real to satisfy an aesthetic need deemed greater than any historical portrayal. The process of ekphrasis that achieved this accessibility to art thus becomes one of interpretation, just as the Pre-Raphaelites reinterpreted Keats's poems in a reverse movement. Ekphrasis is used in Keats's *The Eve of St Agnes* to define location and atmosphere rather than as a means of exploring perception or psychology. This is a reverse ekphrastic poem, one in which instead of bringing a static object to life it takes a live object and transforms it into art so that the latter seems more alive than the characters.[53] By this token Keats attempted his own Pre-Raphaelite painting, not a narrative romance, and this accounts for its mid-century allure. Décor, scenery, and especially colour are predominant in such a reading, not the response of the speaker to any of those things, and this way of animating the backdrop over the human figures is echoed in the various Pre-Raphaelite interpretations of the poem. Under these circumstances it is not surprising that Hunt wrote to Millais recommending it because it was 'brimful of beauties that will soon enchant you', implying again that he saw the poem as a source of objects or images rather than as a complete narrative.[54] This epitomizes the Pre-Raphaelite response; what Keats was doing in words they wanted to achieve in paint, luxuriating in the texture of the medium itself, but especially via decoration and surface detail.[55]

The Eve of St Agnes (1848) by Hunt (figure 19) was the first Keats-inspired painting to be exhibited. It is a very sensuous and tense scene that depicts the escape of the lovers from the castle while guests revel in an adjacent room and guards lie drunk and inert, but are potentially still able to prevent the elopement. Only verse 41 of the poem is recreated; Madeline's seduction and disappointment at finding a real not a dream lover has already happened, but Hunt hints at the moral dilemmas this has thrown up in the mixture of anxiety and innocence on both their faces, the orgiastic scene clearly visible through the arches on the left and

19 William Holman Hunt, *The Eve of St Agnes*, 1848, oil on canvas

the awkward, abandoned sprawl of both guards and dogs amid spilt wine in the foreground.[56] This is also achieved technically through the use of light and shade; the party scene is illuminated more than the figures of the lovers. Arguably, Hunt wanted to put a moral spin on the debauchery of the poetic image as befitting his Victorian context, and this dissipates the eroticism.[57] Hero and heroine are seen about to open an exterior door whose chain has already been released, but danger is everywhere. The door signifies more than a means of escape from a controlling parent whose wealth has established its own social barriers; it also bridges the gap between fantasy and reality, which Keats would have appreciated. Hunt is alluding to the fantasy of Madeline's dream, and as such he glosses over the possibility of her rape and Porphyro's voyeurism. While still in the castle she is also under its protection and this is implied in the shapelessness of her garments. However, once she leaves she will face the reality of his sexuality, expressed in the phallic design of his belt and his short tunic. Just as the poem ends in the death of its two older characters, so in Hunt's picture the lovers will be transformed when they step out of the glowing sensuality of the chamber into nondescript darkness.[58] By way of contrast, Arthur Hughes's 1856 version of the same poem is more romantic and less threatening. His *Eve of St Agnes* is a triptych that uses its frames to get over the passage of time, providing a narrative rather than a commentary upon three key episodes. Once again the actual seduction, so central to the poem, is glossed over; Porphyro's actions are not shown, reinforcing the distance between the ghostly dream-like depictions of the scenes and the reality of Madeline's situation.[59] Darkness is conveyed figuratively and naturalistically, but the awaking Madeline is lit by coldest moonlight which tends to destroy any eroticism and make her an insubstantial figure. This is a more realistic portrayal of Keats's poem than Hunt's, and is more typical of the 1853–70 period of Pre-Raphaelitism with its emphasis on matters being satisfactorily concluded without too much soul-searching.

Millais's *Eve* (1863) was painted when the original PRB had drifted apart and only Hunt remained true to its original tenets. Madeline in this picture is seen undressing in a pool of stark uncompromising moonlight, frozen in apprehension. Most of the picture is in darkness and the space is delineated with verticals which are reminiscent of prison bars: Madeline herself, the heavy picture frames, and the drapes of the bed that dominates the left field. The darkness obliterates the colour found in the poem so that the ghostliness of Hughes's rendition still remains, but unlike the latter this one is loaded with eroticism. The solitary figure is not foregrounded, and the sense of distance this creates ironically increases her power as an object of desire; she is being watched by an unseen Porphyro who could be concealed by the bed hangings. She has an air of innocence, yet her shape is womanly and her dress is pooled around her feet, left to rest where she has allowed it to drop in a quite provocative gesture. The painting explores one moment from the poem and as such it resembles Hunt's reconstruction, but in focusing on Madeline's feelings and emotions as she anticipates union with her dream lover Millais has moved this version beyond what Hunt and Keats envisaged. The narrative of the poem has been set aside to allow the male viewer and the male protagonist to linger over her at will. The voyeurism of Keats's poem is thus retained, but this is clearly not meant as a literal translation, as the vibrant medieval setting, such an integral part of the literary design, has been substituted. As a measure of how Victorians read Keats's text and its sexual subtext fifteen years after Hunt drew it to wider public attention, it is interesting.[60]

Between 1848 and 1850 Hunt and Millais began work on a projected sequence of etchings for *Isabella or The Pot of Basil*, a classic Romantic tale of tragedy in which Lorenzo's love for Isabella is opposed by her brothers, who conspire to murder him. After his death she shows her eternal devotion by rescuing his body and then keeping its head in an urn planted with basil and watered by her tears, but after this is discovered by her brothers she pines away in grief. Millais produced the first drawing to be completed in 1848, and this he elaborated into an oil painting, *Isabella*, exhibited in 1849 as Hunt finished his part of the sequence, *Lorenzo at His Desk in the Warehouse*. In this work Hunt takes the Romantic interpretation of an Early Modern tale and superimposes upon it a number of Pre-Raphaelite narratives. It is a brush, pencil and ink drawing of simplicity and delicacy, taken from verse 14 of the poem, and it shows Isabella arriving to visit her lover who is being closely supervised in his clerical tasks by her brothers. The vertical lines of the picture, the opening door, the carved wooden desk and bookcase containing the ledgers on which Lorenzo works, and the rigid upright figures in the right background all serve to stress the demarcation between the social classes; Lorenzo is a paid employee in his lover's house and another is being reduced to tears behind him. Isabella's kin are hard taskmasters; the warehouse appears crowded and the right foreground is cut away to reveal further workers toiling in a cramped basement which carries more than a suggestion of class exploitation, an appropriate comment in a year of widespread European revolution. Isabella is only timidly pushing open the door, an apologist not a supporter of Lorenzo, and her way is barred by one of two potentially ferocious dogs placed prominently in the scene. The separation of Isabella from her lover is physical, but he is also paying her scant attention, which strengthens their divide. He is daydreaming, biting his pencil, and his legs are pointing away from her and towards the authority figure of her brother which perhaps indicates a desire to be in his position.[61] Hunt's vision of the medieval is very idealistic but this picture is more than merely decorative or escapist, being both a love story and a critique of Victorian working conditions. Keats's poem has been adapted to illuminate the world in different ways and this permits further reinterpretation by Millais, and Hunt himself in 1867.

Hunt painted *Isabella* after the death of his wife Fanny and this arguably allowed him to identify with the character; certainly this work is a far more sentimental envisioning of Keats's poem. A surprisingly healthy-looking heroine in a flowing white diaphanous dress is seen cradling the luxuriant basil plant within her arm and with her hair. There is obvious symbolism in the prominent wilted rose, the death's head mask on the funerary urn, the sanctuary lamp and her bare feet. Yet Isabella thrives at Lorenzo's expense; her love caused his death even if in death he is still worshipped, and the role of her brothers in his tragedy is forgotten. The focus on the iconic woman makes this a saleable piece, and this has been woven into the narrative of the painting through the highly decorated fabrics and marble surfaces, and the exquisite marquetry of the prie-dieu, which all signify great wealth. Ironically, Isabella's vacant stare implies her detachment from such worldly goods, symbolizing Hunt's conflicting motives. Unlike in Millais's 1849 oil, here the central drama is discarded in favour of a depiction of its finale, but this still served to make it a valuable reference point for Keats's work as it enabled the Victorian viewer to visualize the poem. Pre-Raphaelite paintings complemented their sources so that in this symbiotic relationship the artists were not merely taking up subjects for economic exploitation or as vehicles for their expertise, they were promulgating an understanding of their philosophy, as W. M. Rossetti appreciated: 'The power of Keats lies in the transfusion of sight and emotion into sound, in making pictures out of words, or turning words into pictures; of giving a visionary beauty to the closest items of description; of holding all the materials of a poem in a long-drawn suspense of music and reverie.'[62] The combining of several artistic forms, the realization of visual texture and the ability to suspend the audience in imaginative wonder were all essential components of the Pre-Raphaelite narrative painting ethos.

Millais's *Isabella* (figure 20) is similarly loaded with symbolism, but it also echoes the numerous paradoxes found in Keats's

20 John Everett Millais, *Isabella*, 1848–49, oil on canvas

poetry. For example, the love between Lorenzo and Isabella is given its expected early Renaissance setting but the class conflicts of Victorian society are woven into it. The Florentine family and their retainers are seated at a table, close enough for the presence or absence of interaction to be significant. The brothers, robust and awkwardly frozen, sit side by side along one length and are clearly antagonistic towards the pale and demure lovers opposite. The latter are the only two characters in direct communication, although Isabella and the most obviously aggressive of her siblings are almost conjoined by the phallic thrust of his outstretched leg. Conspicuous on the balcony is the pot of basil and Lorenzo is offering Isabella a blood orange, both fateful portents. The entire scene speaks of tension; this is not a relaxed meal, indeed little food is in evidence beyond what is being carelessly spilt, and this focuses attention on the individual preoccupations of the faces seen in profile, and the wealth implied in the fine glass, pottery and silver on the table. A number of other themes in the poem were significant to the Victorians. Economic and social power struggles, as well as those between the sexes and within a family, were relevant to the PRB who consistently argued among themselves in an effort to define their philosophy and direction. Similarly, both Keats and Lorenzo occupied a lowly artistic place in a world dominated by capitalism, and both were in a precarious position requiring self-sacrifice.[63] The paradox between modern nineteenth-century realism and a yearning for the past emerges in the painting in its pastiche of Renaissance and Gothic historicism. Sharp lines and delineation of colour emphasize the contrast between passion and stillness, and different fabrics are used to suggest human characteristics. Contrasting textures further polarize the scene: velvet and silk, metal and flesh, foliage and stone, wood and glass. Of the thirteen people present only four are women, but arguably the most important man, Lorenzo, has been feminized in his dress and downcast facial expression. He is excluded from the groups of males opposite and alongside him, and his weakness can be further observed in his slavish demeanour towards Isabella who paradoxically is paying him scant attention. Neither lover is particularly attractive or healthy-looking, so there is empathy and scorn for both in equal measure; in the same way, the poem parodies them and undermines their serious intent and blinkered introspection.[64] Gender is given disruptive force elsewhere, however; Isabella's brother is kicking her dog and the back legs of his chair are threatening to crush another cowering beneath it. Images telling complex narratives are typical of the Pre-Raphaelites, and in this case Millais has used references in Keats's poem that are pertinent to a Victorian context whilst still recalling the Renaissance story. Pre-Raphaelitism has linked two time periods from the past, but the constricted space given to the scene and its somewhat abnormal rules of perspective also pay homage to its contemporary artistic precepts.[65]

Representation of the physical body in the poems of Siddal and Keats

The poems that inspired these visual images are similarly layered with dichotomy, and paradox underlies both their structure and their emotional and ethical content. *Isabella or The Pot of Basil*,

The Eve of St Agnes, Lamia and 'La Belle Dame Sans Merci' were written between 1818 and 1819, all but the last being published in 1820.[66] *Isabella* tells the story of a doomed love affair that attempts to cross class barriers. Despite its sixty-three octets it is at times very sparing in detail, a poem of stillness and isolation that examines madness and the extremeness of love and the wasting power of romance. The lack of secondary characters and self-evident 'meaning' concentrates and internalizes Isabella's pain so that her reaction to Lorenzo's murder is both tangible and graphic. *The Eve of St Agnes* is the most overtly sensuous but still relies much on the imagination of the reader. It is a work of juxtaposition, and the contrast between two worlds, the real and the visionary. Madeline prepares to 'see' her future husband in a dream; Porphyro arrives to undertake that role in real time in what appears to be a self-fulfilling prophecy, but the text invites multiple interpretations.[67] Compared with the more conformist system in *Isabella* the consistent ababbcbcc rhyming pattern of the Spenserian stanzas creates an illusion of narrative flow while the extra iambic beat in the final line occasionally provides a note of dramatic intensity. *Lamia*, too, depicts the struggle between the mundane and the other-worldly state, while suggesting the impossibility of escape from the reality of the human condition.[68] Lamia is transformed from serpent to human by the god Hermes so she can pursue Lycius, but she is thwarted in her efforts to maintain that illusion by Apollonius, a mere mortal. The question of balance between identity and uncertainty is repeated in a poem that suggests even imagination can be fake. The lack of verse subdivision makes *Lamia* structurally different from the other three poems in this cluster, but slight variants in its pentametric rhythm serve to unsettle the reader and shock narrative expectation, a device Siddal uses regularly. 'La Belle Dame Sans Merci' ostensibly most closely resembles her work. It has twelve sparse quatrains whose rhythms constantly change, save in the last lines of each where three syllables after the anacrusis reinforce the cold finality of the situation of the Knight-at-Arms. Bewitched then abandoned to a recurring nightmare he is aimless and irretrievably lost. This is the most ambiguous of the quartet; it speaks of flawed visionary imagination and the destructiveness of sexuality, but it has no time-frame, which creates an attractive yet ominous ambience. Elusive and illusory, it is certainly as open-ended as Siddal's 'Worn Out', 'Gone' and 'Shepherd Turned Sailor'.

'Worn Out' (1856) consists of five quatrains each with a 4–3–4–3 iambic beat and abab rhyme. The speaker is lamenting their debilitated physical state and asking for comfort as sleep or death approaches. It has an emotional mix: bitterness, sadness and the inevitability of separation. 'Gone' (undated) is also a monologue but lacks the intensity of 'Worn Out' whilst having more of a narrative element. The speaker is facing life alone after her lover has walked away into darkness. It is possible, however, that she may live on in a non-physical form as the focus between the two worlds shifts subtly with each verse. The lyrical ballad 'Shepherd Turned Sailor' (undated) has just two sestets and a simple rhyme and rhythmic structure, yet is the most puzzling of the group. The speaker asks for a burial place in earth rather than water for her lover but why his occupation has changed is not known. All three poems have a pervasive air of transience and disillusion, and there is a change in mood and tempo between verses. Their analysis focuses on one dichotomy that also manifests itself in Keats's work, the dualism between the physical and spectral body. The emerging power struggle has a parallel in Siddal's poems which creates a literary relationship with Keats that exceeds that brought about by her artistic and personal association with the Pre-Raphaelites.

The physical body registers needs. Feasting is common to all four Keats poems together with references to food and hunger. *Isabella* opens with the extended family sitting at table (I:5–6) and early in 'La Belle Dame' the Knight is asked what ails him considering: 'The squirrel's granary is full, / And the harvest's done' (II:3–4). Later the faerie feeds him with delicacies, equating the need for food with need for affection (VII:1–2). There are lustrous descriptions of feasting in *Lamia* (II:173–220) and *The Eve of St Agnes* (XXX–XXI) where spiced treats are presented literally and linguistically as an erotic token to the sleeping Madeline. Her story is set against a backdrop of revelry elsewhere in the castle and its noise impinges on her situation at turning points in the narrative. In *Isabella* Lorenzo's head is fed by a mixture of tears and 'human fears' (LIV:5) that nourish both corpse and ghost, yet ironically Isabella herself feels no hunger (LIX:4). Eating is a very sensuous pastime, not found in Siddal's poems – which tend to be more physically detached by comparison. Her speakers are more introspective, their bodies a measure of the effect of outside stimuli rather than instigators and relishers of sensory experience. Food could be a substitute for the mother Keats lost at puberty, given that women are always present in such scenes.[69] Certainly the need for physical and emotional comfort is obvious, and this is paralleled specifically in 'Worn Out'. The poem begins with a clear statement, but immediately there's a sting in the tail:

> Thy strong arms are around me, love,
>   My head is on thy breast:
> Low words of comfort come from thee
>   Yet my soul has no rest. (1–4)

> Yet keep thine arms around me, love'
>   Until I fall to sleep:
> Then leave me, saying no goodbye
>   Lest I might wake, and weep. (17–20)

The speaker cannot reciprocate the love she is being given, taking refuge instead in sleep that offers a semi-conscious state of non-participation. The same connection emerges in 'Shepherd Turned Sailor', albeit with a more positive slant, as it anticipates the reuniting of physical bodies if the lover dies on land where there can be a final, tangible resting place of 'grey head-stone', 'green moss' and 'clinging grass' (7–9). 'Gone' continues this active/passive dialogue; in the first two verses the speaker tries to touch his lover, but both attempts are futile because her hand is gloved and then because her shadow is, by definition, untouchable. He longs for fleshly contact, and even her covered fingers 'Lifted (his) heart into a sudden song / As when the wild birds sing' (3–4), quite the most euphoric part of the poem and as such a rare penetrating moment in Siddal's work as a whole.

Isabella is overpowered by the need for proximity to Lorenzo's corpse once his grave has been found. Keats describes her ability to see his body through leaf mould as if it were water, and then her sudden, fervent attack on the earth with a knife (XLVI). Her devotion to its head then becomes truly apparent; everything mundane, stars, sky, trees, is forgotten: 'She had no knowledge when the day was done, / And the new moon she saw not: but in peace / Hung over her sweet Basil evermore, / And moisten'd it with tears to the core' (LIII:5–8). Furthermore, she 'will die a death too lone and incomplete' (XLI:7) once separated from the pot. Despite this undercurrent of passion the relationship between Isabella and Lorenzo is centred on a 'tenderer' (II:1) and more innocent love than that found in *Lamia*, *Eve* or 'La Belle Dame'. Their first kiss is a chaste affair (IX), and it comes after weeks of lovesickness (III–IV). Their secret meetings are not described (XI) and the courtly language given to Lorenzo (XXVI) stresses his purity alongside his lowly position. Sexual desire, not companionship, underlies the emotion running through 'La Belle Dame Sans Merci'. The Knight is immediately captivated by the elf, his description sparse but evocative: 'Full beautiful ... / Her Hair was long, her foot was light, / And her eyes were wild' (IV:2–4). That same brevity is applied to the very personal gifts he brings, and to their coition, but it still serves to heighten the sense of physical need: 'I made a garland for her head, / And bracelets too, and fragrant zone; / She look'd at me as she did love, / And made sweet moan' (VI). Similarly, Porphyro deliberately sets out to seduce Madeline in *The Eve of St Agnes* and physical attraction draws together Hermes and the nymph and (with true irony) Hermes and Lamia, for the latter wants human form as a prerequisite to sexual union with a human: 'When from this wreathed tomb shall I awake! / When move in a sweet body fit for life, / And love, and pleasure, and the ruddy strife / Of hearts and lips! Ah, miserable me!' (I:38–41). *Lamia* is alone in setting the narrative in a peopled context, suggesting a need for company that Siddal's characters do not share; even in *The Eve of St Agnes* the revellers are kept at a distance from the main protagonists. By contrast the streets of Corinth are teeming with life (I:350–61) and the extravagant wedding feast with its 'herd' of guests (II:150) is richly described. The Corinthian setting and the focus on Lamia herself within it are significant; the very special form of sexual pleasure associated with the place implies Keats is using worldly needs and pleasures to objectify women. This is indicated by Lycius's aggressive male desire and Lamia's sexual knowledge and expertise, treated with almost scientific physiological precision.[70]

Both Keats and Siddal use the body as a source of meaning production, but there are fewer anatomical references in her work where body parts are generally restricted to the sense organs or those of a non-human, specifically a bird. The latter stresses the changing nature of the body and its escape capability. Such restriction adds to the essentially enigmatic nature of Siddal's work; the reader is allowed freedom of interpretation but the poems guard their privacy and only grudgingly yield their meaning. This metaphorical masking of meaning has a tangible counterpart in 'Gone' where love is mediated not only through the glove on the hand but also through the jewelled ring on the glove. The woman is a passive receiver, her facial beauty is not commented on but is replaced by something inanimate, albeit reflective and precious, that puts up a barrier between her flesh and his. Keats too likens Madeline's body to jewels; as she kneels in prayer in her room the moon catches the colours of the stained glass window and illuminates her hair and silver cross in gold and amethyst. These virtual gems then become real, shed along with her clothes in an erotic display (XXV–XXVI). Porphyro watches, fascinated as much by her 'empty dress' (XXVIII:2) as by Madeline herself. The dress is imprinted with her, is her substitute, just like the ring and gloved hand in Siddal's poem, and all are worshipped. The feeling of distance in 'Gone' also comes from what the reader is not told; the eyes of this woman are not mentioned but the tears (his life is 'full of them' (7)) and watchfulness of the speaker are given prominence. Predictably, the heart is made the centre of emotion but the motif is extended here as 'shadows gather round it' (9), making his response to the absence of his lover more complex and introspective. Similarly, in 'Worn Out' eyes are blinded and weary, full not of tears but pain (14).

Not surprisingly, there are several consecutive references to tears in *Isabella* which drive the narrative and the emotions towards the end of the poem (LI–LIV). Once Isabella has taken her 'prize' home she treats the head as if it were a pampered doll, the lifeless body-part taking on a new and dreadful entity to allow Lorenzo second life:

> She calm'd its wild hair with a golden comb.
> And all around each eye's sepulchral cell

Pointed each fringed lash; the smeared loam
  With tears, as chilly as a dripping well,
She drench'd away:– and still she comb'd ... (LI:3–7)

The tears motif is extended to include other fluids in the same section of the poem; the head is wrapped in silk rich with 'divine liquids with odorous ooze' (LII:3) and the river of oblivion appears twice in an almost-repeated invocation to Melancholy (LV and LXI). Siddal is less graphic in 'Shepherd Turned Sailor' but she also substitutes the animate for the inanimate, a gravestone becoming the reincarnation of a dead lover. Furthermore, the speaker wants to see 'clinging grass' over his breast 'whereon his lambs could bleat' (9–10), which creates an image both of innocent dependency on the part of the young animals and of something far more human. Wet grass can indeed 'cling', but hands grasping to hold a drowning (or even errant) lover can do likewise, and this reading is substantiated when the speaker asks to be buried next to him.

In her illustrations of 'La Belle Dame' Siddal uses hair to signify entrapment, but she doesn't use this trope in her poems, instead citing guile or falsity in 'Love and Hate', Dead Love' and 'The Passing of Love'. The lethal hair metonym became very popular with Dante Rossetti among others but its formulaic aesthetic style lacks the ambiguity of a written text.[71] Keats merely reports that the Lady's hair was 'long' (it was, after all, her eyes that were captivating) which rather proves the point. Neither does he include it in *Isabella* even though hair is used figuratively at pivotal moments. It signifies youthful splendour in Lorenzo whose 'glossy hair ... once could shoot lustre into the sun' (XXXV:3–4), and aged devotion in the nurse who labours with Isabella over his corpse (XLVIII:4). Hair veils the latter's face as she distractedly works (XLVII:7–8) and again when she tries to hide her tears from her brothers once their murderous duplicity has been revealed (LIX). Keats avoids the erotic significance of hair elsewhere but in *Lamia* the motif literally becomes serpentine. Coiled, palpating, hidden but ready to encircle and suffocate, Lamia exudes confident beauty in a different and disturbing form, a complex individual who will inspire complex attitudes towards her (I:45–62). Her transformation is equally vivid and pertinent; she 'writhed about, convulsed with scarlet pain' (I:54) as she sheds her jewel-like colours and markings to emerge as a woman (I:146–68). There are many more references to physicality in *Lamia* than elsewhere, linking the body with the sensuousness, passion and shifting emotions that spring from the text. Even minor characters are given individuality, such as when every guest at the wedding feast decorates their brow with a wreath to signify their personal thoughts (II:215–29). The role of Apollonius is small but crucial to this scene. Lamia accuses him of having a conjurer's eyes (II:277) which he then uses to penetrate her disguise 'Like a sharp spear (that) went through her utterly, / Keen, cruel, perceant, stinging' (II:300–1). This death-blow is the culmination of a passage dominated by references to the eyes that contrasts the determination of Apollonius and the bitter vehemence of Lamia with the weakness of the deceived Lycius (II:277–305), whose immaturity is also made apparent when Lamia at first rejects his marriage proposal: 'His passion, cruel grown, took on a hue / Fierce and sanguineous as 'twas possible / In one whose brow had no dark veins to swell' (II:75–7). His red face shows his embarrassment and there is an implied detumescence; he is not as virile as he wishes to be.

Siddal's poems lack the immediate sensuousness of *Lamia* for example, but the diseased body wasted by sexual attraction whilst remaining erotically powerful is a common theme in her work. Keats shares in this, and images of medicine and disease abound, especially in *Isabella*. Isabella, thin and pale as a young mother with a sick child, hallucinations, pulsing, fever, the compounding of drugs, poisonous flowers, haemorrhage, consumption, amputation, a wormy corpse; all these appear very real and can be seen in opposition to the sentiment of the piece.[72] Lamia too, at her transformation shows signs of sickness: convulsions, foaming at the mouth, fever and pain (I:146–64). In *The Eve of St Agnes* Angela and the Beadsman have stiff and palsied limbs, and Angela later describes herself as a 'feeble soul' and a 'poor, weak palsy-stricken churchyard thing', predicting she will die before midnight (XVIII:1–3). Her prophecy was indeed self-fulfilling; amid the raging storm that covers the escape of the lovers she 'Died palsy-twitch'd, with meagre face deform; / The Beadsman ... slept among his ashes cold' (XLII:7–9). In *The Eve of St Agnes* and 'La

Belle Dame' the first and last verses refer to old age and ill-health and this framing device is made even more poignant in 'La Belle Dame' where almost exact repetition reinforces the bleakness of the entire situation: 'Ah, what can ail thee, wretched wight, / Alone and palely loitering; / The sedge is wither'd from the lake, / And no birds sing' (1–4).

In a poem of emotively Spartan language where every word is significant there are still further references to illness and the effect this can have on mental health. The Knight is fading, feverish, pale, haggard and starved, but also woebegone and anguished. 'Shepherd Turned Sailor' uses a similar technique, although as is generally the case in a Siddal poem the context has to supply meaning to individual words. The 'ten thousand souls' afloat on the sea strike an initial mournful note but should not be considered a finite entity; the failing nature of the physical body is imagined through the stark description of the grave site, but it is the potential reunion of the dead lovers that really draws the attention. In 'Worn Out' the heart is 'failing' (13), symbolic of a dying love. The speaker is 'a startled thing' (5), wounded or damaged, and likened to a bird with a broken wing that ironically must fly away (8). She is weary and unable to register positive emotion. Her body is in decay and withdrawing into sleep as a form of passive resistance. That love is blamed for this becomes more obvious as the poem progresses; she has been 'blinded' and debilitated by it, struck down unwillingly so that now she cannot return it (9–12). Her beauty has gone, leaving only a 'faded mouth'; that such a negative attribute should be considered paramount is a telling image of regret. Love has caused physical losses; sexuality has a unique wasting power. Madeline and Isabella are presented in a similar light, as passively resistant protagonists, very different from the dominant and demonic women in *Lamia* and 'La Belle Dame Sans Merci', but even here sexuality is shown to have a degenerative effect and all these women are considerably more complex than such simple classification might imply. Isabella unwittingly colludes in the emasculation of Lorenzo because as she becomes more sexually aware he is prevented from reaching sexual maturity when the secret of their attachment is discovered.[73] She is part innocent and part temptress, a dualism evident in her transfixed fetishism of Lorenzo's head, and the same dichotomy exists in Lamia, albeit in a more extreme form. Lamia is a creature of opposites, a virgin, but sexually knowing, a baby, yet possessed of a 'sciental' brain. She finds 'bliss and its neighbour pain' inseparable yet she acknowledges the finer points of each (I:185–96).[74] Romance is under siege to cruelty here but both are essential to an erotic aesthetic and both are bound up with pain. How the body deals with pain can indicate its physical and mental state and be a sign of a body in decay. Certainly, the pain of loss runs through all Siddal's work, its manifestation here most apparent in 'Worn Out' and 'Gone'.

Lamia signifies doom for Lycius but she is not just an evil temptress. She has an 'otherness' in terms of her physical description, back-story and language and therefore the poem can be read as being about the alter-ego of a woman as well as a warning against the dangers of desire.[75] There are moral dilemmas in her role, such as the responsibility Lycius may have for his own downfall, or the extent to which she is purely a destroyer of masculine pretension. Whether women are goddesses or enchantresses, and given that sexuality is something to be feared, sexual love becomes a kind of death.[76] Death is seen as fulfilment by Siddal and Keats and is central to all seven of their texts. In 'La Belle Dame' a man 'dies' for love of a pitiless beauty, but death is not necessarily a finite entity; he appears to be still alive after his encounter but his masculinity is wasted and he exists in a half-life because passion has a transformative effect. A mere glimpse of beauty has led to a diminished reality in which the spectral nature of the self achieves predominance.[77] Siddal's poems share this concept of posthumous existence. Lorenzo is so diminished by his declaration of love that a sudden rush of blood renders him speechless and threatens to kill him (VI). After he is murdered he then appears as a ghost (XXXV–XLL) and then as a severed head. Lamia transforms herself to facilitate love. Madeline may be said to die a little after she wakes from her dream of Porphyro (XXXVI), and their combined fate is shrouded in mystery as they abruptly dissolve into the storm at the end of the poem (XLII:1–2). All these figures are differently possessed by love but its intensity will ultimately lead to death beyond which fulfilment will only come in a dream world, another concept familiar in Siddal's works.

Keats's fascination with things medical is not surprising given his training as an apothecary and surgeon and his personal familiarity with tuberculosis. He arguably also had worries over the general condition of his body, hiding his small stature behind descriptions of the physique and daring of Porphyro.[78] *Isabella* has been read in an associated but extrapolated light, as an exploration of the contention that energies could be wasted not only by a female lover but by the art of poetry itself.[79] There is evidence of this in Keats's correspondence; in February 1819 he wrote to his brother wondering whether to continue with his physician's training as he was not taking kindly to it. That said, he felt it could be no worse than writing poems and then facing potentially critical reviews.[80] Ruskin wrote of Keats as a 'sick poet', with a mind of 'fine make' but with no fixed faith or power of self-command, plunging into sin and unable to avoid the dreams of terror which sin conjures up. He maintained Keats's mind threw itself into examining and expressing those dreams, which accounted for the whole treatment of *Isabella* and the despair in *The Eve of St Agnes*. Ruskin believed physical weakness arose from mental over-exertion in which 'irregular habits of life lead to painful visions of imaginary beings which then have violent physical manifestation in the poet, proportional with those visions'. *Lamia*, he said, came from such an episode.[81] His analysis of Keats's mental state is similar to the opinion of Robert Bree, Keats's doctor, who stated he had no organic complaint, only 'anxiety'. It is quoted here in the context of Siddal's visit in 1855 to Dr Henry Acland who came to the conclusion she too was suffering from a psychosomatic condition, 'mental power long spent up and lately over-taxed'.[82] In a semiotic construction of Siddal she is signifier to Rossetti's signified, denied an independent sexuality by his artistic vision. Siddal then becomes a site of literal and figurative consumption, an object of exchange in which her ailing body leads to his gain; Rossetti becomes more artistically virile as she declines in the images he creates.[83] There is a parallel with Keats here; in literature consumption is associated with females, and in the light of his diagnosis this gives him a feminine and subordinate role in the Victorian context, his convulsions also making him more attractive to women.[84] Siddal and Keats are constructs of disease, sexuality and death just as their poems intertwine these things to create images of loss and the viability of spectral existence.

Power struggle and transformation

The physical body changes and lacks identity and very often these changes are registered in the voice and its relationship with silence. Lamia takes on human form in reversal of a death motif. She has been human before (I:17) and her emotions have remained human, making the poem an examination of fluid external identity as well as the most overt discourse on the physical body, worked against a background of spectral transformation. With a new body comes a new voice (I:167) that will speak a new language of seduction and deception (I:189–99), such as when she reassures Lycius she is no dream (I:295–309). Lycius later has to ask her name, still half-believing her to be 'of heavenly progeny' (II:84–9). When she begins to transform again under Apollonius's gaze (II:260–70) his power ultimately rests in his voice as at the operative moment he only needs to speak two words in an undertone, 'A Serpent!' (II:305), to make her vanish. This is a neat inversion at the end of a poem in which the constant undercurrent of noise is muted and where only at pivotal moments is the voice heard above the silence. The 'quiet cacophony' in *Lamia* is a good example of Lycius's boyish imagination trying to locate his manly, mature voice.[85] When Lycius proposes his adult voice gets the better of him, propelling him into rash speech in an effort to shed his childish image, and this matches a transformative phase in Keats's work that is visible in these later poems. Their male protagonists are unconvincing heroes who cannot deal with the change to virile adulthood, and their confusion is mirrored in the sexual dilemmas facing Keats who saw himself as being between man and boy and also uncertain of his poetic direction. This is an aspect of 'negative capability' in that it allows for dialogue between critic and reader and their open-ended responses to the poems.[86] Siddal's poems likewise defy definitive interpretation and rely on such dialogue. They also exhibit a desire to withdraw from the complexities of relationships.

There is a form of transformation in each Siddal poem, notably from human to bird. In 'Gone' the move equates to a shift in mood from ecstasy to the depths of despair. Silence takes on a negative aspect, the surviving lover finding it impenetrable like a 'darkened wood' (6), and the bird is a dove, a symbol of purity leaving earthly pleasures in search of renewed innocence. There is an interesting balance between active and passive here, from touching to watching, from being adored to making an escape: 'I watch the shadows gather round my heart, / I live to know that she is gone – / Gone gone for ever, like the tender dove / That bravely left the Ark alone' (9–12). Perhaps the Ark was too confining, a notion more confidently read into 'Worn Out'. Here the speaker 'must fly' (8) because she can no longer engage with her lover, and her reincarnation as a bird-figure stresses her fragility and impermanence as well as her ability to remove herself from too complex a position. Having established this new identity, it is reinforced by her lack of human responses: she 'cannot smile and may not laugh again' (15–16). Absence or variation of voice can therefore be a metre of change, a way of measuring the significance of speech in a given literary situation. In *The Eve of St Agnes* there are many images of sexual excitement and fulfilment but all are presented in silence; the sexuality is largely visual, seen in descriptions of colour, history and spectacle.[87] The whole poem may be read as being about speech, language, communication and their unreliability, the balance between quoted and unquoted speech, and the amount of whispering and falsehoods indicating that Keats was concerned with fractured speech.[88] The voices of guests and kinsmen (and trumpets) contrast with the silence outside the castle (IV) and Madeline's isolation within it (VIII). Such a reading could also apply to *Isabella* in which silence is vital to the structure: people not speaking out create the tragedy. The human voice is altered or substituted for non-human sound to emphasize fracturing. In 'Worn Out' low words of comfort are no use to the speaker and in 'La Belle Dame' the Lady speaks in 'language strange' (VII:3), suggesting a voice that can be heard but not fully understood. Music has a voice of its own in *The Eve of St Agnes*; speech cannot wake Madeline but music can (XXXIII) and it has a 'golden tongue' (III:2). It follows then that direct speech carries its own importance when it occurs. Siddal doesn't use quoted speech but 'Worn Out' like 'La Belle Dame' is a monologue so the reader still receives the subjective and uncertain viewpoint of the protagonist. Keats uses it to draw attention to crucial moments in the narrative. The conversation between Porphyro and Angela expiates his plan for Madeline and anticipates the moral dilemmas this will usher in (XI–XIV), and later his words, the longest passage of direct speech in the poem, are needed to persuade Madeline to run away with him (XXXVIII–XXXIX).

The physical body can be ungendered, or blur the lines of sexuality. There is nothing in 'Gone', 'Worn Out', or 'Shepherd Turned Sailor' to precisely identify either speaker or receiver by name, and it is only a presumption that the first is delivered by a man, or that the others indicate heterosexual relationships. The sentiments in 'Shepherd Turned Sailor' could readily be those of a male lover and whereas 'clinging grass' has quite a feminine ring much of the poem is androgynous. Lesbian love is suggested in 'Worn Out' by the bird simile and the muted vocal comfort offered at its start, and the same can be inferred from 'Gone' where the gloved hand has not actually been kissed, more a courtly male gesture, only touched and adored. However, if Siddal is writing as a man then this poem could be an exploration of male emotion as well as a deliberate anti-autobiographical device, as the middle verse speaks of impotence as well as loss: 'To touch her shadow on the sunny grass, / To break her pathway through the darkened wood, / Filled all my life with trembling and tears / And silence where I stood' (5–8). Siddal makes her narratives less clear by not specifying names or gender and Keats confuses sexuality by making the behaviour of his characters less stereotypical: men are less manly, or become so, and women more dominant. This adds to the enigmatic quality of 'La Belle Dame' in which the Knight is already 'in thrall' (X) and destitute as the poem begins. He is associated with flowers and along with the ghostly warriors is femininely pale. The latter also have 'starv'd lips (XI:1) that imply diminution through consumptive disease, significant in a gendered nineteenth-century context.[89] The roles of Lamia and Lycius, and Lorenzo and Isabella are inverted; Lamia is proactive and in control of the destinies of the nymph, Hermes and Lycius, whereas Lycius can only 'shriek' (II:269) when exposed as a 'fool' by a contemptuous Apollonius for allowing himself to become a 'serpent's prey' (II:291–99). Lorenzo appears timid and pallid, easily deceived by Isabella's brothers, and Isabella has to be lovesick before he dares to declare his love (V). Finally, she has to take the initiative to break the impasse and even then embarrassment stifles him (VI:4). He is but a ghost while she finds the courage to avenge his death and become his half-life force (XLIII–L).

The physical body can register emotion and sensation, but this is strangely absent in 'La Belle Dame'. The narrative takes place in a form of lyric silence akin to that in 'Shepherd Turned Sailor' so the reader doesn't know why events have occurred, and the sparse language creates a picture of detachment from reality. Together these point to the possibility of the spectral body as a metacentre of living. There is little physical contact in the poem and very little description of either character, instead plants and foods are given prominence. Most of the sensory experience of the Knight is therefore channelled via dead or non-human beings; he sees little while riding with the lady (V:2) and sleeps through much of his encounter with her, but he can taste 'honey and manna dew' (VII:2). He is in limbo, so his physical body is becoming less important. The reader learns more about his nightmare than of his relationship with the creature who seems to have created it, and this emotional separation from the living is bound up in his limited sensory awareness. By comparison *The Eve of St Agnes* is a work of great sensuousness in which both protagonist and reader can share. Porphyro's actions and motives are cloudy so the reader is left to imagine the exact nature of his liaison with Madeline and her compliance with it, but it is still a scene of warmth and intensity, made more so by the immediate return to outside chill afterwards. The rich medievalism renders the setting almost tactile; architectural detail, cold statuary, garments, textiles, cobwebs and candlelight come together with religion and superstition to build a haunting context for the drama between the lovers. Madeline herself is blind to it, lost in prayer, but the reader becomes Porphyro's eyes as he sees her room, then her and her undressing (XXIV–XXVI). The reader also listens for her breathing as he does (XXVIII) and tastes the morsels he lays before her. There is combined emotional involvement too; Porphyro acknowledges his fear by having to do all his seeing in secret and the reader is forced to consider their guilty role in his voyeurism.[90]

Nothing in Siddal's poems equates to the bedroom scene in *The Eve of St Agnes* or to the marriage feast in *Lamia* but her protagonists clearly register emotion and are connected to their physical context. 'Gone' looks at the difference between real and imaginary touch; touching a glove brings euphoria but trying to touch a shadow, or watching them gather around the heart brings desolation. Touching and watching are important as signs of heightened sensory perception and Siddal uses them to explore the emotional response to the possibility that life and death are not mutually exclusive. She also uses them as transmitters of feelings, vital in poems that are very short and where language is economical. 'Worn Out' turns its back on sensation and this correspondingly enhances the paralysis of loss. A need for comfort frames the poem, and despite the withdrawal that characterizes the verses in between, the woman still requests this and believes it relevant as she fades into sleep or possible death: 'Yet keep thine arms around me, love, / Until I fall to sleep; / Then leave me, saying no goodbye / Lest I might wake, and weep' (17–20). 'Shepherd Turned Sailor' has a much more physical ring because its subject matter is largely tangible and recognizable:

> Now Christ ye save you bonny shepherd
>   Sailing on the sea:
> Ten thousand souls are sailing there
>   But they belong to Thee.
> If he is lost then all is lost
>   And all is dead to me.
>
> My love should have a grey head-stone
>   And green moss at his feet
> And clinging grass above his breast
>   Whereon his lambs could bleat,
> And I should know the span of earth
>   Where some day I might sleep.

The 'ten thousand souls' may not have quite the same finite presence but they do 'belong' (4) to Christ, giving them a sense of location less obvious in 'Gone' and 'Worn Out'.

The physical body can be used as a metaphor for the structure of Siddal's poems and their chameleon-like variations in tense, rhyme, rhythm and form. The poems are quite fractured in places and this corresponds to the weakening of the body as well as to the broken relationships of which they speak. The body changes over time as have her poems, leading to a metaphorical struggle between Siddal's poetic voice and her earliest editors. There are structural shifts between verses in all three poems but they are more obvious in 'Shepherd Turned Sailor' and 'Gone'. They come when emphasis changes to the non-physical body and they create gaps in the narrative which allow obscured or withheld meaning, making it difficult to decide when and if death has occurred. There are slight changes in rhythm and rhyme in 'Gone' which leave poetic stumblings at operative moments. Verses 1 and 2 have an identical pattern in both respects, with one exception: 'Lifted my heart into a sudden song' (3) drops the initial iambic beat and draws attention to the injection of optimism. The climactic third verse is rather different; the rhyming pattern has gone and the rhythmic sequence is irregular in the middle two lines, arguably the most poignant in the poem. These lines may be a work in progress but their form makes an intriguing diversion, especially when every verse still ends with the same three strong beats that suggest finality. Christina Rossetti liked this arrangement and approved of its usage in a poem about restrained grief and consolation.[91] Tenses also change in this poem; the first couplet in the initial verses can be read as both present and past, which allows for the continuation of physical life referred to there. In 'Shepherd Turned Sailor' there is a change from present indicative to present subjunctive, expressing a wish for the future also found at the end of 'Worn Out'. All these subtleties are mirrored in the alternation between active and passive; in 'Worn Out' for example the speaker appears to be almost inert but she still has control of her own body because she has the means to escape and she has chosen the mask of sleep.

Inhabiting the spectral body

The spectral body allows for an extended range of emotions and the exploration of experience beyond the physical, and this develops the power of imagination which emerges in the use of colour and texture in language. Desire drives imagination in Keats's poems and because colour is central to aesthetic perception it leads all other sensations at pivotal or ecstatic moments such as the seduction of Madeline or the transformation of Lamia. Conversely, absence of colour can still achieve the same effect. In 'La Belle Dame' it is largely absent and then only used to describe foliage which acts as a foil for the danger of chilling 'on the cold hillside' (XI:4). Colour is seen through a filtering agency, mist, trees, sleep or hair, and this creates a half-light and shadows, allowing the imagination to become more active since without colour, truth is not absolute. Ordinary things are made to seem full of colour when presented veiled to the mind, and senses are heightened by the act of imagining.[92] 'La Belle Dame' is constructed around visionary imagination; the Knight has experienced it and the reader needs it because the language of the poem is so sparse. Despite its 'paleness' its visionary impact is surprisingly vivid, and the brevity of Siddal's poems, 'Gone' especially, have a similar ability to heighten visual perception. Even darkness can be affected by colour which penetrates it and fuses with it. The contrast between the two is central to the chamber scene in *The Eve of St Agnes* where imagination and reality clash in Madeline's dream. Her imaginings are made real, all she knows and all she needs to know, because they are surrounded by things unknown, like death, darkness and cold, yet these very surroundings make this reality illusory and transitory.[93] Porphyro, hidden in the darkness, watches Madeline as if he were a spirit not a human and in that state he can fully appreciate her beauty (XXV). As the dark is pierced by moonlight coloured by the 'innumerable stains and splendid dyes' (XXIV:5) of the windowpanes, so he uses colour in his mind to warm his image of Madeline whose beauty makes him 'lustrous' like the dishes he sets before her (XXXII:5). All his senses are heightened at the moment of orgasm (XXXVI) and colour matches his arousal. Desire drives Porphyro and their imaginations but it also drives the poetry via a linguistic chain of sensory pleasures from the point when Madeline shuts the door on herself and her lover.[94]

Colour is transportive; its role in the imaginative process takes the physical body into an other-worldly state. Lamia, hugely colourful, can imagine herself into a different form and send her spirit wherever she wants in the physical and Olympian world, and she can do the same to others. She keeps the nymph invisible so she will remain unloved by mortals whilst still sensing life around her (I:94–109). The nymph fades after her meeting with Hermes but is reborn as an immortal spirit, able to experience life on an ethereal plane. The wedding guests are transported by the sensory excesses of the feast; drink leads them to an altered state in which they experience everything in glorious colour with 'bright eyes double bright' (II:203–14), and this elevation is indicative of the rising emotional tension between Lamia, Lycius and Apollonius that results in tragedy when imagination impacts on reality.[95] Extended sensory and emotional awareness are structurally important in 'Gone' and 'Shepherd Turned Sailor'. 'Gone' begins with the tangible but then moves into the realms of imagination and the subconscious. The speaker is seeing what cannot be seen and to do this must stand outside the body. The emotional response to this, and the loss that has precipitated it, is acute and reaches a climax in the middle verse after which a greater air of resignation overtakes the speaker. 'Shepherd Turned Sailor' is worked in reverse; it begins with the possibility of total and irretrievable loss but modulates into speculation of something that may be borne, almost as if such intense emotion cannot be sustained for long. Both verses are laden with fear but the first is more chilling, with its implication that this could be the new permanence. There would appear to be little hope of comfort in spectral existence on this occasion.

The spectral body creates an elusive or dreamy otherness that equates to being half-alive and allows for escape from the self. These concepts run throughout Siddal's work but are particularly striking in 'Gone' and 'Worn Out' where from the outset instability is made evident. The soul has 'no rest' (4), and the speaker 'must fly', although to what extent she intends to leave is unclear. She is in theory capable of flight but in practice she is disabled (7); she could be exhorting herself to flee a regrettable situation, or her tone could be purely wistful, recognizing that she ought to go rather than actually being about to do so. This sense of being in two places at once and a non-participant in both is cemented in the last verse where the loss of the physical body becomes almost too much, yet there is a reluctance to withdraw from it completely. To commit to either existence is to acknowledge a range of emotion that is not always possible or desirable. There is greater physical distance between the two characters in 'Gone' and the bird has already flown, but ambiguities remain. The speaker survives but is crippled by regret and introspection and is therefore not a whole person. The dove may have died, or merely abandoned her lover. 'To break her pathway through the darkened wood' (6) can be read in several ways and this adds to the feeling of uncertainty: perhaps she was being prevented from going, or she was being followed along the path, or it was being marked or made easier for her. Here, as in 'Shepherd Turned Sailor', the unknown whereabouts of a lover has forced the speaker into a semi-functioning existence. The location of both parties is clear in 'Worn Out'; instead, the poem explores the possibility of existing more fully, half-alive. Siddal is therefore looking at the idea of escape from two perspectives, its desirability and its impact, and this adds to the fluidity inherent in her poetics.

In two letters to Benjamin Bailey in 1817 Keats describes himself as 'abstracted', unable to feel passion or affection for a week or even a month at a time and questioning the genuineness of his feelings in between.[96] Writing to John Reynolds the following year he speaks of his sensations being 'deadened'; so fearful was he of marriage, for himself and others, he had 'not been unwilling to die'.[97] Specific circumstances pertain to all three letters but their generic sentiments can be found in these poems. La Belle Dame sings without words and leaves a potent legacy; she brings about drastic change and provokes disturbing dreams. Her Knight, meanwhile, inhabits a timeless wasteland which is more spectral than physical. Madeline, in a half-sleep state, experiences visions that catch her between imagination and reality. Porphyro offers her a way out of her imprisonment in the castle and towards sexual fulfilment of the legend on which she is fixated, but this is imprisonment of her own making and she can also facilitate her own escape.[98] Madeline and Porphyro eventually disappear leaving no impression on their surroundings, unlike Angela and the Beadsman whose mortal remains are plain, yet even these two characters are half-dead as the poem begins. The time shifts in *The Eve of St Agnes* are indicative of the idea that time traps those who are alive or dead so that humans are frozen in a kind of purgatory here on earth where religion isn't working.[99] Certainly, the Beadsman seems quite isolated and detached from the action around him, like a ghostly commentator.

Isabella is only half-alive after Lorenzo is killed because grief disables her and pushes her into 'gradual decay' (XXXII:8). 'Piteous she'd look on dead and senseless things, / Asking for her lost Basil amorously' (LXII:1–2), a double irony as she could expect no reply and she was little more than dead and senseless herself. Lamia is by nature contradictory and illusive, and only half-human. Lycius is in a love-trance when he is with her until the reality of her persona intervenes (II:240). She escapes her serpent body but Lycius also escapes her entrapment, suggesting that Keats considered the desire to do so was ungendered.

Given the many references to an other-worldly state it is not surprising that both Keats and Siddal explore dreams and the concept of sleep in their poems. Their dream worlds can be visions of utopia and they can affect the future, but they can also be painful and full of suffering. Sleep can bring respite but it can also be a mask and a means of manipulation; as such sleep and dreams can be seen as aspects of 'negative capability' because they bring associated benefits and dangers. 'Shepherd Turned Sailor' illustrates this complexity; the speaker longs for sleep, but only if her lover has to die. She has dreamed of where she wants his grave to be with enough clarity for it to be a self-fulfilling prophecy. Sleep, death and living are also enmeshed in 'Worn Out' where the edges between the three states are blurred, which allows for the possibility of posthumous existence, or a vision of it. This poem has a further element of self-determination; sleep may be an artifice, feigned as a means of avoiding the reality of a lover's betrayal or a barrier against unwanted sexual advances, or the reverse, or a way of eliciting sympathy. Madeline daydreams of meeting her lover in her sleep (VI–VIII) and this then becomes her reality. At first she 'dreams awake' (XXVI:7), 'in a sort of wakeful swoon' but 'poppied' sleep then soothes away physical sensation like a drug and replaces it with something far more erotic, 'As though a rose should shut and be a bud again' (XXVII). In contrast to her dreams Madeline sleeps as a virgin 'In blanched linen, smooth, and lavender'd' (XXX:2) as Porphyro lays his feast before her. He attempts to rouse her physically and sexually but she remains 'Impossible to melt as iced stream', 'the steadfast spell' too powerful for him to penetrate (XXXII). He joins her in a drowsy interlude, and the shared sleep motif continues as she wakes 'but still beheld, / ... the vision of her sleep' (XXXIV:1–2). This pains her because her vision of him is at odds with his reality; his physical body is pale and cold like the statues of the castle whereas his spectral body was vibrant and lusty. As the confusion between the two states continues Porphyro makes love to her by 'melting' into her dream (XXXVI:5) but once fully awake and with the spell of St Agnes' Eve broken Madeline must face the consequences of her de-flowering. Her dream has brought rather more than the legend promised and she is now 'a deceived thing; / A dove, forlorn and lost with sick, unpruned wing' (XXXVII:8–9), lines Siddal almost writes in 'Worn Out'.

Like Siddal Keats blurs the boundaries between sleep and wakefulness to enable extended perception and experience, but he also uses dreams as a catalyst for change. The ghostly Lorenzo appears to Isabella in a dream and she then endures in that state looking for forgetfulness while resisting it (LXI:4–9). In 'La Belle Dame' the Knight puts the faerie to sleep but it's his dreams the reader shares. They are ghastly and transforming, they carry answers but he cannot unlock them despite the dreams remaining with him. Here as in *Lamia* sleep and dreams become a danger, and not the refuge Siddal wants them to be. There can be too much investment in illusion, and there is no escape from the human condition along this path.[100] The last verse of 'La Belle Dame' reveals why the Knight is wandering alone: he is only half-alive after his bewitching so cannot rejoin society. Constant revisiting of his encounter with the elf condemns him to permanent withdrawal and grieving, and grief can only be managed through separation, even if separation is its cause. Madeline is disillusioned by Porphyro's actions and is still 'beset with fears' (XL:1) as she escapes the castle, which signifies her doubts about her present and future. She makes no verbal response to his urgent pleas to leave, implying that she can only reflect on her experience once she has distanced herself from her previous life, but as the storm raging outside could well be portentous her thoughts and their fate are open to question. Lamia isolates herself to lament her loss of female form (I:35–41) and she then inhabits a non-human, quite simplistic world where anything is admissible. From there she waits, having rationalized her predicament, ready to exploit the chance Hermes' adoration of the nymph affords her. She and Lycius hide their faces from his acquaintances but it is Apollonius, the signifier of Lycius's doubts over his hasty proposal whom they both fear (I:362–74). Away from his eyes in a place unknown to any but themselves they consider their strategy: Apollonius was not to be invited to this particular marriage feast (II:164–9).

Siddal's poems end with an acceptance of sadness and an implied lack of anger at betrayal. Grief is more readily dealt with passively, which is at odds with the drama of *Isabella, Lamia* and *The Eve of St Agnes*. Siddal's speakers have agonized over their loss and believe themselves impotent in the face of it, but their languidness suggests more than just resignation, it is a means of survival. The physical body will decay but the spectral will endure. Siddal sees suffering as the inevitable consequence of relationships; it has to be borne even though the speaker is its victim and not its perpetrator. Taking this stance doesn't make the speaker physically stronger but it can empower by providing a way of adapting to adversity. It is easy to read these poems as being overwhelmingly negative but this is not necessarily the case; they anticipate that life will continue in some form and they contain signs not just of acceptance, but of optimism. 'Worn Out' hints at escape and adaptation; the lambs in 'Shepherd Turned Sailor' give religious inference to the poem and are its prevailing image. The brave dove, the symbol of peace leaving the ark for a new life, does the same in 'Gone'. Siddal's speakers may be withdrawing, but they are not suicidal.

The spectral body allows the masking of emotion and the creation of an alter-ego; like the physical body it can therefore also be transformative. All artistic production pertains to a process of masking that is detected in the contrast between the existence of the writer before and after creating a poem during which the old being is covered by a new and radiant one. Byron and Milton appreciated this but in Keats it assumed its most defined and essential form, a conversion of a felt inadequacy in the self into a visage that would appeal to the reading public of the time. The self becomes repressed and can then be stripped or evacuated, and by donning a mask another body can be filled. Personality does not emerge until the mask is in place which means Keats the man is purely a reading of his poems, a literary construct, a text, an object of readers' attention.[101] As Porphyro is also a figure defined by sexuality it follows that he becomes Keats's mask, a way of defining the antithesis of Keats as a sexual being. *The Eve of St Agnes* is therefore a way of banishing and negating Keats's sexual frustration.[102] The Knight, released from love but nomadic and depressed, is also a mask, put on while Keats struggled with his love for Fanny Brawne.[103] In *Isabella* the lovers are forced to keep their emotions secret (V, VI, XI), and love transforms them. Lorenzo is shown alive and dead and he is the antithesis of Isabella's two brothers even to the extent that when he blooms in the knowledge of Isabella's love they become 'sick and wan' as they lure him to the forest (XXVII:5–7). Like Lamia, and unlike male protagonists, Isabella undergoes multiple mental and physical changes after Lorenzo goes missing and these are linked symbolically with changes in the natural world. She declines with autumn (XXXII), grows in strength with the 'native lilies of the dell' (XLVI:6), abandons herself to the seasons in her grief (LIII), and withers like a felled palm (LVI:7–8), all the while fixated on a pot of basil. Such complexity of metamorphosis suggests Keats attributed a wider range of emotion to women even if it was destructive or withheld, and Siddal's poems tend to echo this, even allowing for their putative gendering. There is certainly detachment in 'Worn Out' where emotion cannot be supplied or felt and the speaker only tolerates the physical proximity of her lover on her own terms. All the poems bear witness to a fear that love is only transient, that when it is declared it leads to tragedy, and this is illustrated in 'Gone' where after the proclamation of joy in verse 1 there comes a sudden shift of emphasis towards a state of mourning which is indicative of the power struggle between the physical and the spectral.

The spectral body, by very definition, has to allow for posthumous existence, and this is obvious in *Isabella* where Lorenzo's head becomes his whole earthly body and an extension of his earthly function. He returns to describe his fate to Isabella and to set the path to retribution, and to settle his soul: 'the taste of earthly bliss' stolen when speaking to her warms his grave 'as though I had / A seraph chosen from the bright abyss / To be my spouse' (XL:3–6). He describes his burial place, in a verse remarkably similar to the second in 'Shepherd Turned Sailor':

Saying moreoever, 'Isabel, my sweet!
Red whortle-berries droop above my head,
And a large flint-stone weighs upon my feet;
Around me beeches and high chestnuts shed
Their leaves and prickly nuts: a sheep-fold bleat
Come from beyond the river to my bed:
Go, shed one tear upon my heather-bloom,
And it shall comfort me within the tomb. (XXXVIII)

Both pieces argue for the importance of permanence for the physical body, vital for a fulfilled relationship despite its failing or otherness. Madeline and Porphyro 'glide' as 'phantoms' (XLI:1–2) as they exit the castle and they then survive as a memory, their story 'ages old' (XLII:1). Something similar pertains in 'Gone' where memory takes the form of a dove, and in 'Worn Out' where it becomes a 'restless soul' (4). 'I have a habitual feeling of my real life having past, and that I am leading a posthumous existence', Keats wrote to Charles Brown in 1820 when he was too low in mind and body to 'summon up feeling for light and shade, all that's needed for a poem'.[104] Joseph Severn, describing Keats's death, reported how each day Keats tried to get from the doctors how long he would live: 'How long will this posthumous life of mine last?'[105] Siddal's poems do not always share this sense of regret; 'Worn Out' welcomes a move to semi-existence, and Siddal herself was largely defined after 1869 by her exhumation and the publication of the manuscript poems Dante Rossetti had retrieved on that occasion. Where and how poets are buried plays a significant part in their textual afterlife. Keats's corpse was regarded as dangerous and attempts to repatriate it became a defence of his remains, his reputation and his poetic corpus. *Lamia, Isabella, The Eve of St Agnes and Other Poems* was published in July 1820 and this coincided with a recommendation by his doctors to go to Italy if he were to survive tuberculosis. Keats writes in letter in August that he is convinced he will die, that he will write no more poems and that he will be immortalized purely via his publications.[106] Arguably, Siddal did not desire or anticipate similar immortalization as her poems were a secret, unpublished undertaking, but ironically she achieved this in the contemporary myth that her hair continued to grow after she died until it filled her coffin. It is ironic too that had

Rossetti not requested her exhumation he like her could have been an unpublished poet.

The spectral body allows for and encourages an awareness of uncertainty or a version of 'negative capability'. Keats described this conception of the receptivity necessary for the process of poetic creativity as being when a man was capable of being uncertain and willing to suspend disbelief, was doubtful and not looking for absolute truth. He regarded Shakespeare as the prime example of negative capability, attributing to him the ability to identify completely with his characters, and to write about them with empathy and understanding, and he contrasts this with the more partisan and egotistical stance of Milton and Wordsworth. Negative capability tempers the active pursuit of rational knowledge and philosophy with wise and informed passiveness, and belief in it means unresolved issues take on positivity, ambiguity can be celebrated and the whole idea of simple hard choice can be questioned. This applies to *Isabella*, *Lamia* and *The Eve of St Agnes*, but especially to 'La Belle Dame' in which Keats does not give the reader a simple villain/victim binary but instead complicates the motives of the characters and the responses of the readers. This poem, like much of Siddal's work, has an unfinished feel and nothing is quite as it seems. Her poems are full of uncertainty, and doubt clouds the future in all three, but there is an acceptance of this, not the anger that might be expected. They present opposites in consecutive verses and may therefore be seen as being essentially fractured; unlike Keats's poems they have been heavily reworked and could be more a collection of fragments rather than incomplete wholes.[107] They may not have been intended as finished copies and if the latter ever existed they could have been purposely destroyed. Siddal did not have them printed or circulated. The surviving manuscripts are almost illegible in places, and all three have been the subject of revision. There is undoubted individual significance to each of the changes recorded in Trowbridge's 2018 edition but collectively they illustrate the general point that these poems are capable of analysis despite the many issues that surround their provenance and subsequent handling and that their shifting editorial context is an essential element within the process of their restitution.

Siddal's poems had their own spectral existence during her lifetime, only acquiring a physical presence thirty years after her death and then not as one complete entity or in the form she would have recognized.[108] As such they represent the power struggle between the physical and the spectral around which this chapter has hinged. It emerges in the internal polarities, dualisms and conflicts that disguise meaning and reflect the tension between reality and illusion, public and private, structure and non-structure. It also emerges in a desire for artistic and poetic individualism and in her refusal to share her work, which indicates a resistance to interpretation by others and a reaction to artistic interference from Ruskin and Dante Rossetti. Siddal's poetics of withdrawal placed her in both physical and spectral worlds and the sometime lack of coherent transition between the two is signified by breaks or turning points in her poems that mirror breaks in imagination and experience, and in an awareness of the potential of the self to host two conflicting spirits. Siddal's sketch *A Woman and a Spectre*, the 'wraith drawing', allows for this second concept and has its most striking Keatsian parallel in 'La Belle Dame sans Merci' in which the eponymous faerie is paradoxically both a malevolent and a nurturing figure and therefore possessed of a good/evil genius as understood in nineteenth-century terms. W. M. Rossetti claimed this work, along with five Odes, was 'the cream' of Keats's poetry, 'the highest point of romantic imagination in dealing with human and quasi-human persons', 'the highest level of simplicity along with completeness of art'.[109] 'La Belle Dame' was the product of both imagination and belief; in 1817 Keats wrote to Benjamin Robert Haydon: 'I remember your saying that you had notions of a Good Genius presiding over you – I have of late had the same thought.'[110] *A Woman and a Spectre* graphically encapsulates this dualism and the power struggle between spirit and body evident in Siddal's poems, and it is fitting that it should do so considering it is often the visual image that first emerges from such enigmatic literary works.

Notes

1 Marsh, *Sheffield*, p. 69.
2 Taylor, 'Beatrix/Creatrix', p. 34.

3 Isabelle Williams, 'Elizabeth Siddal: The Health Issue', *The Journal of Pre-Raphaelite Studies*, Vol. 5 (Spring 1996), 53–70, p. 69.
4 Alfred Lord Tennyson, *Poems*, ed. Christopher Ricks (London and Harlow: Longmans, Green and Co. Ltd, 1969), pp. 552–4.
5 William Michael Rossetti, *The Life of Keats* (London: George Allen, 1887), p. 209.
6 Hassett, *Christina Rossetti*, p. 30.
7 Roe, *Rossetti's Faithful Imagination*, pp. 34–42.
8 Marsh, *Legend*, pp. 66–7.
9 W. M. Rossetti, *Burlington*, p. 273, and *Family Letters with a Memoir*, Vol. II, p. 173.
10 Margaret Homans, 'Keats Reading Women, Women Reading Keats', *Studies in Romanticism*, Vol. 29, No. 3 (Fall 1990), 341–70.
11 *Ibid.*, p. 346.
12 *Ibid.*, pp. 347–8.
13 Parkins, *Jane Morris*, p. 67.
14 *Ibid.*, p. 70.
15 *Ibid.*, pp. 74–7 has a detailed analysis of the Rossetti/Morris correspondence.
16 Alison Chapman, *The Afterlife of Christina Rossetti* (Basingstoke: Macmillan Press Ltd, 2000), pp. 58–9.
17 Marsh, *Sheffield*, p. 51 points to an alternative title for one sketch, *Three Figures at a Fountain*.
18 J. B. Bullen, *Rossetti: Painter and Poet* (London: Frances Lincoln Ltd, 2011), p. 185 quotes Elizabeth Gaskell making this remark.
19 Elisabeth G. Gitter, 'The Power of Women's Hair in the Victorian Imagination', *PMLA*, Vol. 99, No. 5 (October 1984), 936–54, p. 936.
20 *Ibid.*, p. 939.
21 *Ibid.*, pp. 946–7.
22 G. M. Matthews, ed., *Keats. The Critical Heritage* (London: Routledge & Kegan Paul, 1971), pp. 1–37 has concise coverage of Keats's publication history and reaction to it.
23 *Ibid.*, p. 30.
24 Arthur Hallam, 'On Some of the Characteristics of Modern Poetry, and on the Lyrical Poems of Alfred Tennyson', *Englishman's Magazine* (August 1831), 616–21, reprinted in Matthews, *Ibid.*, pp. 264–72.
25 Matthews, *Critical Heritage*, p. 2.
26 Sarah Wootton, 'Keats in Early Pre-Raphaelite Art', *Keats Shelley Review*, Vol. 12 (1998), 3–14, p. 10.
27 John Keats, *Letters 1814–21*, 2 vols, ed. Edward Hyder Rollins (Cambridge: Cambridge University Press, 1958), Vol. I, No. 45,

pp. 191–4. The letter was sent to his brothers after Keats had been to see a painting by a friend.
28 Julie Codell, 'Painting Keats: Pre-Raphaelite Artists Between Social Transgressions and Painterly Conventions', *Victorian Poetry*, Vol. 33, Nos 3–4 (Autumn–Winter 1995), 341–70, p. 342.
29 *Ibid.*, p. 366.
30 *Ibid.*, pp. 362–3.
31 W. M. Rossetti, *Life of Keats*, pp. 45–6.
32 Codell, 'Painting Keats', p. 346.
33 Matthews, *Critical Heritage*, p. 10.
34 W. M. Rossetti, *Dante Gabriel Rossetti. His Family Letters with a Memoir*, Vol. 1, p. 100.
35 *Ibid.*, Vol. II, pp. 39–40.
36 Published as George Milner, 'On Some Marginalia made by Dante Gabriel Rossetti in a Copy of Keats', *The Manchester Quarterly*, Vol. II (1883), 1–11.
37 George H. Ford, *Keats and the Victorians. A Study in His Influence and Rise to Fame 1821–95* (London: Archon Books, 1962), pp. 121–45 looks at Keats's influence on Rossetti, and at developments in Rossetti's style suggesting Rossetti conceals much of the former so that his poetry is a paradoxical mixture of his own work and that derived from Keats.
38 *Ibid.*, p. 142.
39 W. M. Rossetti, *Dante Gabriel Rossetti. His Family Letter with Memoir*, Vol. I, p. 420.
40 Ford, *Keats and the Victorians*, pp. 109–19 explores all these shared and transferred poetic concepts and beliefs.
41 Wootton, *Consuming Keats*, p. 32.
42 *Ibid.*, pp. 86–8 explores the Rossetti–Caine relationship via Caine's unpublished letters 1879–81 held in the Manx National Heritage Library.
43 T. Hall Caine, *Recollections of Dante Gabriel Rossetti* (London: Elliot Stock, 1882), p. 84.
44 Ford, *Keats and the Victorians*, p. 109.
45 W. Holman Hunt, *Pre-Raphaelitism and the Pre-Raphaelite Brotherhood*, 2 vols (London: Macmillan and Co. Ltd, 1905 and 1913), Vol. II, p. 159.
46 *Ibid.*, Vol. I, p. 106.
47 *Ibid.*, Vol. I, pp. 70–80.
48 *Ibid.*, Vol. I, p. 85.
49 *Ibid.*, Vol. I, pp. 87–9.

50 *Ibid.*, Vol. I, p. 103.
51 *Ibid.*, Vol. I, p. 106.
52 Grant F. Scott, *The Sculpted Word. Keats, Ekphrasis and the Arts* (Hanover and London: University Press of New England, 1994), pp. 14–20 looks at Keats's ekphrasis in a classical and Romantic context and explores its binaries and situates it within his aesthetic.
53 *Ibid.*, pp. 86–95.
54 Hunt, *Pre-Raphaelitism and the PRB*, Vol. I, p. 80.
55 Scott, *Sculpted Word*, p. 87.
56 Codell, 'Painting Keats', p. 351.
57 Wootton, 'Keats in Early Pre-Raphaelite Art', p. 4.
58 Paul Barlow, 'Pre-Raphaelitism and Post-Raphaelitism: The Articulation of Fantasy and the Problem of Pictorial Space', in Marcia Pointon, ed., *Pre-Raphaelites Re-Viewed* (Manchester and New York: Manchester University Press, 1989), pp. 66–82, p. 71.
59 Lynne Pearce, *Woman/Image/Text. Readings in Pre-Raphaelite Art and Literature* (Hemel Hempstead, Hertfordshire: Harvester Wheatsheaf, 1991), pp. 108–9.
60 Codell, 'Painting Keats', p. 356.
61 Wootton, 'Keats in Early Pre-Raphaelite Art', p. 10.
62 W. M. Rossetti, *The Life of Keats*, p. 183.
63 Codell, 'Painting Keats', pp. 346–8.
64 Wootton, 'Keats in Early Pre-Raphaelite Art', p. 9.
65 Tim Barringer, *Reading the Pre-Raphaelites* (New Haven and London: Yale University Press, 1998), p. 9.
66 The texts of all four poems are those in *John Keats, The Complete Poems*, ed., Paul Wright (Ware, Hertfordshire: Wordsworth Editions Ltd, 1994).
67 Jack Stillinger, *Reading The Eve of St Agnes. The Multiples of Complex Literary Transaction* (Oxford and New York: Oxford University Press, 1999), pp. 39–77.
68 *Lamia* was illustrated in 1905 and 1909 by John William Waterhouse, not strictly a Pre-Raphaelite artist.
69 Robert Gittings, *John Keats: The Living Year 21 September 1818 to 21 September 1819* (London: William Heinemann Ltd, 1954), p. 173.
70 John Whale, *Critical Issues. John Keats* (Basingstoke: Palgrave Macmillan, 2005), pp. 82–4.
71 Wootton, *Consuming Keats*, p. 116.
72 Jack Stillinger, *The Hoodwinking of Madeline and other Essays on Keats's Poems* (Chicago: University of Illinois Press, 1971), pp. 37–9.

Siddal, Keats and Pre-Raphaelite relations of power   255

73 Whale, *Critical Issues*, pp. 57–8.
74 Stillinger, *The Hoodwinking of Madeline*, p. 55.
75 Wootton, *Consuming Keats*, p. 109.
76 John Barnard, *John Keats* (Cambridge: Cambridge University Press, 1987), p. 71.
77 Whale, *Critical Issues*, p. 65.
78 Thomas McFarland, *The Masks of Keats. The Endeavours of a Poet* (Oxford and New York: Oxford University Press, 2000), p. 33.
79 Whale, *Critical Issues*, p. 57.
80 Keats, *Letters 1814–21*, ed. Rollins, Vol. II, No. 159, p. 70. Other letters follow that indicate this was an ongoing concern.
81 John Ruskin, 'Appendix to MSS of Modern Painters Vol. II', in E. T. Cook and Alexander Wedderburn, eds, *The Works of John Ruskin Vol. IV Modern Painters, Vol. II containing Part III Sections I and II of the Imaginative and Theoretical Faculties* (London: George Allen, 1903), pp. 363–83, pp. 379–80.
82 Quoted without precise reference in Grylls, *Portrait of Rossetti*, p. 49.
83 Deborah Cherry and Griselda Pollock, 'Woman as Sign in Pre-Raphaelite Literature: A Study of the Representation of Elizabeth Siddall', *Art History*, Vol. 7 No. 2 (1984), pp. 206–27, p. 221 argues this purely in artistic terms and with reference to his adoption of a more robust style of oil portraiture in which principally Fanny Cornforth and not Siddal sat as model. No extrapolated claim is made, nor could be substantiated.
84 Wootton, *Consuming Keats*, p. 7.
85 Richard Marggraf Turley, *Keats's Boyish Imagination* (London: Routledge, 2004), pp. 68–71.
86 *Ibid.*, pp. 48–9.
87 Whale, *Critical Issues*, p. 73.
88 Stillinger, *Reading The Eve of St Agnes*, p. 70.
89 An alternative reading may be found in Jacqueline Schoemaker, 'Female Empathy to Manliness: Keats in 1819', in C. C. Barfoot, ed., *Romantic Keats and Romantic Carlyle. The Fusions and Confusions of Literary Periods* (Amsterdam and Atlanta, GA: Rodopi B. V., 1999), pp. 79–94, pp. 85–7. The lady is not dominant because the reader only learns of her through him, and the extent to which she has blinded him is unclear.
90 Christopher Ricks, *Keats and Embarrassment* (London and Oxford: Oxford University Press), pp. 90–1.
91 Hassett, 'Elizabeth Siddal's Poetry', p. 460.

92 Allan C. Christensen, 'Newtonian and Goethean Colour in the Poetry of Keats', in Barfoot, ed., *Romantic Keats and Romantic Carlyle*, pp. 53–62.
93 Ricks, *Keats and Embarrassment*, p. 96.
94 The etymological relationships in this sequence are expounded in Helsinger, *Poetry and the Pre-Raphaelite Arts*, pp. 96–8.
95 Barnard, *John Keats*, p. 6 speculates that Keats equated Lamia with poetic imagination, meaning that a poet may fall victim to it. Ruskin, given his verdict on Keats's mental state, appears to have arrived at the same conclusion.
96 Keats, *Letters*, Vol. I, No. 39, p. 173 and Vol. I, No. 43, p. 186.
97 *Ibid.*, Vol. I, No. 96, p. 325.
98 Schoemaker, 'Female Empathy to Manliness', p. 83.
99 Whale, *Critical Issues*, p. 68.
100 Stillinger, *The Hoodwinking of Madeline*, p. 53.
101 McFarland, *The Masks of Keats*, pp. 1–25.
102 *Ibid.*, pp. 26–8.
103 *Ibid.*, pp. 55–6.
104 Keats, *Letters*, Vol. II, No. 310, p. 359.
105 *Ibid.*, Vol. II, No. 318, p. 378.
106 Matthews, *Poetical Remains*, pp. 115–17.
107 Stillinger, *Reading The Eve of St Agnes*, p. 9 quotes Keats as favouring the 'magic' of spontaneous creativity, but also recognizes the existence of multiple texts: drafts and fair copy manuscripts and editorially variant versions.
108 Barnard, *John Keats*, pp. 68–9, 84, 88 argues that in the final texts of *Isabella* and *The Eve of St Agnes* Keats struggled to achieve a balance between sentimentality and an appeal to contemporary taste, and that changes made by J. H. Reynolds and Richard Woodhouse resulted in versions not necessarily what Keats would have wanted.
109 W. M. Rossetti, *The Life of John Keats*, pp. 192–4.
110 Rollins, *The Letters of John Keats*, Vol. I, No. 26, p. 142. Keats thought his presiding figure was Shakespeare and he refers elsewhere to the 'Genius of Poetry that must work out its own salvation in a man ... by sensation and watchfulness in itself'. *Ibid.*, No. 110, p. 373.

Conclusion:
Contextualizing Elizabeth Siddal

Siddal's poems seek to explore and rationalize paradoxes and dualisms. They evaluate and balance opposing ideas to create a pathway to self-knowledge, so that in the dichotomy between voice and silence Siddal points the reader towards the liberating nature of communication with the self, or between women, or beyond death or through the use of non-speech text. Similarly, in their attempt to reconcile mid-century feminism with the demands of the patriarchal society it was challenging, Siddal's poems commend the opportunities presented by female self-determination and autonomy, such as financial and moral independence and the ability to access the transformative potency of women's poetry. Siddal contends that a woman's persona is subject to the demands of two conflicting entities, the spectral and the physical body, but her poems postulate that the preponderance of the spectral self presents a viable means of experiencing an extended range of emotion, of coping with grief and loss, of escaping the self and creating an alter-ego. In the power struggle between human and divine love the solution is less clear-cut. Spiritual love is perceived as being more significant than a sexual relationship or worship of physical beauty, but none of these bring the security and fulfilment Siddal's speakers find in the self-reliance and autonomy that emerge during and from conscious debate with the self.

These dualisms emanate from contexts that are themselves paradoxical. Dante Rossetti's iconic depictions of female beauty and sexuality are at odds with the mid-Victorian Evangelical and Anglo-Catholic revivals; reluctant to engage with the demands of the established church, he instigated a cult of beauty that required allegiance to its own system of ethics and beliefs. He worshipped Siddal, yet their powerful, complex and emotive association is itself dualistic as she was not his only muse. His sonnet sequence played a decisive part in the development of the genre, but it returned to Renaissance precedent and perpetrated a stereotypical image of dependent Victorian womanhood, one which Siddal forcibly rejected. Swinburne and Siddal both engaged with a ballad tradition that had its roots in medieval society, yet they were extending and developing it during a period of concentrated and unprecedented economic and social change. Swinburne was Siddal's closest friend yet knew nothing of her poetry writing. The ballad is essentially an oral medium but Siddal's speakers have fractured voices. Siddal was connected to the Langham Place Group but not by virtue of any overt feminist sympathy; the relationship came about because of her association with Rossetti and Ruskin, whose perceptions of women and their creativeness varied from the paternal to the surprisingly reactionary. The position of middle-class women was being openly questioned amid demands for their financial, legal, educational and even political parity with men at a time when Siddal was forced to accept male patronage to pursue her artistic ambitions, women were not allowed to attend the Royal Academy, and models were regarded as little better than prostitutes. Keats was feted by the PRB as their most significant literary influence, yet like Siddal he became their construct, designed to support their individual philosophies. His poems inspired numerous images, but it is these and not his poetic texts that signified 'Keats' to Victorian audiences. Keats's poems of sensation represented a yearning for the past at a time of emerging scientific realism and progress. They constituted an element of escape that found its equivalent in Siddal's sporadic physical and emotional withdrawal from Pre-Raphaelite society and her desire to make her interpretations of Keats's work both individual and ambiguous.

Paradox, however, runs deeper than its manifestation in Siddal's poems and the contexts that provoked their writing. It signifies the essence of what it means to recover or uncover a female poet whose poetics was structured around the ambiguous and the enigmatic, and whose work was literally a secret. Context is vital to the understanding of meaning in these poems but in order to

Conclusion: Contextualizing Elizabeth Siddal 259

avoid a biographical reading these contexts need to go beyond the biographic. Siddal is inextricably fixed into the Pre-Raphaelite narrative upon which she is dependent as an artist at least, but such dependence gives her an assumed identity while smothering her own. Her poetic voice ceases to be individual as long as the reader is reminded of her Pre-Raphaelite context and her relationship with so colourful a figure as Dante Rossetti, making it difficult to separate Siddal from her life-story, especially as she is made tangible by the fantasy Pre-Raphaelitism weaves around her. Siddal was an appendage to the Pre-Raphaelite circle from which she was excluded by her gender whilst, ironically, being worshipped for her beauty and valued as a muse. The recovery of her art and poetry is therefore bound up in an ideology that simultaneously produced and silenced her work.[1] Most commentators consider her art and poems not only Pre-Raphaelite, but autobiographical, an opinion reinforced by the regular inclusion of biographical material based on anecdotal evidence in the preface to publications of her work. The myth of her rescue from poverty and semi-illiteracy by Rossetti continues to be spread, which strengthens the case for her representation not as a person but as a permanent legend, an absent figure just as she appeared in life. This does nothing to aid understanding of Siddal the individual and arguably influences too much the way her texts have been read. Victorian women's poetry was supposedly written out of a sentimental tradition which limited female creativity to a private and domestic sphere of experience and emotion. If biographical discourse is exclusively relied upon it overflows into readings which then reiterate Victorian gender ideology and discourage analysis of motivation, reasoning and methodology. Siddal the person is constantly brought to the surface, stressing the very thing recovery of her poetic voice is aiming to counter. Emphasis on Siddal as a producer of art tends to be negated by the presence of Rossetti as her mentor, but establishing a history beyond the influence of the Pre-Raphaelites is problematic. To compound the issue, as their aesthetic created hers it will automatically be recycled if and when her history is uncovered, and this counterproductive move stops Siddal ever being considered as an artist in her own right.[2]

Logically, Siddal cannot be completely isolated from the Pre-Raphaelites, especially as they make up that part of her history for which the most factual evidence exists, but their presence is diluted if her visual and poetic texts are distanced from an obvious biographical influence that continues to silence and instead are read as a means of understanding why she, in common with all Victorian women poets, was silenced in the first place. Her voice then becomes more a generic response to the frustration spawned by the attitudes of a patriarchal society in denial of the extent to which women were capable of creative, independent thought, and less likely to be mined for autobiographical inference. Most current Siddal scholars focus on her as a producer of art, something already public and therefore open to interpretation as part of the Pre-Raphaelite canon even while she was alive. This book has concentrated on her poems, secret thoughts that can be non-conformist and pursue a deeply personal agenda, and in order to look beyond the manuscript and printed word has subjected them to a more concentrated close reading than has been attempted before. Moreover, new contexts for the elucidation of meaning have been established. Siddal's biographical involvement with the men at their epicentres is *de facto*, but by emphasizing them as producers it moves each context further away from the one in which she is portrayed as a secondary figure because of her gender and their elevated literary status. Pre-Raphaelitism cannot and should not be ignored, but it can be decentred by placing it in the wider sphere of nineteenth-century culture and society. Read within these contexts Siddal's poems assume a different mantle. They need no longer be seen as slight, self-indulgent and predicated on loss and disillusionment, but rather as enabling and extending explorations of specific poetic and personal concerns like those broached by the acclaimed male poets whose texts have been examined here.

In the late 1960s feminist critics began to consider whether such a thing as "women's writing" existed, and if so whether it should be given a distinct entity. Essentialists believe there is a fundamental distinction, arising from social and economic factors rather than biological determination, whereas this book has embraced the opposite, relativist, approach: the analysis of work by men and women by male and female authors and the avoidance of separate anthologies can mitigate against the marginalization of women's voices encouraged by existing social patriarchy and gender bias.

A by-product of the wider discussion has been the discovery of a tradition of women's writing, specifically numerous nineteenth-century works temporarily forgotten or ignored, whose writers provide Siddal with another context. They fell out of favour as the twentieth century brought new social and political climates that devalued the ideals they represented; jingoism, prudery, colonialism, sentimentality, religious fervour and an acceptance of a woman's secondary role were now deemed inappropriate, the modern reader wanting irony and analysis not florid description delivered in archaic language. Victorianism would be popular again but amid a simultaneous return to traditional patriarchy its women writers didn't automatically resurface. It is only since the 1980s that the feminist debate has become more self-critical and differentiated, encompassing elements of psychoanalysis, gynocriticism, Marxism, post-structuralism and new historicism to readmit more than a hundred women poets to the nineteenth-century canon. A new historicist approach does not focus on the aesthetic value of a text but researches the contexts of its production, consumption and status. It argues that literature cannot be appreciated without knowing its historical bearings, how, why and by whom it came to be written. It resists dogmatic assertions and offers itself as a more suggestive approach to criticism, using contexts to elucidate and explain textual references, and this has helped to put flesh on the ostensibly meagre bones of Siddal's poems, to extrapolate influences and possible motives, to reinterpret her experience as a writer and suggest new readings for her work – readings that challenge how women are supposed to think, act and feel.

Siddal did not intend to have a public voice so presumably did not want to be heard, using her poems instead purely as a means of conversing or struggling with her inner self. The holding up of her private thoughts to intense scrutiny exposes the final paradox. Whether read as autobiography or literary exploration these poems and any conclusions drawn from them constitute perhaps the most solid body of evidence likely to be gathered about one who appears to have fashioned herself into a reclusive observer rather than participant, deliberately choosing to be enigmatic and withdrawn, sickly and only half-alive.[3] They, and the critical reception they garner, are now a matter of public record and cannot help but inform attitudes towards their creator, because published documents are rhetorical statements with multiple meanings imposed on them by the reader. The relationship between poet and reader can be problematic if the image presented is one the reader takes literally. Any deviation could be then regarded as hypocrisy, as in the case of L. E. L. and Hemans who needed to publish to support families, yet whose supposedly untoward personal lives at times attracted more interest than their work. Their search for a poetic identity became bound up in public reception and the fame that came with it once the spread of literacy and printing allowed their work to be commented on more widely than ever before. The mystery that surrounded both women most likely increased reader numbers but Hemans was the more influential as the century wore on; her heroines epitomized domestic virtue, courage, tenacity and religious conviction, qualities synonymous with 'Victorian values'. Domestic duty and fame, however, did not create the perfect fit. Artistic achievement was the ultimate goal, but to indulge it meant taking the poet out of the domestic sphere which many women still believed to be the higher calling. Fame, albeit encourage by her mother, didn't bring Hemans happiness as it destroyed her marriage. Barrett Browning was able to balance the two but her personal circumstances were very different. Rossetti was deeply committed to her writing career but as a single woman, part of a notable scholastic family and an associate of the PRB, she was facilitated in making it her profession. She, Barrett Browning, Hemans *et al.* wrote poetry that was aimed outwards, towards wider British society, post-Napoleonic Europe and beyond. They commented on the revolutionary transformation of the old order into modern, more liberal states and showed an awareness of other cultures and literatures. They sought a readership in order to make a living and to voice social, political and aesthetic ideologies, whereas Siddal was the total opposite. She was entirely inward, her poems stateless and timeless and seemingly not intended for the public domain. By all accounts she shunned the limelight, not even exploiting the recognition she gained in her lifetime for her artwork. Her influence as a poet cannot be measured according to sales or contemporary critical reception, and neither contemporaries nor immediate successors had the benefit of seeing her in print. By the time her poems

Conclusion: Contextualizing Elizabeth Siddal

were made public the cultural landscape was very different, making it so important that they be read and judged today within her mid-Victorian contexts.

This book hinged upon reading Siddal alongside some of the most illustrious nineteenth-century male poets, but contextualizing Siddal with women writers has also been illuminating. Tragedy, loss, betrayal and desertion are themes common to all, but ambiguity and structural simplicity, dualism and elusiveness mark Siddal's poems out as something more unusual. Hers was a truly lost voice compared with those that were once known but fell from fashion to be rediscovered or reinvigorated later. Writing in secret allowed it to be more direct, reflecting women's anger at their lack of effective speech and the double standards that pertained regarding permissible sexual behaviour. Siddal was not part of a dialogue about the role and position of women, the relative importance of romantic love or the significance of faith, but her private participation in such debates is obvious. She was responding to changes in society that were in turn influencing the prevailing aesthetic and refashioning what constituted femininity and religious experience, making these poems valuable historical documents in their own right. They also have intrinsic merit, realized through a comprehensive analysis of Siddal's technique, concerns and influences, always with awareness of the prevailing political and socio-cultural contexts. And this methodology could have further application, regardless of gender, oeuvre or time period. Siddal, Swinburne, Keats, Tennyson and Rossetti would once have been considered unlikely bedfellows, but brought together they have thrown light on a collection previously overlooked or undervalued, and removed Siddal further from a life-history that compromised her literary worth. Other 'lost' voices might yet be similarly retrieved.

Notes

1 Chapman, *The Afterlife of Christina Rossetti*, p. 38.
2 *Ibid.*, p. 42.
3 Elisabeth Bronfen, *Over Her Dead Body. Death, Femininity and the Aesthetic* (Manchester: Manchester University Press, 1992), p. 168.

Bibliography

Manuscript sources

Ashmolean Museum, Oxford, Western Art Print Room.
Bryson Bequest 1977.182, Rossetti Family Letters of DG, WM and Christina Rossetti, and Poems and some Drawings by Elizabeth Siddal. Including Bryson 2599c–2599j, Bryson 2915 and 2916, fair copies by D. G. and W. M. Rossetti.
Brotherton Library, University of Leeds, Special Collections
  MS.19C Swinburne. Handlist 154, Literary Manuscripts of A. C. Swinburne together with some transcriptions of other works and some related material 1851–1999, 94 items, 79 bound 15 unbound.
Girton College Library and Archive, Cambridge University.
GCPP Parkes 5, correspondence between Bessie Rayner Parkes and Barbara Leigh Smith Bodichon.
GCPP Parkes 9, correspondence between Bessie Rayner Parkes and Dante Gabriel Rossetti and John Ruskin *et al*.
GCPP Parkes 11, newspaper articles about the relationship between Elizabeth Siddal and Dante Gabriel Rossetti.
GCPP 15, Crompton, Margaret, Prelude to Arcadia (*c*.1970), unpublished biography of the early life of Bessie Rayner Parkes.

Poetry editions

Arnold, Matthew, *Poems 1840–1866*, ed. R. A. Scott-James (London: J. M. Dent and Co., 1908).
Barrett Browning, Elizabeth, *Poetical Works in Six Volumes*, Vol. IV (London: Smith Elder and Co., 1890).
Barrett Browning, Elizabeth, *Aurora Leigh and other Poems*, ed. Cora Kaplan (London: The Women's Press, 1978).
Barrett Browning, Elizabeth, *Sonnets from the Portuguese and other Poems* (New York: Dover Publications Inc., 1992).

Barrett Browning, Elizabeth, *Selected Writings*, eds Josie Billington and Philip Davies (Oxford: Oxford University Press, 2014).
Browning, Robert, *Pippa Passes, with an introduction by Arthur Symons* (London: Forgotten Books, 2012 [1906]).
Child, Francis James, ed. *The English and Scottish Popular Ballads*, 5 vols (New York: Cooper Square Publishers Inc., 1962 [3rd edn 1882]).
Hemans, Felicia, *Selected Poems, Letters, Reception Materials*, ed. Susan J. Wolfson (Princeton and Oxford: Princeton University Press, 2000).
Hemans, Felicia, *Selected Poems, Prose and Letters*, ed. Gary Kelly (Canada: Broadview Literary Texts, 2002).
Keats, John, *Complete Poems*, ed. Paul Wright (Ware, Hertfordshire: Wordsworth Editions Ltd, 1994).
Landon, Letitia Elizabeth, *The Improvisatrice*, ed. Jonathan Wordsworth (Poole and New York: Woodstock Books, 1996).
Rossetti, Christina, *The Complete Poems*, ed. R. W. Crump (London: Penguin Books, 2001).
Rossetti, Dante Gabriel, *The House of Life. A Sonnet Sequence*, ed. Paull Franklin Baum (Cambridge, Mass.: Harvard University Press, 1928).
Rossetti, Dante Gabriel, *Poems*, ed. Oswald Doughty (London: J. M. Dent and Sons Ltd, 1957).
Rossetti, Dante Gabriel, *Selected Poems and Translations*, ed. Clive Wilmer (Manchester: Carcanet Press Ltd, 1991).
Rossetti, Dante Gabriel, *Collected Poetry and Prose*, ed. Jerome McGann (New Haven and London: Yale University Press, 2003).
Rossetti, Dante Gabriel, *The House of Life. A Sonnet Sequence*, Variorum Edition, ed. Roger C. Lewis (Cambridge: Boydell & Brewer, 2007).
Scott, Sir Walter, *Minstrelsy of the Scottish Border 1802–3*, 4 vols, ed. T. F. Henderson (London and Edinburgh: Oliver & Boyd, 1932).
Siddal, Elizabeth, *Poems and Drawings*, eds Roger C. Lewis and Mark Samuels Lasner (Wolfville, Nova Scotia, Canada: Wombat Press, 1978).
Siddall, Elizabeth, *My Ladys Soul. The Poems of Elizabeth Siddall edited with an introduction and notes by Serena Trowbridge* (Brighton: Victorian Secrets Ltd, 2018).
Swinburne, Algernon Charles, *Posthumous Poems*, eds Edmund Gosse and Thomas James Wise (London: William Heinemann, 1917).
Swinburne, Algernon Charles, *Ballads of the English Border*, ed. William A. MacInnes (London: William Heinemann, 1925).
Swinburne, Algernon Charles, *Poems and Ballads and Atalanta in Calydon*, ed. Kenneth Haynes (Harmondsworth: Penguin Books Ltd, 2000).
Swinburne, Algernon Charles, *Major Poems and Selected Prose*, ed. Jerome McGann and Charles L. Sligh (Newhaven: Yale University Press, 2004).
Tennyson, Alfred Lord, *Poems*, ed. Christopher Ricks (London and Harlow: Longmans, Green and Co. Ltd, 1969).

Tennyson, Alfred Lord, *Tennyson. A Selected Edition*, ed. Christopher Ricks (Harlow: Pearson Education Ltd, revised edn, 2007).

(Principally) nineteenth-century sources

Belloc (née Parkes), Bessie Rayner, *A Passing World* (London: Ward and Downey Ltd, 1897).

Brown, Ford Madox, *Diary*, ed. Virginia Surtees (New Haven and London: Yale University Press, 1981).

Burne-Jones, Georgiana, *Memorials of Edward Burne-Jones*, 2 vols (London: Macmillan and Co. Ltd, 1904).

Caine, T. Hall, *Recollections of Dante Gabriel Rossetti* (London: Elliot Stock, 1882).

Hallam, Arthur, 'On Some of the Characteristics of Modern Poetry, and on the Lyrical Poems of Alfred Tennyson', *Englishman's Magazine* (August 1831), 616–21.

Howitt, Mary, *An Autobiography*, edited by her daughter Margaret Howitt (London: Isbister and Co. Ltd, 1889).

Hunt, W. Holman, *Pre-Raphaelitism and the Pre-Raphaelite Brotherhood*, 2 vols (London: Macmillan and Co. Ltd, 1905).

Keats, John, *Letters 1814–21*, 2 vols, ed. Edward Hyder Rollins (Cambridge: Cambridge University Press, 1958).

Milner, George, 'On Some Marginalia made by Dante Gabriel Rossetti in a Copy of Keats', *The Manchester Quarterly*, Vol. II (1883), 1–11.

Rossetti, William Michael, *The Life of Keats* (London: Walter Scott, 1887).

Rossetti, Dante Gabriel, *The Letters to William Allingham 1854–70*, ed. George Birkbeck Hill (London: T. Fisher Unwin, 1897).

Rossetti, Dante Gabriel, *Letters*, 4 vols, eds Oswald Doughty and John Robert Wahl (Oxford: Clarendon Press, 1965).

Rossetti, Dante Gabriel, *Correspondence with Jane Morris*, ed. John Bryson in association with Janet Crump Troxell (Oxford: Clarendon Press, 1976).

Rossetti, William Michael, ed. *Dante Gabriel Rossetti. His Family Letters with a Memoir*, 2 vols (London: Ellis and Elvey, 1895).

Rossetti, William Michael, ed. *Ruskin: Rossetti: Pre-Raphaelitism. Papers 1854–62* (London: George Allen, 1899).

Rossetti, William Michael, 'Dante Rossetti and Elizabeth Siddall', *Burlington Magazine*, No. 1 (May 1903), 273–95.

Rossetti, William Michael, *The PRB Journal. Diary of the Pre-Raphaelite Brotherhood 1849–53 together with other Pre-Raphaelite Documents*, ed. William E. Fredman (Oxford: Clarendon Press, 1975).

Ruskin, John, *Works*, eds E. T. Cook and Alexander Wedderburn, 39 vols (London: George Allen, 1903–12).
——, Vol. IV *Modern Painters Vol. II containing Part III of the Imaginative and Theoretical Faculties* (1903).
——, Vol. V *Modern Painters Vol. III* (1903).
——, Vol. VI *Modern Painters Vol. IV containing Part V of Mountain Beauty* (1904).
——, Vol. VII *Modern Painters Vol. V containing Leaf Beauty, Cloud Beauty and Ideas of Relation* (1905).
——, Vol. XIV *Academy Notes. Notes on Prout and Hunt and other Art Criticisms 1855–88* (1904).
——, Vol. XV *The Elements of Drawing and The Elements of Perspective and The Laws of Fésole* (1904).
——, Vol. XVIII 'Of Queens' Gardens' in *Sesame and Lilies* (1865), *The Ethics of Dust* (1866), *The Crown of Wild Olives* (1866), pp. 109–44 (1905).
——, Vol. XXXIII *The Bible of Amiens. Valle Crucis. The Art of England. The Pleasures of England* (1908).
——, Vol. XXXIV *The Storm-Cloud of the Nineteenth Century. On the Old Road. Ruskiniana* (1908).
——, Vol. XXXV *Praeterita and Dilecta* (1908).
——, Vol. XXXIV *Letters 1827–69* (1909).
Ruskin, John, *Diaries 1848–73*, eds Joan Evans and John Howard Whitehouse (Oxford: Clarendon Press, 1958).
Ruskin, John, *Sublime and Instructive. Letters to Louisa, Marchioness of Waterford, Anna Blunden and Ellen Heaton*, ed. Virginia Surtees (London: Michael Joseph Ltd, 1972).
Sharp, William, *Dante Gabriel Rossetti. A Record and a Study* (London: Macmillan and Co., 1882).
Swinburne, Algernon Charles, *Lesbia Brandon*, ed. Randolph Hughes (London: Falcon Press, 1952).
Swinburne, Algernon Charles, *Letters*, 6 vols, ed. Cecil Y. Lang (Newhaven: Yale University Press, 1959–62), Vol. I, 1854–69.
Swinburne, Algernon Charles, *New Writings by, or Miscellanea Nova et Curiosa. Being a Medley of Poems, Critical Essays, Hoaxes and Burlesques*, ed. Cecil Y. Lang (New York: Syracuse University Press, 1964).
Swinburne, Algernon Charles, *A Year's Letters*, ed. Francis Jacques Sypher (New York: New York University Press, 1974).
Watts-Dunton, Clara, *The Home Life of Swinburne* (London: A. M. Philpot, 1922).

Later sources

Abse, Joan, *John Ruskin. The Passionate Moralist* (London, Melbourne and New York: Quartet Books, 1980).
Adams, Eli, 'Woman Red in Tooth and Claw: Nature and the Feminine in Tennyson and Darwin', in Rebecca Stott, ed. *Tennyson* (London and New York: Addison Wesley Ltd, 1996), pp. 87–111.
Amigoni, David, *Victorian Literature* (Edinburgh: Edinburgh University Press, 2011).
Anderson, John M., 'The Triumph of Voice in Felicia Hemans's *The Forest Sanctuary*', in Nanora Sweet and Julie Melnyk, eds, *Felicia Hemans: Reimagining Poetry in the Nineteenth Century* (Basingstoke: Palgrave, 2001), pp. 55–72.
Angeli, Helen Rossetti, *Dante Gabriel Rossetti. His Friends and Enemies* (London: Hamish Hamilton Ltd, 1949).
Armstrong, Isobel, *Victorian Poetry. Poetry, Poetics and Politics* (London and New York: Routledge, 1993).
Armstrong, Isobel, and Bristow, Joseph with Sharrock, Cath, eds, *Nineteenth-Century Women Poets. An Oxford Anthology* (Oxford: Clarendon Press, 1996).
Armstrong, Isobel, 'The Pre-Raphaelites and Literature', in Elizabeth Prettejohn, ed., *The Cambridge Companion to the Pre-Raphaelites* (Cambridge: Cambridge University Press, 2012), pp. 15–31.
Arseneau, Mary, *Recovering Christina Rossetti. Female Community and Incarnational Poetics* (Basingstoke and New York: Palgrave Macmillan, 2004).
Avery, Simon, and Stott, Rebecca, *Elizabeth Barrett Browning* (Edinburgh: Pearson Education Ltd, 2003).
Avery, Simon, ''Twixt Church and Palace of a Florence Street: Elizabeth Barrett Browning and Italy', in Simon Avery and Rebecca Stott, *Elizabeth Barrett Browning* (Edinburgh: Pearson Education Ltd, 2003), pp. 156–80.
Barfoot, C. C., ed., *Romantic Keats and Romantic Carlyle. The Fusions and Confusions of Literary Periods* (Amsterdam and Atlanta, GA: Rodopi B.V., 1999).
Barlow, Paul, 'Pre-Raphaelitism and Post-Raphaelitism: the articulation of fantasy and the problem of pictorial space', in Marcia Pointon, ed., *Pre-Raphaelites Re-viewed* (Manchester and New York: Manchester University Press, 1989), pp. 66–82.
Barnard, John, *John Keats* (Cambridge: Cambridge University Press, 1987).
Barringer, Tim, *Reading the Pre-Raphaelites* (New Haven and London: Yale University Press, 1998).

Barringer, Tim, Rosenfeld, Jason, and Smith, Alison, eds, *The Pre-Raphaelites. Victorian Avant-Garde* (London: Tate Publishing, 2012).
Barton, Anna, *Tennyson's Name. Identity and Responsibility in the Poetry of Alfred Lord Tennyson* (Aldershot: Ashgate Publishing, 2008).
Bell, Quentin, *A New and Noble School. The Pre-Raphaelites* (London: Macdonald and Co. Ltd, 1982).
Bentley, D. M. R., '"La Bocca mi Baciò": The Love Kiss in the Works of Dante Gabriel Rossetti', *The Journal of Pre-Raphaelite Studies*, Vol. 16 (Spring 2007), 31–44.
Berg, Maggie, 'A Neglected Voice: Elizabeth Siddal', *Dalhousie Review* (1980–81), 151–6.
Billone, Amy Christine, *Little Songs: Women, Silence and the Nineteenth Century Sonnet* (Columbus: Ohio State University, 2007).
Birch, Dinah, ed., *Ruskin and the Dawn of the Modern* (Oxford: Oxford University Press, 1999).
Birch, Dinah, and O'Gorman, Francis, eds, *Ruskin and Gender* (London: Palgrave, 2002).
Blain, Virginia, ed., *Victorian Women Poets. A New Annotated Anthology* (Harlow: Pearson, 2001).
Bronfen, Elisabeth, *Over Her Dead Body. Death, Femininity and the Aesthetic* (Manchester: Manchester University Press, 1992).
Buchanan, Lindal, '"Doing Battle with Forgotten Ghosts": Carnival, Discourse and Degradation in Tennyson's *The Princess*', *Victorian Poetry*, Vol. 39, No. 4 (Winter 2001), 573–95.
Bullen, J. B., *Rossetti: Painter and Poet* (London: Francis Lincoln Ltd, 2011).
Burlinson, Kathryn, *Christina Rossetti* (Plymouth: Northcote House Publishers, 1998).
Campbell, Matthew, 'The Victorian Sonnet', in A. D. Cousins and Peter Howarth, eds, *The Cambridge Companion to the Sonnet* (Cambridge: Cambridge University Press, 2011), pp. 204–24.
Chapman, Alison, *The Afterlife of Christina Rossetti* (Basingstoke: Macmillan Press Ltd, 2000).
Chapman, Alison, 'Sonnet and Sonnet Sequence', in Richard Cronin, Alison Chapman and Antony H. Harrison, eds, *A Companion to Victorian Poetry* (Oxford: Blackwell Publishers Ltd, 2002), pp. 99–114.
Cherry, Deborah, *Painting Women. Victorian Women Artists* (London and New York: Routledge, 1993).
Deborah Cherry, 'Elizabeth Eleanor Siddall (1828–62)', in Elizabeth Prettejohn, ed., *The Cambridge Companion to the Pre-Raphaelites* (Cambridge: Cambridge University Press, 2012), pp. 183–95.
Cherry, Deborah, and Pollock, Griselda, 'Woman as Sign in Pre-Raphaelite Literature: A Study of the Representation of Elizabeth Siddall', *Art History*, Vol. 7, No. 2 (1984), 206–27.

Christensen, Allan C., 'Newtonian and Goethean Colours in the Poetry of Keats', in C. C. Barfoot, ed., *Romantic Keats and Romantic Carlyle. The Fusions and Confusions of Literary Periods* (Amsterdam and Atlanta, GA: Rodopi B.V., 1999), pp. 53–62.

Clapp-Intyre, Alisa, 'Marginalized Musical Interludes: Tennyson's Critique of Conventionality in *The Princess*', *Victorian Poetry*, Vol. 38, No. 2 (Summer 2000), 227–48.

Codell, Julie F., 'Painting Keats: Pre-Raphaelite Artists Between Social Transgressions and Painterly Conventions', *Victorian Poetry*, Vol. 33, Nos 3–4 (Autumn–Winter 1995), 341–70.

Connor, Patrick, *Savage Ruskin* (London and Basingstoke: Macmillan Press Ltd, 1979).

Cousins, A. D., and Howarth, Peter, eds, *The Cambridge Companion to the Sonnet* (Cambridge: Cambridge University Press, 2011).

Cronin, Richard, *Romantic Victorians: English Literature 1824–1840* (Palgrave: Basingstoke and New York, 2001).

Cronin, Richard, Chapman, Alison, and Harrison, Antony H., eds, *A Companion to Victorian Poetry* (Oxford: Blackwell Publishers Ltd, 2002).

Cruise, Colin, *Pre-Raphaelite Drawing* (London: Thames & Hudson Ltd, 2011).

Cruise, Colin, 'Pre-Raphaelite Drawing', in Elizabeth Prettejohn, ed., *The Cambridge Companion to the Pre-Raphaelites* (Cambridge: Cambridge University Press, 2012), pp. 47–61.

D'Amico, Diane, 'Christina Rossetti and the English Women's Journal', *The Journal of Pre-Raphaelite Studies*, No. 3 (Spring 1994), 20–4.

Distiller, Natasha, *Desire and Gender in the Sonnet Tradition* (Basingstoke: Palgrave Macmillan, 2008).

Dunicliff, Joy, *The Traveller on the Hill-top. Mary Howitt the Famous Victorian Authoress* (Leek, Staffordshire: Churnet Valley Books, 1998).

Eagleton, Terry, 'Tennyson: Politics and Sexuality in *The Princess* and *In Memoriam*', in Rebecca Stott, *Tennyson* (London and New York: Addison Wesley Longman Ltd, 1996), pp. 76–86.

Ehnenn, Jill R., '"Strong Traivelling": Re-visions of Women's Subjectivity and Female Labour in the Ballad-Work of Elizabeth Siddal', *Victorian Poetry*, Vol. 52, No. 2 (Summer 2014), 251–76.

Ehrenpreis, Anne Henry, 'Swinburne's Edition of Popular Ballads', *Publications of the Modern Language Association of America (PMLA)*, Vol. 78 (December 1963), 559–71.

Ehrenpreis, Anne Henry, ed., *The Literary Ballad* (London: Edward Arnold Ltd, 1966).

Flint, Kate, *The Victorians and Visual Imagination* (Cambridge: Cambridge University Press, 2000).

Fuller, Jean Overton, *Swinburne. A Critical Biography* (London: Chatto & Windus, 1968).
Ford, George. H., *Keats and the Victorians. A Study of his Influence and Rise to Fame 1821–95* (London: Archon Books, 1962).
Foucault, Michel, *The History of Sexuality*, 3 vols (New York: Vintage Press, 1990).
Gaunt, William, *The Pre-Raphaelite Tragedy* (London: Jonathan Cape, 1942).
George, J.-A., 'Poetry in Translation', in Richard Cronin, Alison Chapman and Anthony H. Harrison, eds, *A Companion to Victorian Poetry* (Oxford: Blackwell Publishers Ltd, 2002).
Giebelhausen, Michaela, 'The Religious and Intellectual Background', in Elizabeth Prettejohn, ed., *The Cambridge Companion to the Pre-Raphaelites* (Cambridge: Cambridge University Press, 2012), pp. 62–75.
Gilbert, Sandra M., and Gubar, Susan, *The Madwoman in the Attic. The Woman Writer and the Nineteenth-Century Literary Imagination* (New Haven and London: Yale University Press, Second Edition, 2000).
Gitter, Elizabeth G., 'The Power of Women's Hair in the Victorian Imagination', *PMLA*, Vol. 99, No. 5 (October 1984), 939–54.
Gittings, Robert, *John Keats: The Living Year 21 September 1818 to 21 September 1819* (London: William Heinemann Ltd, 1954).
Gosse, Edmund, *The Life of Algernon Charles Swinburne* (London: Macmillan and Co. Ltd, 1917).
Grylls, Rosalie, *Portrait of Rossetti* (Carbondale, Ill.: Illinois University Press, 1964).
Hardy, Maximillian, 'John Keats and the Pre-Raphaelite Brotherhood', *The Review of the Pre-Raphaelite Society*, Vol. XII, No. 1 (Spring 2004), 1–16.
Harris, Jose, 'Ruskin and Social Reform', in Dinah Birch, ed., *Ruskin and the Dawn of the Modern* (Oxford: Oxford University Press, 1999), pp. 7–33.
Harrison, Anthony H., *Christina Rossetti in Context* (Brighton: Harvester Press, 1988).
Harrison, Antony H., 'Arthurian Poetry and Medievalism', in Richard Cronin, Alison Chapman, and Antony H. Harrison, eds, *A Companion to Victorian Poetry* (Oxford: Blackwell Publishers Ltd, 2002), 246–61.
Hassett, Constance W., 'Elizabeth Siddal's Poetry: A Problem and Some Suggestions', *Victorian Poetry*, Vol. 35, No. 4 (1997), 443–70.
Hassett, Constance W., *Christina Rossetti. The Patience of Style* (Charlottesville and London: University of Virginia Press, 2005).
Hawksley, Lucinda, *Lizzie Siddal. The Tragedy of a Pre-Raphaelite Supermodel* (London: André Deutsche, 2004).

Helsinger, Elizabeth K., *Poetry and the Pre-Raphaelite Arts. Dante Gabriel Rossetti and William Morris* (New Haven and London: Yale University Press, 2008).
Henderson, Philip, *Swinburne: The Portrait of a Poet* (London: Routledge & Kegan Paul, 1974).
Herstein, Sheila R., *A Mid-Victorian Feminist, Barbara Leigh Smith Bodichon* (New Haven and London: Yale University Press, 1985).
Hill, Robert W. Jnr, ed., *Tennyson's Poetry* (New York: W.W. Norton and Co. Inc., 1999).
Himmelfarb, Gertrude, 'Household Gods and Goddesses', in Robert W. Hill Jnr, ed., *Tennyson's Poetry* (New York: W. W. Norton and Co. Inc., 1999), pp. 667–75.
Hilton, Timothy, *The Pre-Raphaelites* (London: Thames & Hudson, 1970).
Hilton, Timothy, *Keats and His World* (London: Thames & Hudson, 1971).
Hilton, Tim, *John Ruskin. The Early Years 1819–59* (New Haven and London: Yale University Press, 1985).
Hilton, Tim, *John Ruskin. The Later Years* (New Haven and London: Yale University Press, 2000).
Holmes, John, *Dante Gabriel Rossetti and the Late Victorian Sonnet Sequence* (Aldershot: Ashgate Publishing Ltd, 2005).
Homans, Margaret, *Women Writers and Poetic Identity. Dorothy Wordsworth, Emily Brontë and Emily Dickinson* (New Jersey: Princeton University Press, 1980).
Homans, Margaret, 'Keats Reading Women, Women Reading Keats', *Studies in Romanticism* (Boston University), Vol. 29, No. 3 (Fall 1990), 341–70.
Hood, James, *Divining Desire. Tennyson and the Poetics of Transcendence* (Aldershot, Hampshire and Burlington, Vermont: Ashgate Publishing Ltd, 2000).
Hunt, John Dixon, *The Wider Sea. A Life of John Ruskin* (London, Melbourne and Toronto: J. M. Dent and Sons Ltd, 1982).
Hunt, Violet, *The Wife of Rossetti. Her Life and Death* (London: Bodley head, 1932).
Hyder, Clyde K., 'Swinburne and the Popular Ballad', *PMLA*, Vol. 46 (March 1934), 295–309.
Hyder, Clyde K., ed., *Swinburne. The Critical Heritage* (London: Routledge & Kegan Paul, 1970).
Joseph, Gerhard, *Tennyson and the Text* (Cambridge: Cambridge University Press, 1992).
Kaplan, Cora, *Questions for Feminism. Sea Changes, Culture and Feminism* (London: Verso, 1986).

Kaplan, Cora, 'Language and Gender', in Dennis Walder, ed., *Literature in the Modern World. Critical Essays and Documents* (Oxford: Open University Press, 1990), pp. 310–16.

Killham, John, *Tennyson and The Princess. Reflections of an Age* (London: The University of London Athlone Press, 1958).

Kozicki, Henry, 'Tennyson's "Tears, Idle Tears": The Case for Violet', *Victorian Poetry*, Vol. 24, No. 2 (Summer 1986), 99–113.

Lacey, Candida Ann, ed., *Barbara Leigh Smith Bodichon and the Langham Place Group* (New York and London: Routledge & Kegan Paul, 1987).

Lang, Cecil Y., ed., *The Pre-Raphaelites and their Circle* (Chicago and London: University of Chicago Press, 1975).

Levine, Phillipa, *Victorian Feminism 1850–1900* (London: Hutchinson Education, 1987).

Macleod, Diane Sachko, *Art and the Victorian Middle Class: Money and the making of Cultural Identity* (Cambridge: Cambridge University Press, 1996).

Marsh, Jan, *Pre-Raphaelite Sisterhood* (London: Quartet Books, 1985).

Marsh, Jan, *Pre-Raphaelite Women. Images of Femininity in Pre-Raphaelite Art* (London: Weidenfeld & Nicolson, 1987).

Marsh, Jan, *The Legend of Elizabeth Siddal* (London: Quartet Books, 1989).

Marsh, Jan, and Nunn, Pamela Gerrish, *Women Artists and the Pre-Raphaelite Movement* (London: Virago Press Ltd, 1989).

Marsh, Jan, *Elizabeth Siddal. Pre-Raphaelite Artist 1829–62* (Sheffield: Ruskin Gallery, 1991).

Marsh, Jan, and Nunn, Pamela Gerrish, *Pre-Raphaelite Women Artists* (London: Thames & Hudson Ltd, 1998).

Marsh, Jan, *Dante Gabriel Rossetti. Painter and Poet* (London: Phoenix Paperback Edition, 2005).

Matthews, G. M. ed., *Keats. The Critical Heritage* (London: Routledge & Kegan Paul, 1971).

Matthews, Samantha, *Poetical Remains. Poets' Graves, Bodies and Books in the Nineteenth Century* (Oxford: Oxford University Press, 2004).

Maxwell, Catherine, *Swinburne* (Tavistock, Devon: Northcote House Publishers Ltd, 2006).

Maxwell, Catherine, *Second Sight. The Visionary Imagination in Late Victorian Literature* (Manchester: Manchester University Press, 2008).

Maxwell, Catherine, 'Algernon Charles Swinburne (1837–1909)', in Elizabeth Prettejohn, ed., *The Cambridge Companion to the Pre-Raphaelites* (Cambridge: Cambridge University Press, 2002), pp. 233–49.

Maynard, John, 'Sexuality and Love', in Richard Cronin, Alison Chapman and Antony H. Harrison, eds, *A Companion to Victorian Poetry* (Oxford: Blackwell Publishers Ltd, 2002), pp. 543–66.

McFarland, Thomas, *The Masks of Keats. The Endeavour of a Poet* (Oxford and New York: Oxford University Press, 2000).
McGann, Jerome J., *Swinburne. An Experiment in Criticism* (Chicago and London: The University of Chicago Press, 1972).
McGann, Jerome J., *Dante Gabriel Rossetti and the Game That Must be Lost* (New Haven and London: Yale University Press, 2000).
McGann, Jerome J., 'The Poetry of Dante Gabriel Rossetti (1828–82)', in Elizabeth Prettjohn, ed., *The Cambridge Companion to the Pre-Raphaelites* (Cambridge: Cambridge University Press, 2012), pp. 89–102.
McSweeney, Kerry, *What's the Import? Nineteenth-Century Poems and Contemporary Critical Practice* (Montreal and Kingston: McGill-Queens' University Press, 2007).
Melnyk, Julie, 'Hemans's Later Poetry. Religion and the Vatic Poet', in Nanora Sweet and Julie Melnyk, eds, *Felicia Hemans: Reimagining Poetry in the Nineteenth Century* (Basingstoke: Palgrave, 2001), pp. 74–92.
Mermin, Dorothy, 'The Damsel, the Knight and the Victorian Woman Poet', *Critical Enquiry*, Vol. 13, No. 1 (Autumn 1986), 64–80.
Mermin, Dorothy, *Elizabeth Barrett Browning. The Origins of a New Poetry* (Chicago and London: The University of Chicago Press, 1989).
Miller, Lucasta, *The Brontë Myth* (New York: Alfred A. Knopf, 2004).
Millett, Kate, 'The Debate over Women. Ruskin vs. Mill', in Martha Vicinus, ed., *Suffer and Be Still. Women in the Victorian Age* (London: Methuen and Co. Ltd, 1980), pp. 121–39.
Montefiore, Jan, *Feminism and Poetry: Language, Experience, Identity in Women's Writing* (London, Chicago, Sydney: Pandora, 2004).
Motion, Andrew, *Keats* (London: Faber & Faber, 1997).
Nicolson, Harold, *Swinburne* (London: Macmillan and Co., 1926).
Nunn, Pamela Gerrish, 'Ruskin's Patronage of Women Artists', *Women's Art Journal*, Vol. 2 (1981), 8–13.
Parkins, Wendy, *Jane Morris. The Burden of History* (Edinburgh: Edinburgh University Press, 2013).
Pearce, Lynne, *Woman/Image/Text. Readings in Pre-Raphaelite Art and Literature* (Hemel Hempstead, Hertfordshire: Harvester Wheatsheaf, 1991).
Perry, Seamus, *Alfred Tennyson* (Tavistock, Devon: Northcote House Publishers Ltd, 2005).
Peterson, Linda, H., 'The Feminist Origins of 'Of Queens' Gardens', in Dinah Birch and Francis O'Gorman, eds, *Ruskin and Gender* (London, Palgrave, 2002).
Pointon, Marcia, ed., *Pre-Raphaelites Re-viewed* (Manchester: Manchester University Press, 1989).
Prettejohn, Elizabeth, *Rossetti and his Circle* (London: Tate Gallery Publishing, 1997).

Prettejohn, Elizabeth, *Beauty and Art 1750–2000* (Oxford: Oxford University Press, 2005).
Prettejohn, Elizabeth, *The Art of the Pre-Raphaelites* (London: Tate Gallery Publishing, 2007).
Prettejohn, Elizabeth, ed., *The Cambridge Companion to the Pre-Raphaelites* (Cambridge: Cambridge University Press, 2012).
Prins, Yopie, *Victorian Sappho* (Princeton, New Jersey: Princeton University Press, 1999).
Reynolds, Margaret, ed., *The Sappho Companion* (London: Vintage, 2001).
Reynolds, Margaret, *The Sappho History* (Basingstoke: Palgrave Macmillan, 2003).
Ricks, Christopher, *Tennyson* (New York: The Macmillan Company, 1992).
Ricks, Christopher, *Keats and Embarrassment* (London and Oxford: Oxford University Press, 1974).
Ridd, Jenny, *A Destiny Defined. Dante Gabriel Rossetti and Elizabeth Siddal in Hastings* (Pett, East Sussex: Edgerton Publishing Services, 2008).
Riede, David, 'The Pre-Raphaelite School', in Richard Cronin, Alison Chapman, and Antony H. Harrison, eds, *A Companion to Victorian Poetry* (Oxford: Blackwell Publishers Ltd, 2002), pp. 305–20.
Roe, Dinah, *Christina Rossetti's Faithful Imagination: The Devotional Poetry and Prose* (Basingstoke: Palgrave Macmillan, 2006).
Rooksby, Rikky, *A. C. Swinburne: A Poet's Life* (Aldershot: Scolar Press, 1997).
Rummons, Constance, 'The Ballad Imitations of Swinburne', *Poet Lore*, Vol. 33, No. 1 (Spring 1922), 58–84.
Schoemaker, Jacqueline, 'Female Empathy to Manliness: Keats in 1819', in C. C. Barfoot, ed., *Romantic Keats and Romantic Carlyle. The Fusions and Confusions of Literary Periods* (Amsterdam and Atlanta, GA: Rodopi B.V., 1999), pp. 79–94.
Scott, Grant F., *The Sculpted Word. Keats, Ekphrasis and the Visual Arts* (Hanover and London: University Press of New England, 1994).
Scott, Grant F., 'The Fragile Image. Felicia Hemans and Romantic Ekphrasis', in Nanora Sweet and Julie Melnyk, eds, *Felicia Hemans: Reimagining Poetry in the Nineteenth Century* (Basingstoke: Palgrave, 2001), pp. 36–54.
Sedgwick, Eve Kosofsky, 'Tennyson's *Princess*: One Bride for Seven Brothers', in Rebecca Stott, ed., *Tennyson* (London and New York: Addison Wesley Longman Ltd, 1996), pp. 181–96.
Simpson, Claude, M., *The British Broadside and its Music* (New Brunswick: Rutgers University Press, 1966).

Sinfield, Alan, *Alfred Tennyson* (Oxford: Basil Blackwell Ltd, 1986).
Smith, Alison, *The Victorian Nude. Sexuality, Morality and Art* (Manchester: Manchester University Press, 1996).
Smith, Alison, ed., *Exposed. The Victorian Nude* (London: Tate Publishing, 2001).
Smith, Lindsay, *Victorian Photography, Painting and Poetry. The Enigma of Visibility in Ruskin, Morris and the Pre-Raphaelites* (Cambridge: Cambridge University Press, 1995).
Smith, Lindsay, *Pre-Raphaelitism: Poetry and Painting* (Tavistock, Devon: Northcote House Publishers Ltd, 2013).
Sonstroem, David, *Rossetti and the Fair Lady* (Middletown, Conn.: Wesleyan University Press, 1970).
Spear, Jeffrey L., *Dreams of an English Eden. Ruskin and his Tradition in Social Criticism* (New York: Columbia State University Press, 1984).
Spiller, Michael R. G., *The Development of the Sonnet. An Introduction* (London and New York, Routledge, 1992).
Starzyk, Lawrence J., 'Elizabeth Siddal and the "Soulless Self-Reflections of Man's Skill"', *The Journal of Pre-Raphaelite Studies*, Vol. 16 (Fall 2007), 8–26.
Stephenson, Glennis, 'Letitia Landon and the Victorian Improvisatrice. The Construction of L. E. L.', *Victorian Poetry*, Vol. 30, No. 1 (Spring 1992), 1–17.
Stillinger, Jack, *The Hoodwinking of Madeline and Other Essays on Keats' Poems* (Chicago, Illinois: University of Illinois Press, 1971).
Stillinger, Jack, *Reading The Eve of St Agnes. The Multiples of Complex Literary Transaction* (Oxford and New York: Oxford University Press, 1999).
Stone, Marjorie, *Elizabeth Barrett Browning* (Basingstoke: Macmillan, 1995).
Stott, Rebecca, ed., *Tennyson* (London and New York: Addison Wesley Longman Ltd, 1996).
Stott, Rebecca, 'Where Angels Fear to Tread: Aurora Leigh', in Simon Avery and Rebecca Stott, eds, *Elizabeth Barrett Browning* (Edinburgh: Pearson Education Ltd, 2003), pp. 181–209.
Strachan, John, ed., *The Poems of John Keats. A Sourcebook* (London and New York: Routledge, 2003).
Sturrock, June, 'Literary Women of the 1850s and Charlotte Mary Yonge's *Dynevor Terrace*', in Nicola Diane Thompson, ed., *Victorian Women Writers and the Woman Question. Cambridge Studies in Nineteenth-Century Literature and Culture* (Cambridge: Cambridge University Press, 1999), pp. 116–34.
Sweet, Nanora and Melnyk, Julie, eds, *Felicia Hemans: Reimagining Poetry in the Nineteenth Century* (Basingstoke: Palgrave, 2001).

Taylor, Beverly, 'Beatrix/Creatrix: Elizabeth Siddal as Muse and Creator', *The Journal Of Pre-Raphaelite Studies*, Vol. 4 (Spring 1995), 29–50.

Thain, Marion, *'Michael Field'. Poetry, Aestheticism and the Fin de Siècle* (Cambridge: Cambridge University Press, 2007).

Thompson, Nicola Diane, ed., *Victorian Women Writers and the Woman Question. Cambridge Studies in Nineteenth-Century Literature* (Cambridge: Cambridge University Press, 1999).

Tickner, Lisa, *Dante Gabriel Rossetti* (London: Tate Publishing, 2003).

Treuherz, Julian, Prettejohn, Elizabeth and Becker, Edwin, *Dante Gabriel Rossetti* (London: Thames & Hudson, 2003).

Turley, Richard Marggraf, *Keats's Boyish Imagination* (London: Routledge, 2004).

Van Remoortel, Marianne, *Lives of the Sonnet, 1787–1895. Genre, Gender and Criticism* (Farnham, Surrey: Ashgate Publishing Ltd, 2011).

Vicinus, Martha, ed., *Suffer and Be Still. Women in the Victorian Age* (London: Methuen and Co. Ltd, 1980).

Walder, Dennis, ed., *Literature in the Modern World. Critical Essays and Documents* (Oxford: Open University Press, 1990).

Walker, Kirsty Stonell, *Stunner: The Fall and Rise of Fanny Cornforth* (Spacecreate.com, 2006).

Whale, John, *Critical Issues. John Keats* (Basingstoke: Palgrave Macmillan, 2005).

Williams, Isabelle, 'Elizabeth Siddal: The Health Issue', *The Journal of Pre-Raphaelite Studies*, Vol. 5 (Spring 1996), 53–70.

Williams, Raymond, *Culture and Society 1780–1950* (London: Chatto & Windus, 1960).

Williams, Raymond, *Culture* (London: Fontana Paperbacks, 1981).

Wootton, Sarah, 'Keats in Early Pre-Raphaelite Art', *Keats-Shelley Review*, Vol. 12 (1998), 3–14.

Wootton, Sarah, *Consuming Keats. Nineteenth-Century Representations in Art and Literature* (Basingstoke and New York: Palgrave Macmillan, 2006).

Zonana, Joyce, 'Swinburne's Sappho: The Muse as Sister Goddess', *Victorian Poetry*, Vol. 28, No. 1 (Spring 1990), 39–50.

General Index

Ackland, Henry 170
addiction 2, 8, 26, 42
aesthetics 31, 61, 215, 219, 263
Allingham, William 20
Anglican Church 51
Anglican Sisterhoods 153
aphonia 113
Arnold, Matthew 23, 82
autobiographical readings of poems 5, 9, 67–8, 258–61

Bailey, Benjamin 244
ballad tradition 12–13, 93, 100–24, 128, 131, 135–7, 258
'Beatrice persona' 34–5
beauty, concepts of 35–45, 257–8
the Bible 52
Blackfriars Bridge 19
Blackwood's Magazine 210–11
Blake, William 72
Blind, Matilda 6
Boccaccio, Giovanni 42
bodies
　physical 225–36
　spectral 241–51, 257
Boyce, George 30
Brawne, Fanny 213, 248
Brett, John and Rosa 166
Brown, Charles 249
Brown, Ford Madox 1, 16
Browning, Elizabeth Barrett 5–7, 50–3, 57–60, 96, 105–6, 112, 143–4, 149, 173, 177, 179, 185, 206, 262
Browning, Robert 16, 20, 50, 149, 154, 176
Bryan, Mary 60
Buchanan, Robert 49, 101

Burden, Jane *see* Morris, Jane
burial of poets 249
Burne-Jones, Edward 25, 37
Burne-Jones, Georgiana 27
Byron, Lord George Gordon 216, 247

Caine, Thomas Hall 215
Chaucer, Geoffrey 4
Cheyne Walk circle 37
Child, Francis 104, 110
Christianity 9, 50–5, 81, 116, 153, 167
'civil death' concept of 150
Coleridge, Samuel Taylor 216
Collinson, James 51
colour, use of 125, 241–2
context and contextualization 10–14, 260–3
Cornforth, Fanny 19–20, 26, 30–2, 35, 42, 53
Craig, Isa 152, 154

Dante Alighieri 4, 10, 24, 29, 32–4, 40, 53
Darwinian theory 50
Deverell, Walter 24, 204
Dickens, Charles 46
divorce 150
Donati, Gemma 34
double standard of morality 150, 263
dreams 128, 135, 142, 182–3, 187, 219–21, 226, 234, 242, 245–7

Edinburgh Review 210–11
education 163, 167–8, 173
ekphrasis 11–12, 63, 73, 217–19
The English Women's Journal 152, 155

The Englishman's Magazine 211
epic poetry 186
equality
   between women and men 258
   social 153
eroticism 13, 23, 38, 52, 77, 179, 208, 220–1

Faithfull, Emily 154
feminine appearance 35
feminine strengths and virtues 7, 153
femininity 5, 115, 154–5, 207, 263
feminism 5–10, 13, 52, 127, 131, 143, 149–58, 165, 173–81, 190–1, 257–60
Field, Michael 176
flesh painting 37, 42

Gaskell, Elizabeth 151
genius, concept of 2, 98, 156–7, 164, 170, 198, 200, 210, 251
Gladstone, William 46
Gordon, Mary 95
Greenwell, Dora 53, 176
grief 47, 61, 125, 127, 181, 184, 200, 222, 241, 245–8, 257

hair, women's as a trope 198–9, 208–10, 231, 249
Hallam, Arthur 211–13
Hastings 156
Haydon, Benjamin Robert 251
Heaton, Ellen 163–5, 171
Hemans, Felicia 6–8, 53–7, 60, 96, 104, 111, 176, 189–90, 217, 262
Hill, Octavia 151
historical romances, writers of 206
history painting 155–6
Holland Park circle 37
Homer 4, 186
Howell, Charles 28
Howitt, Mary 20, 144, 150–1, 154–61
The Howitt Journal 151
Hughes, Arthur 221
Hunt, Holman 18, 24, 51, 199, 203–7, 212–13, 216–22

Illustrated London News 37
incest 8, 118, 135
'inclusiveness', concept of 50–1
Ingelow, Jean 7, 53, 154, 176, 204
intertextuality 11

Jesus Christ 216
journalism produced by women 6

Keats, John 4, 9–13, 176, 198–251, 258, 263
   death of 249
   fascination with things medical 234–6
   polarization of opinion about 210
   Pre-Raphaelite interpretation of the poems of 217–25
Kelmscott Manor 31
Kinloch, George Ritchie 89, 91
kissing 119–20

laments in ballad style 137
Landon, Letitia (L. E. L.) 6–8, 96–7, 104, 111–12, 176, 262
Langham Place Group 144, 148–63, 185, 190, 198, 258
La Touche, Rose 172
L. E. L. *see* Landon, Letitia
Leonardo da Vinci 4
lesbianism 8
Levy, Amy 176
'living death', concept of 125–6
'lost' voices 263
love, concepts of 13, 20, 23–4, 29, 35, 45–9, 58, 61–75, 178–9, 183, 257
   see also religious love

magnetism 54
male dominance *see* patriarchal society
Malory, Sir Thomas 52
Married Women's Property Acts 150–1
Martineau, Harriet 151
Mary Magdalene 55, 57
masculine view of women 6
mesmerism 53
middle-class women 62, 149–52, 206, 258
Millais, John Everett 24, 51, 156, 170, 199–207, 212, 216–18, 221–5
Milnes, Richard Monkton 211, 213–14
Milton, John 4, 247, 250
Morley, John 101
Morris, Jane 28–35, 48, 206
Morris, William 25, 31, 102–3, 203
Moxon, Edward 143, 200, 202

negative capability 51, 200, 205, 212, 236, 245, 250
new historicism 7, 261
Nightingale, Florence 156
Norton, Caroline 60, 96
nudes 37

obscenity laws 37
Oxford Union 25, 93

Palgrave, Francis Turner 214
Parkes, Bessie 144, 150–9, 163, 185
patriarchal society 53, 149–50, 153–5, 167–8, 188, 191, 257, 260–1
pet names 149, 172
Petrarch and Petrarchanism 4, 57, 59
philosophical considerations 14, 50, 116
Pope, Alexander 210
pornography 37
Portfolio Society 9, 154–5, 176
Portland School 163
posthumous reworking of Siddal's poems 200
Pre-Raphaelitism 2–5, 8–13, 23–4, 33–6, 51–2, 55, 92, 106, 109, 125, 143–6, 155, 159, 163–4, 176, 188, 198–212, 216–25, 258–62
  feminine appearance associated with 35
Procter, Adelaide 7, 152, 154, 176
prostitution 18, 20, 46, 153, 179

Quarterly Review 210–11

Raphael 4
religion 23
'religion of beauty' 10, 36
religious love 50–6, 81–2
repetition, incremental and modulated 124
Reynolds, John 244
Romantic movement 5, 7, 198, 219
Rossetti, Christina 5–8, 52–3, 57–9, 96, 105, 112, 126–7, 152–3, 176, 203, 206–10, 214, 241
Rossetti, Dante Gabriel 1–3, 8–14, 18–24, 28–42, 52–60, 66, 79–82, 93, 98–100, 143, 149, 151, 155–9, 169–70, 176, 199, 203–18, 235, 249–51, 257–9, 262–3

drawings and paintings by 25–7, 46, 158, 162, 171
poetry by 32, 45–50, 70–2, 76, 78
public persona of 9
Rossetti, William Michael 3, 9, 12, 24–5, 45, 52–5, 97, 100, 102, 170, 199, 205, 213–14, 223, 251
Rossetti family 2
Royal Academy 218, 258
Ruskin, John 3, 10–13, 20, 34, 38, 52, 55, 131, 143–4, 148–9, 154–7, 161–74, 183–5, 198, 208, 235, 251, 258
  patronage of Siddal and others 148, 165–70

Sappho and Sapphic culture 95–7, 185, 206
Scott, Walter 89, 91, 94, 100, 104, 110
self-knowledge and self-understanding 14, 23, 51, 60
sentimental tradition regarding women's writing 259
Severn, Joseph 249
sexuality 9, 38, 46, 49–50, 54, 63, 97, 220–2, 233, 238
Shakespeare, William 4, 174, 216, 250
Shelley, Percy Bysshe 211, 216
Siddal, Elizabeth
  apparent negativity of literary work 247
  as an artist and creative force 3, 11, 113, 259, 262
  attitude to death 34, 48, 54, 61, 77, 93, 113, 123, 126, 130, 133, 178, 234–5, 236, 240, 245, 257
  death of 1–2, 26, 94–5
  drawings and paintings by 4, 8, 11, 14, 22, 45, 89–93, 148, 155, 164–5, 176, 196, 201–2, 214–15
  exhumation of 28–9, 38, 249–50
  handwriting of 3
  illnesses and other challenges faced by 10, 26, 156–61, 164, 170, 206–7
  love of art and poetry 176
  love of theatre 98–9
  marriage and financial position of 93–100, 151–6, 205, 216, 258
  as model and muse 28, 158, 185, 205, 258–9

non-publication of 14, 155, 159, 177, 200, 208, 249–51, 258, 261–3
personality and life-history of 1–3, 11, 14, 23, 29, 158, 165, 259, 263
physical appearance of 25–6, 41, 60, 146, 158–62, 171, 196, 209, 259
poetry by 3–5, 8–14, 22–3, 45, 48, 50–1, 61–82, 99–100, 108–37, 149–52, 167, 172–202, 207, 214–15, 225–51, 257–63
posthumous reputation of 29–30, 97, 200
pregnancies of 1–2, 26
public persona of 9, 14, 159, 262
as a reclusive observer of rather than a participant in the art world 261
religious faith 54–5
spoken of as a genius 156–7, 164, 170
Smith, Barbara Leigh 144, 150–60, 163, 185
Society for Promoting the Employment of Women 152, 154
sonnets and sonnet sequences 57–61, 76, 258
'soul sleep' 127
spiritualism 53
Swedenborg, Emanuel 54
Swinburne, Algernon Charles 1–2, 10, 12, 38, 45, 89–112, 118–37, 258, 263
  ballads 100–10, 119–20, 129, 134
Swinburne, John Edward 107
symbiosis 10

Tennyson, Alfred Lord 4, 10–13, 143–6, 149, 161, 172–3, 176, 179–81, 189–91, 200–4, 211–16, 263

Tighe, Mary 60
Titian 36
Tractarianism 112
Trevelyan, Lady Pauline 95, 163–4
Turner, Joseph Mallord William 165, 170

Victorian culture and society 7, 33, 50, 57–62, 76, 97, 105–6, 115–16, 126–8, 143–4, 148, 152–5, 175, 188, 207, 209, 213, 224, 258–62
visual impression of poems 11
voice, denial of 111, 131, 209, 259–60
voyeurism 221

Waterford, Marchioness of 163–4
Watts-Dunton, Clara 107, 109
Webster, Augusta 6–7, 46, 59, 153, 176
Wollstonecraft, Mary 173
'Woman Question' 13, 143–4, 149, 172–3
womanhood
  celebration of 14
  ideal of 33
  types of 17–18
women
  adoration of 61
  as artists 143, 156, 165–6
  D. G. Rossetti's depictions of 35–44
  employment of 152
  poetry by 5–7, 12, 55–60, 95–6, 111, 126, 154–5, 172–6, 185, 188–9, 257–63
  role and status of 36, 145, 150–5, 162–3, 166–7, 173–5, 182, 188, 261, 263
women's movement 6, 152–3, 163
women's rights 151–3
Wordsworth, William 4, 176, 216, 250
Working Ladies Guild 163

Index of individual poems, pictures and collections

'After Death' (C. Rossetti) 203
'After Death' (Swinburne) 109–10, 115, 120–1, 124–6, 131–4
'Ask me no more' (Tennyson) 173, 182
Astarte Syriaca (D. G. Rossetti) 42–4
'As through the land at eve we went' (Tennyson) 173, 181
'At Home' (C. Rossetti) 203
'At Last' (Siddal) 100, 108–12, 118, 123–34, 207
Aurora Leigh (Barrett Browning) 46, 172–5, 179, 184–5, 191

Beata Beatrix (D. G. Rossetti) 33, 38–40, 63
'Bertha in the Lane' (Barrett Browning) 106
'The Birth-Bond' (D. G. Rossetti) 63, 71, 73
The Blessed Damozel (D. G. Rossetti) 49
Boadicea Brooding over her Wrongs (Howitt) 155
Bocca Baciata (D. G. Rossetti) 30, 42
The Bridesmaid (Millais) 208
'Burd Helen' (border ballad) 110

'Casabianca' (Hemans) 104
'A Castaway' (Webster) 46
'The Chamois Hunter's Love' (Hemans) 190
Clerk Saunders (Siddal) 45, 89–93, 103, 113, 133, 145
'The Cry of the Children' (Barrett Browning) 112

'Come down oh Maid' (Tennyson) 173, 179, 190
'A Curse for a Nation' (Barrett Browning) 112

'The Dark Glass' (D. G. Rossetti) 63–4, 69–70, 73, 78
'Dead Love' (Siddal) 174–8, 181–3, 187–90
'Divided' (Ingelow) 204
'Dream Land' (C. Rossetti) 203–4
'Duriesdyke' (Swinburne) 109, 117–18, 121, 124, 129

'Early Death' (Siddal) 64–5, 77, 81
Ecce Ancilla Domini! (D. G. Rossetti) 39
Elizabeth Siddall (Howitt) 160
Elizabeth Siddall (Smith) 161
Elizabeth Eleanor Siddal (D. G. Rossetti) 24–5

'The Factory' (Landon) 104
'The Fause Lover' (border ballad) 110
The Forest Sanctuary (Hemans) 111
Found (D. G. Rossetti) 18–20, 30

The Gay Goshawk (Siddal) 113
'Genius in Beauty' (D. G. Rossetti) 63, 69, 79
'Gladys and Her Island' (Ingelow) 154
Goblin Market (C. Rossetti) 8, 105, 112, 126, 209
'Gone' (Siddal) 199, 207, 228–30, 237–44, 248–9

Index of individual poems, pictures and collections 283

'He and She and Angels Three' (Siddal)
  108, 113, 120–2, 127–30, 133–4
'Heart's Compass' (D. G. Rossetti) 63,
  69, 71, 75–7
'Heart's Hope' (D. G. Rossetti) 62–3,
  69, 75–6
'Her Gifts' (D. G. Rossetti) 63, 69, 72,
  77
'Home they brought her warrior, dead'
  (Tennyson) 143–4
The House of Life (D. G. Rossetti) 18,
  22, 28–9, 32, 45–50, 57–62, 66,
  68, 72–3, 76, 80

Isabella (Hunt) 223
Isabella, or The Pot of Basil (Keats)
  236–51
Isabella (Millais) 223–5

Jenny (D. G. Rossetti) 46–7
'Johnie Scot' (border ballad)
  110

'The King's Daughter' (Swinburne)
  109–10, 115, 118–21, 124,
  129–31, 134–5
'The Kiss' (D. G. Rossetti) 63, 66, 71,
  75, 78

'La Belle Dame Sans Merci' (Keats)
  209–10, 215, 226–7, 231–4,
  238–9, 242–6, 250–1
La Belle Dame Sans Merci (Siddal)
  207–8
Lady Clare (Siddal) 143–9, 176
'Lady Geraldine's Courtship' (Barrett
  Browning) 105–6
Lady Lilith (D. G. Rossetti) 42
Lamia (Keats) 214, 226–36, 240, 246,
  248
'The Landing of the Pilgrim Fathers in
  New England' (Hemans) 104
'Lord May I Come?' (Siddal) 61, 65–8,
  73–80, 112, 127
Lorenzo at His Desk in the Workhouse
  (Hunt) 222–3
'Love and Hate' (Siddal) 51, 105,
  174–85, 188, 190
'Love Enthroned' (D. G. Rossetti) 62,
  68–9, 72, 76
'Love-Sweetness' (D. G. Rossetti) 63,
  69–70, 77–80

Lovers Listening to Music (Siddal) 44–5
'Love's Lovers' (D. G. Rossetti) 63,
  71–2, 76, 78
'The Lust of the Eyes' (Siddal) 36,
  61–9, 73–7, 100, 207
'Lyke Wake Dirge' (border ballad) 110

Madonna and Child (Siddal) 56
'May Janet' (Swinburne) 109–10, 115,
  118–19, 124–5, 130, 133–4
Monna Innominata (C. Rossetti) 8–9,
  58–9
Monna Vanna (D. G. Rossetti) 209
Mother and Daughter (Webster) 59

'Night Blowing Flowers' (Hemans) 104
'Night at Sea' (Landon) 111–12
'Noble Sisters' (C. Rossetti) 105
'Now sleeps the crimson petal'
  (Tennyson) 173, 179
'Nuptial Sleep' (D. G. Rossetti) 63, 65,
  71, 77–80

'Ode on a Grecian Urn' (Keats) 218
'O Swallow, Swallow' (Tennyson) 173
'Our enemies have fallen' (Tennyson)
  184

'The Passing of Love' (Siddal) 105,
  174–5, 180–5, 188, 190
'Passion and Worship' (D. G. Rossetti)
  63, 71, 75–8
Pippa Passes (Siddal) 16–20, 46
Poems (1870) (D. G. Rossetti) 28, 49
'The Poor Ghost' (C. Rossetti) 127,
  209–10
'The Portrait' (D. G. Rossetti) 63,
  69–74
Portrait of Elizabeth Siddal Reading
  (D. G. Rossetti) 24–6
The Princess (Tennyson) 10, 13, 131,
  144, 149, 172–9, 182
*Profile Portrait of Elizabeth Siddal with
  Irises in her Hair* (D. G. Rossetti)
  162
'Properzia Rossi' (Hemans) 217

'The Queen of Hearts' (C. Rossetti) 112

Rachael and Leah (D. G. Rossetti) 164
'Remember' (C. Rossetti) 127
'Repining' (C. Rossetti) 204

Rossetti Sitting to Elizabeth Siddal
(D. G. Rossetti) 26–7

'St Agnes' Eve' (Tennyson) 200–1
'The Sea-Swallows' (Swinburne)
    109–10, 117–21, 124–5, 131, 134
Self Portrait (Siddal) 41–2
'Shepherd Turned Sailor' (Siddal) 199,
    228, 231–3, 238–45, 248–9
'A Silent Wood' (Siddal) 61, 64–77
Sister Helen (D. G. Rossetti) 20–1
Sister Helen (Siddal) 20–2
'A Song of the Ragged Schools of
    London' (Barrett Browning) 105
'Song: 'When I am Dead, My Dearest'
    (C. Rossetti) 127
'Songs of the Cid' (Hemans) 104
'A Sonnet is a Moment's Monument'
    (D. G. Rossetti) 62
Sonnets from the Portuguese (Barrett
    Browning) 58
'Speechless' (Siddal) 106, 110, 114–16,
    120, 123–30, 133–5, 207
'The Stream's Secret' (D. G. Rossetti)
    209
Study for St Agnes' Eve (Siddal) 201–4
'Sweet and low' (Tennyson) 173, 181

'Tears, idle tears' (Tennyson) 173, 189
The Eve of St Agnes (Hunt) 219–21

The Eve of St Agnes (Keats) 199, 203,
    206–7, 236–51
The Eve of St Agnes (Millais) 221–2
'Thy voice is heard through rolling
    drums' (Tennyson) 143
'True Love' (Siddal) 100, 109–10, 113,
    116, 120, 123–30, 133–5, 207
'The Twa Corbies' (border ballad)
    110

'Uphill' (C. Rossetti) 9

'A Vision of Poets' (Barrett Browning)
    96

A Woman and a Spectre (Siddal) 196–9,
    251
'A Woman's Last Word' (Browning)
    154
'A Woman's Question' (Procter) 154
'The Worm of Spindlestonheugh'
    (Swinburne) 109–10, 119–21,
    129–35
'Worn Out' (Siddal) 199, 227–33,
    237–41, 244–9

'A Year and a Day' (Siddal) 99, 106,
    109, 116–20, 124, 127–30,
    133–5, 207

EU authorised representative for GPSR:
Easy Access System Europe, Mustamäe tee 50,
10621 Tallinn, Estonia
gpsr.requests@easproject.com

www.ingramcontent.com/pod-product-compliance
Lightning Source LLC
Chambersburg PA
CBHW051603230426
43668CB00013B/1965